www.ingramcontent.com/pod-product-compliance
Lightning Source LLC
Chambersburg PA
CBHW060235240426
43663CB00041B/2872

TABLE OF CONTENTS

NOTES ON LANGUAGE 2

PREFACE 3

KABBALAT SHABBAT: RECEIVING THE SABBATH 6

SHACHARIT: THE DAWNING PRAYER 94

TORAH SERVICE 174

BLESSINGS FOR HEALING 182

MINCHAH: AFTERNOON PRAYERS 200

HALLEL 207

HAVDALAH: FAREWELL TO SHABBAT 210

TEKUFOT: EQUINOXES AND SOLSTICES 213

ROSH CHODESH: NEW MOON CEREMONY 214

TABLE BLESSINGS 218

GRACE AFTER MEALS 229

CREDITS 233

SONG INDEX 234

NOTES ON LANGUAGE

In both Hebrew and English, our siddur uses multiple names, designations, and grammatical forms for God where Adonai would usually appear—as well as multiple names, designations, and grammatical forms for humans, expressing a variety of ideas. Our siddur most typically uses Shekhinah, Divine Presence, to refer to deity. We invite you to use the language that most speaks to you and fits your spiritual practice.

The ancient biblical custom was to refer to God in the majestic plural (i.e. eloheinu). Our siddur uses eloheinu (plural masculine "our God") and eloteinu (plural feminine "our Goddess") to refer to deity.

Biblical and liturgical texts in the siddur may be originally masculine in their grammar, or originally feminine. Where the text is originally masculine, our siddur often feminizes the text or offers a non-binary option and sometimes leaves the text in its original form.

When multiple options for addressing God appear in that same prayer,

> ☐ a square indicates language that is grammatically feminine,
> △ a triangle indicates language that is grammatically masculine, and
> ⊖ a bisected circle indicates language that is nonbinary

— readers can choose one. Our nonbinary language comes from the Nonbinary Hebrew Project created by Lior Gross and Eyal Rivlin (https://www.nonbinaryhebrew.com/) and Siddur Davar Ḥadash (https://inclusivesiddur.com/).

For help in pronouncing the transliteration, readers may refer to this guide:

kh OR ch	ch as in achtung
tz	ts as in cats
a	short a as in cot
ei	long a as in save
ai	long i as in my
o	long o as in phone

NOTE ON MUSIC

Chants and melodies for many of the prayers appear on the *Siddur haKohanot* companion album as well as on the albums of Taya Shere, Shoshana Jedwab, Shir Meira Feit, and others. Please visit kohenet.com or hebrewpriestess.bandcamp.com to find this music.

PREFACE

You are holding a Jewish prayerbook with a myriad of possibilities for connecting with the Source of Life, however you understand or experience that source. In *Siddur haKohanot: A Hebrew Priestess Prayerbook*, you'll find creative and traditional rituals and prayers, and explore an earth-honoring, feminist spirituality with deep roots in Jewish tradition. *Siddur haKohanot* includes *Kabbalat Shabbat* and *Maarivah* (evening), *Shacharit* (morning), *Minchah* (afternoon), and Holiday services that balance traditionally-inspired liturgy and creative language and readings.

We generally use feminine-gendered Hebrew God-language and person-language, and non-binary and masculine language also appear here. Names for Goddess/Goddexx/God change throughout the siddur as the prayers unfold. This reflects our devotion to Shekhinah—Divine Presence, a term used by Jews throughout the ages for the feminine divine—in Her many guises, and our commitment to the paths through which She is embodied in our lives. The siddur also reflects our spiritual connection to the planet, the four elements of earth, water, air, and fire, as well as the four worlds of kabbalistic tradition.

Why do we use the term kohenet, or Hebrew priestess? Long ago, as evidenced by inscriptions and other items discovered by archaeologists, and as suggested by many biblical texts, priestesses served the Jewish people through ritual, song, and dance. This prayerbook understands itself to follow in that tradition.

We are grateful to all those who have given us permission to use their work in this prayerbook. Siddur haKohanot was originally created for students in the Kohenet Hebrew Priestess Institute's (2005-2023) training program. We are delighted that it is now used by people of all genders who wish to honor the divine feminine.

We rejoice to be part of a movement reclaiming and evolving an embodied, earth-honoring Judaism and are honored to connect with you in a circle of prayer. May Siddur haKohanot bring inspiration, meaning, and expansive possibilities and depth into your prayer experiences and spiritual life.

Jill Hammer and Taya Shere

ABOUT SIDDUR HAKOHANOT

Siddur HaKohanot can be used for daily, Sabbath, and festival prayer, and also for meditation and ritual at any moment. *Siddur HaKohanot* differs from a traditional siddur (prayerbook) in our inclusion of feminine and masculine and non-binary language for the divine and for people; names for God/Goddess/Goddexx that are drawn from mysticism, contemporary liturgy, and other sources; and elemental imagery and ritual that reflects a concept of the universe as holy.

GOD/DESS/GODDEXX LANGUAGE

In the conception of *Siddur HaKohanot*, Goddess is the source of being and the sum total of being. She/he/they is also called God, Goddexx, Universe, Fountain of Being, or Tree of Life. We call Her Goddess when we imagine Her in a female or femme form, or when we seek to remember ways we are made in Her image. To name God She, or Zhe, does not presume to give God a permanent gender identity, but rather to summon up ancient archetypal images: womb, earth, blood, mother, lover, moon.

Goddess/Goddexx, as She/Zhe appears in the lives of many today, is holistic, embodied in nature, present in the cycle of life, and non-dual. She/Zhe is one and many; and whether She/Zhe is one or many is not the most important thing about Her; because for the Goddess, the state of oneness and the state of multiplicity coincide. She is one full with the many, or the many woven into one.

She may call to us as Divine Mother or Holy Origin. Zhe may call to us as earth, sea, and sky.

The most common God/Goddess/Goddexx name used in this siddur is Shekhinah, which means "indwelling." In the Jewish understanding, Shekhinah is the divine presence that inheres in all matter and all life. The mystics depict Shekhinah as moon, bride, queen, mother bird, dark oceanic force, and the earth itself. This siddur honors that depiction and also expands it to include many ways that we experience God/dess/dexx.

Other terms for Goddess/Goddexx we use throughout the siddur are *Havaya* (Being), *Shaddai* (Almighty, but also meaning Breasted One), *Immah* (Mother), *Tzimtzemai* (the One who Makes Space), and *Malkat haShamayim* (Queen of Heaven, a name used for goddesses in the ancient Near East). At times we call Her *Asherah*, a name ancient Israelites used for the Goddess, or *Chochmah* (Wisdom), and *Etz Chayyim* (Tree of Life)—names for the divine feminine from the Book of Proverbs.

Most of our language in the siddur is feminine, in accordance with the original practice of the Kohenet Institute, but we also have included some nonbinary and masculine language options.

Many new translations of Jewish prayers avoid the words "lord" (*Adonai*) and "king" (*melekh*) because of their hierarchical and patriarchal significance. We have chosen to use these names for the Divine masculine some of the time. This reflects our awareness that "king" or "lord" can be a name for the masculine as lover of the Goddess. In her essay "Speaking of Goddess," Julia Watts Belser notes that the king in the Song of Songs is not an authoritarian king but a consort for a divine woman. We also use inclusive gender-neutral terms like *Ma'yan Chayim* (Wellspring of Life), *Ruach* (Divine Wind), and *Yah* (Divine Breath).

The choices we make seek to honor myriad paths of prayer language and also the importance of honoring many faces of God through prayer. In the kabbalistic world-view, many divine faces can embody multiple genders.

We invite you to explore prayer language and names for God/Goddess/Goddexx that may be new for you. And, it's fine to place the divine names you find most resonant into the prayers shared here, even if that is different from how we've written it. Feel welcome to pray with God/Goddess/Goddexx language that is meaningful and holds vitality for you.

KOHENET / THE HEBREW PRIESTESS

Kohenet is the Hebrew word for priestess. In reclaiming the role of *kohenet*, we highlight models of sacred service based on ways Jewish women and non-binary people served in spiritual leadership throughout the centuries, from biblical prophetess-priestesses to talmudic healers and magicians to kabbalistic dream interpreters to modern feminist ritualists. And, we reclaim paradigms of embodied experiences of the sacred. By opening to the sacred feminine in Jewish sources, in the world around us, and in our own lives, we evolve an embodied, earth-based, and feminist Jewish practice.

The word priestess (singular Hebrew, *kohenet*; plural Hebrew, *kohanot*) frequently appears in this siddur, along with the non-binary / gender neutral word priestexx, and can be understood to mean one in sacred ritual connection to God/dess/dexx.

> The priestess reveals through her being and doing the presence of Shekhinah: the mystery of embodiment of sacred place, time, and body/soul.
> *Jill Hammer*

> Priestexxes love the liminal and embody the sacred. Through ritual, prayer, creativity, relationship and action, how we meet each moment is an expression of devotion. We engage life as sacred practice— embracing the earth and her cycles and immersing in embodied expressions of the sacred, right here and now.
> *Taya Shere*

Kohanot work intensively within an embodied and immanent paradigm of Judaism and spirituality. Mainstream modern (post 1650) rabbis by and large have been connected with the transcendent as it is applied to social organization, ethics, philosophy and Jewish peoplehood… We know that during the last 300 years of rabbinic history in the West, rationalism has damaged the trust Jews have in the immanent and embodied aspects of Jewish spirituality. Kohanot seek to radically restore the bond to the Goddess of Being in Judaism and beyond.
Shoshana Jedwab

THE ALTAR

Siddur HaKohanot can be engaged toward prayer anywhere. And, one powerful way to work with this siddur is around an altar. An altar is a ritual space where sacred objects are placed to indicate the connection between the worlds; between divine and human, between one soul and another. You might craft an altar by gathering objects of meaning onto a table or shelf or sacred place in your home, or in nature near where you live. When gathering in community, you might invite those with you to bring something of meaning to them for a central altar: a candle, a stone, a picture of an ancestor, a healing herb, or another sacred object. In this way, sacred space is co-created. When gathering in nature, a lake, a fire pit, a rock or a tree may become the altar—honor the sacred where you are.

Altars are an ancient sacred tool—a delineated sacred space used for making offerings. In the book of Exodus, the Hebrew people are asked to make "an altar of earth" and "an altar of stones" for God. The biblical Tabernacle had an altar for animal sacrifice and an altar for incense. The Temple in Jerusalem also had these two central altars. In addition to the central altar in the Temple, the early Hebrews worshiped at shrines called bamot, or high places. We know from archaeology that local altars existed throughout the land at the time of the Bible, and represented an important part of Israelite custom. The Temple altar ceased operating in 70 CE, in Roman times, when the Temple was destroyed and the Jews went into exile for the second time. The Shabbat or holiday table in many homes until today can be considered a symbolic altar, as the blessings over wine and bread hearken back to the rituals of the Temple.

Altars also represent the cosmos. An altar connects the world we live in to the upper and lower worlds, and to the past and future. The Zohar teaches us that the altar represents the earth itself: Shekhinah's body. We encourage the building of altars as part of worship in the Kohenet mode.

THE DRUM

Thousands of years ago, priestesses around the ancient Near East used drums, and appeared with drums in art. Drums were a way of creating music, calling to community, or inducing a trance state. The book of Psalms and the book of Exodus both speak of women drumming as part of ritual song. The Levites, a component of the male priestly class in ancient Israel, also used drums to make music. Thousands of years later, Jewish women in Middle Eastern and Sephardic culture continue to use the drum as a companion to their songs.

Today, drums are still an important part of ritual in many cultures, and across the world, a huge variety of drums sound the beat. Though Jewish prayer music traditionally did not use instruments as a sign of mourning for the Temple's destruction, that principle has changed for many Jewish communities. While a generation ago few Jewish prayer services used drums as an instrument, today the drum is a popular instrument in liberal synagogues to enliven and bring joy to prayer.

The beat of the drum is an important element of our chants, spirit journeys, and rituals. As Layne Redmond notes in *When The Drummers Were Women: A Spiritual History of Rhythm*, the drum reminds us of the first sound any of us ever heard: the sound of the heartbeat when we were in the womb. We feel the drum as a heartbeat of sacred circle and of ceremony. We encourage drumming to accompany, support and deepen experiences of personal and communal prayer.

THE FOUR ELEMENTS

The four elements of earth, water, air, and fire are a fundamental building block of many spiritual traditions, from the kabbalists to the Babylonians, from the ancient Greeks to the Tibetans and Japanese. Many indigenous peoples across the Americas understand the four directions—connected to the elements—as a spiritual navigation system. Modern earth-based traditions including Wicca work with the elements as well. Many traditions also acknowledge a fifth element—spirit, void, or ether.

A thousand years ago, the philosopher Maimonides followed the Greeks and posited that God had created four elements as the foundation of the world. The Zohar sees the four elements as fundamental depictions of divine attributes. Sixteenth-century kabbalist Isaac Luria sees earth, water, air, and fire as symbols of the four worlds: *assiyah, yetzirah, beriyah,* and *atzilut,* loosely understood as doing, feeling, thinking, and being. Contemporary Jewish earth-based teachers use the four winds, four worlds, and four directions in healing work, and the Jewish Renewal movement maintains an awareness of the four worlds through prayer and meditation.

For us, the four elements are a core part of ritual. Our altars frequently are crafted with them, and *Sidddur HaKohanot* includes invocations and chants honoring them. We use the spiritual systems of mystical books like the Zohar to associate the four elements with the four directions and with different faces of God. While traditional kabbalah perceives the worlds as hierarchically ordered from most corporeal (lowest) to most ethereal (highest), we perceive them as interlocking circles, no one more important than the next.

The image of the four elements is an image of the Goddess as She separates into the substances of the world. They are a reminder of the sacredness of the corporeal— the holiness of real bodies that exist in real time. Gathering the four separate entities together is a symbolic reconstitution of the oneness of creation. So too, the symbolic parts of the self—body, heart, mind, spirit—are a ritual building of the human whole.

And, honoring the four elements is not only symbolic. Engaging them in physical form with awareness, or with reverence, is a pathway of attuning to the sacred. As we place a stone (earth) on our altar, as we immerse in a river (water), as we bring our awareness to our breath (air), as we light a candle (fire), we experience and honor the sacred in life all around us, in life within us and in Life that sustains us.

THE BODY

Dance as an embodied expression of praise appears throughout Jewish tradition. In the book of Exodus, Miriam takes out her timbrel and guides the women in song and dance. The judge Jephthah is welcomed home by his daughter with dancing, and when King Saul and David return from battle, the women meet them with joyful song and dance. Circular movements (*hakafot*) are danced on celebratory occasions including the holidays of Sukkot and Simchat Torah and on the holiday of Tu b'Av, young women danced together in the fields as a way of finding their beloved. The Baal Shem Tov, the founder of Chassidism, spoke of dancing as a form of prayer that has a place at the center of Jewish life.

We pray in ways that honor the body as sacred, and we often engage movement as a practice of devotion. In morning prayer, we give thanks for the gift of our bodies through the Morning Blessings (*Birkot haShachar*), through the Openings (*Asher Yaztar*) chant and more. We may dance when the spirit moves us as a way to express joy, to raise energy or to deepen in prayer. And particularly, we may dance during the Lecha Dodi prayer on Friday night, hearkening to the stories of Jewish mystics going out and dancing in the fields while welcoming Shabbat; when we offer the words of Psalm 149 "Praise God with timbrels and dance" and when we sing Mi Chamocha, the Song of the Sea. We may *shuckle*—the Yiddish term for back-and-forth swaying that at times accompanies Jewish prayer—as a repetitive motion that can be both soothing and transportive. Those who are able may bow, as described in Psalms and Talmud—perhaps at our knees, waist or simply with our heads, during prayers including *Barchu* call to worship, certain blessings of the Amidah, and with the closing stanza of *Lecha Dodi*. We may prostrate, laying belly to the earth, as a way of humbling ourselves or of connecting more deeply to earth as Source.

As you engage the prayers in this siddur, we invite you to move in ways that feel good for your body, knowing that needn't look any particular way. Regardless of experience or ability, feel welcome to follow body's needs into meaningful prayer. As Julia Watts Belser says in *Loving Our Own Bones: Disability Wisdom and the Spiritual Subversiveness of Knowing Ourselves Whole*, you might "trace the lines of the palms of [your] own hands," and find, feel and claim "the holiness of [your] own bones."

THE WHEEL OF THE YEAR

The Jewish calendar is a many-layered masterpiece of time. It is both lunar and solar, both myth-based and history-based. Its sacred days have natural, historical, communal and mystical components. Its most ancient holidays are connected to the Sumerian and Babylonian calendars, while its most recent occasions relate to events in the last century. We invite deep encounter with the Jewish calendar as part of the use of this siddur.

We understand the Jewish calendar as a way of experiencing nature as a spiritual practice. Passover, or Pesach, is not only a holiday of freedom but the beginning of the grain harvest. During this spring festival, the seed frees itself from the ground as the people free themselves from Egypt. Chanukah, the winter holiday that memorializes a victory over the Syrian-Greeks, is not only a tale of national self-determination but also a dark-of-the-moon winter solstice holiday. As we move through the year, we note the ways that the calendar teaches us the rhythms of the earth.

We also experience the calendar as an encoding of Goddess wisdom. On Tu b'Shevat, we celebrate Goddess as Tree and remember that the earliest goddess of the Hebrews, Asherah, was revered in and through trees. On Purim, when Jews read the book of Esther, we consider the connections between Esther and her namesake, the goddess Ishtar. On Passover, we think of the crossing of the Sea as a birthing of the people through the watery birth canal of the Divine Mother.

We celebrate Shabbat, the Sabbath, in a variety of ways, from relatively traditional observance to a more freeform remembering of the day. We embrace Shabbat as a time of rest, communion with nature, and awareness of our connection with the earth and all her creatures. Like the Jewish mystics of Safed, we imagine Shabbat as the time when Shekhinah enters the world in the fullest way.

THE *NETIVOT*: WAYS OF BEING

Netivah (plural *netivot*) is a Hebrew word for path or way of being. In the book of Proverbs, we hear of Wisdom that all "her ways are pleasant, and all her paths (netivot) are peace." We use this word netivah to refer to priestess/Goddess paths: ways of being that embody a particular form of the sacred feminine.

Interactions with wise women, spirit-workers, mothers, healers, queens, and temple-keepers have shaped the stories of the Jewish people, even though those interactions have been reshaped or repressed to fit the text's agenda. We feel that spiritual leaders of all genders have the right to know and respect their earliest history, and have worked to both recover and re-imagine these roles through study, ritual, movement, music, spirit journey and experiential learning. These pathways are archetypes which guide our reclaiming the priestess/exxhood. The *netivot* help to structure our siddur, and we encourage you to engage or encounter them in prayer and meditation space. You'll find them named on page 112/113 and explored in-depth in our book *The Hebrew Priestess: Ancient and New Visions of Jewish Women's Spiritual Leadership*.

This is the original wheel of the *netivot* that we first used in the Kohenet community. Some of the terminology today we use today is slightly different. We continue to use this wheel in honor of Yosefa R'faela haKohenet of blessed memory, who created it.

Tree of Life, you are seared stump

and seed. Weaver and stoneworker,

you spin the thread of life

and carve the channel through to death.

Womb of ice and sun, you scatter snow

and melt the fishponds.

Gate and boundary, you are a door to the stars

and a wall between atoms.

You are the dance floor and the eulogy,

From umbilical cord to umbilical cord, you weave.

You are the skin we wrap around our hollows,

and you are the marrows of our bones.

You are the infused oil of memory,

and the blood that forgets again, again, again.

You flow through us when we

bathe the child and dip the bride and wash the dead.

In all the worlds we say your names.

Jill Hammer

עוֹמֶק רוֹם וְעוֹמֶק תָּחַת
עוֹמֶק מִזְרָח וְעוֹמֶק מַעֲרָב
עוֹמֶק צָפוֹן וְעוֹמֶק דָרוֹם
וְהֵיכַל הַקוֹדֶשׁ מְכֻוָּן בָּאֶמְצַע

omek rom ve'omek tachat
omek mizrach ve'omek ma'arav
omek tzafon ve'omek darom
veheichal hakodesh mechuvan be'emtza

A depth of above and a depth of below
A depth of east and a depth of west
A depth of north and a depth of south
And the holy shrine in the center

Sefer Yetzirah 1:7

KABBALAT SHABBAT
RECEIVING THE SABBATH

On the Sabbath eve, in tradition, the psalms and poems of Kabbalat Shabbat (receiving the Sabbath) precede the evening prayers. According to the Talmud, the sages of the Gemara would put on their best clothes on Friday as the sun was setting and say "Come, o bride." The kabbalists of Sfat in the 16th century established the custom of going out into the fields on Friday evening to welcome the bride, the Shekhinah, embodied in the Sabbath. This custom evolved into the psalms and poems of Kabbalat Shabbat. Sephardic Jews recite the Song of Songs, considered to be a love poem between God and the Jewish people, at this time.

The kabbalists dedicated Kabbalat Shabbat to the union between Shekhinah and the Holy One of Blessing—the immanent/feminine and transcendent/masculine aspects of God described in kabbalistic lore. Ethiopian Jews have understood Shabbat to be God's beloved daughter. Some may choose to adopt these understanding of Kabbalat Shabbat, while others may prefer less traditional readings. At Kohenet, one way we choose to think about Kabbalat Shabbat is as a moment of union between the one and the many, between the multitude of separate beings and Being itself.

KNOWER OF SECRETS

Blessed Wisdom Pool of Blessing
Water of Life
Spirit of the World
Come from North South East and West
Tree of Life
Living and Evergiving Well
Divine Weaver
Her Ways are Paths of Peace
Tzimtzemai, Knower of Secrets, Come

Yocheved Landsman

EIT DODIM

עֵת דּוֹדִים כַּלָּה בּוֹאִי לְגַנִּי
פָּרְחָה הַגֶּפֶן הֵנֵצוּ הָרִמּוֹנִים
נְרַנְּנָה נְזַמְּרָה
עֵת שִׂמְחָה וְעֵת אַהֲבָה
בּוֹאִי לְגַנִּי

eit dodim kalah bo'i legani
parcha hagefen heineitzu harimonim
neranena nezamera
eit simcha ve'eit ahavah
bo'i legani

It is the time of love, my beloved/my bride,
come into my garden.
The grapevine has flowered,
the pomegranates have blossomed.
Let us sing and rejoice.
A time of joy, a time of love,
come into my garden.

Shalom Shabazi, adapted from Song of Songs

BEHOLD HOW GOOD!

הִנֵּה מַה טּוֹב וּמַה נָּעִים
שֶׁבֶת אַחִים/אֲחָיוֹת גַּם יָחַד

hinei mah tov u'mah na'im
shevet achim/achayot gam yachad

Behold how good this is!

Taya Shere, from Psalm 133

SHABBAT HAMALKAH

הַחַמָּה מֵרֹאשׁ הָאִילָנוֹת נִסְתַּלְּקָה
בּוֹאוּ וְנֵצֵא לִקְרַאת שַׁבָּת הַמַּלְכָּה
הִנֵּה הִיא יוֹרֶדֶת הַקְּדוֹשָׁה הַבְּרוּכָה
וְעִמָּהּ מַלְאָכִים צְבָא שָׁלוֹם וּמְנוּחָה
בּוֹאִי בּוֹאִי הַמַּלְכָּה
בּוֹאִי בּוֹאִי הַכַּלָּה
שָׁלוֹם עֲלֵיכֶם מַלְאֲכֵי הַשָּׁלוֹם

hachamah meirosh ha'ilanot nistalkah
bo'u venetzei likrat shabbat hamalkah
hinei hi yoredet hakedoshah haberuchah
ve'imah malachim tzvah shalom umenuchah
bo'i bo'i hamalkah, bo'i bo'i hakallah
shalom aleichem, malachei hashalom.

The sun looks out from the tops of the trees.
Come gather to greet Shabbat the queen.
She comes down to us holy and blessed,
And with Her, Her angels of peace and of rest.
Come, o queen. Come o bride.
Blessings to you, o angels of peace.

Hayyim Nachman Bialik

PEACE TO YOU ANGELS
(SHALOM ALEICHEM)

Peace to you angels, angels of peace (x2)
Come in peace, angels,
bless us with peace, angels,
and when you go, angels,
go in peace!

Taya Shere

PEACE BE WITH YOU
(SHALOM ALAYICH)

shalom alayich adamah	שָׁלוֹם עָלַיִךְ אֲדָמָה
shalom alayich levanah	שָׁלוֹם עָלַיִךְ לְבָנָה
shalom aleichem kochavim	שָׁלוֹם עֲלֵיכֶם עֲנָנִים
shalom aleichem tzemachim	שָׁלוֹם עֲלֵיכֶם צְמָחִים
shalom aleichem domemim	שָׁלוֹם עֲלֵיכֶם דוֹמְמִים
shalom aleichem ruchei chayim	שָׁלוֹם עֲלֵיכֶם רוּחוֹת חַיִּים
shalom aleichen nishmot adam	שָׁלוֹם עֲלֵיכֶן נִשְׁמוֹת אָדָם
shalom aleichem mei hayam	שָׁלוֹם עֲלֵיכֶם מֵי הַיָּם
shalom alayich shekhinah	שָׁלוֹם עָלַיִךְ שְׁכִינָה
shalom alecha almah	שָׁלוֹם עָלֶיךָ עָלְמָא

Peace be with you, earth!
Peace be with you, moon!
Peace be with you, clouds!
Peace be with you, trees and plants!
Peace be with you, stones!
Peace be with you, living things!
Peace be with you, human people!
Peace be with you, waters of the sea!
Peace be with you, Shekhinah!
Peace be with you, World!

Jill Hammer

◻ FEMININE

שָׁלוֹם עֲלֵיכֶן shalom aleichen
מַלְאֲכִיּוֹת הַשָׁרֵת malachiot hashareit
מַלְאֲכִיּוֹת עֶלְיוֹנָה malachiot elyona
מִמַלְכַּת מַלְכוֹת הַמְּלָכוֹת mimalkat malchot hamlachot
עִלָּאָה בְּרוּכָה הִיא ila'ah beruchah hi

בּוֹאֲכֶן לְשָׁלוֹם boachen leshalom
מַלְאֲכִיּוֹת הַשָּׁלוֹם malachiot hashalom
מַלְאֲכִיּוֹת עֶלְיוֹנָה malachiot elyona
מִמַלְכַּת מַלְכוֹת הַמְּלָכוֹת mimalkat malchot hamlachot
עִלָּאָה בְּרוּכָה הִיא ila'ah beruchah hi

בָּרְכוּנִי לְשָׁלוֹם barchuni leshalom
מַלְאֲכִיּוֹת הַשָּׁלוֹם malachiot hashalom
מַלְאֲכִיּוֹת עֶלְיוֹנָה malachiot elyona
מִמַלְכַּת מַלְכוֹת הַמְּלָכוֹת mimalkat malchot hamlachot
עִלָּאָה בְּרוּכָה הִיא ila'ah beruchah hi

צֵאתְכֶן לְשָׁלוֹם tzeitchen leshalom
מַלְאֲכִיּוֹת הַשָּׁלוֹם malachiot hashalom
מַלְאֲכִיּוֹת עֶלְיוֹנָה malachiot elyona
מִמַלְכַּת מַלְכוֹת הַמְּלָכוֹת mimalkat malchot hamlachot
עִלָּאָה בְּרוּכָה הִיא ila'ah beruchah hi

Bless us with peace
messengers of peace
messengers of the Highest One
you who have come from the ruler of rulers
the Blessed Holy One

Depart in peace
messengers of peace
messengers of the Highest One
you who have come from the power of powers
the Blessed Exalted One

△ MASCULINE

שָׁלוֹם עֲלֵיכֶם	shalom aleichem
מַלְאֲכֵי הַשָּׁרֵת	malachei hashareit
מַלְאֲכֵי עֶלְיוֹן	malachei elyon
מִמֶּלֶךְ מַלְכֵי הַמְּלָכִים	mimelekh malachei ham'lachim
הַקָּדוֹשׁ בָּרוּךְ הוּא	hakadosh baruch hu
בּוֹאֲכֶם לְשָׁלוֹם	boachem leshalom
מַלְאֲכֵי הַשָּׁלוֹם	malachei hashalom
מַלְאֲכֵי עֶלְיוֹן	malachei elyon
מִמֶּלֶךְ מַלְכֵי הַמְּלָכִים	mimelekh malachei ham'lachim
הַקָּדוֹשׁ בָּרוּךְ הוּא	hakadosh baruch hu
בָּרְכוּנִי לְשָׁלוֹם	barchuni leshalom
מַלְאֲכֵי הַשָּׁלוֹם	malachei hashalom
מַלְאֲכֵי עֶלְיוֹן	malachei elyon
מִמֶּלֶךְ מַלְכֵי הַמְּלָכִים	mimelekh malachei ham'lachim
הַקָּדוֹשׁ בָּרוּךְ הוּא	hakadosh baruch hu
צֵאתְכֶם לְשָׁלוֹם	tzeitchem leshalom
מַלְאֲכֵי הַשָּׁלוֹם	malachei hashalom
מַלְאֲכֵי עֶלְיוֹן	malachei elyon
מִמֶּלֶךְ מַלְכֵי הַמְּלָכִים	mimelekh malachei ham'lachim
הַקָּדוֹשׁ בָּרוּךְ הוּא	hakadosh baruch hu

Peace be to you
messengers of peace
messengers of the Highest One
you who have come from the king of kings
the Blessed Holy One

Come in peace
messengers of peace
messengers of the Highest One
you who have come from the queen of queens
the Blessed Exalted One

WELCOMING THE ELEMENTS

From the four ethereal elements
all the hidden worlds were created,
and these are the four letters of the divine name.

Hayyim Vital, Sha'arei Kedushah 1:1

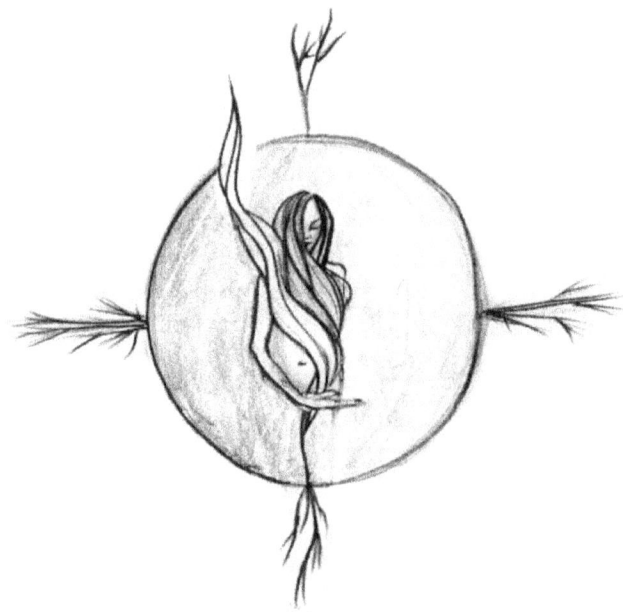

ANGELS OF FIRE

Angels of fire,
light our way through time's labyrinth
to its center.

Angels of wind,
breathe with us till we find the stillness
inside the breath.

Angels of water,
swim with us to the depths of the well
where the world drinks.

Angels of earth,
arise from the soil, bow down with us
to the day's end.

Jill Hammer

BIRTH OF THE ELEMENTS

הַמַּיִם הָרוּ וְיָלְדוּ אֲפֵלָה hamayim haru veyaldu afeilah
הָאֵשׁ הָרָה וְיָלְדָה אוֹר ha'eish harah   veyaldah or
הָרוּחַ הָרָה וְיָלְדָה חָכְמָה haruach harah veyaldah chochmah
הֶעָפָר הָרָה וְיָלְדָה חַיִּים he'afar harah   veyaldah chayim

In the beginning,
Water conceived and gave birth to darkness.
Fire conceived and gave birth to light.
Wind conceived and gave birth to wisdom.
Earth conceived and gave birth to life.

Adapted from Exodus Rabbah 13:3

ELEMENTAL MEDITATION

Call forth a moment of earth:
wood, stone, soil.

Call forth a moment of water:
ocean, stream, rain.

Call forth a moment of air:
wind, song, breath.

Call forth a moment of fire:
candle, sun, lightning.

Let these moments ground you
as you open your heart to pray.

Jill Hammer

LA ORASION DE LA MUJER

Kun estas kandelas	With these candles
Arrogamos al Dio	We pray to God
El Dio de muestros madres	The God of our mothers
Sara, Rifka, Lea i Rachel	Sarah, Rebecca, Leah and Rachel
Ke muz de vida saludoza	To grant a good, whole life
A todus miz keriduz	To all my dear ones
I al mundo intero	And the whole world
Kun estas kandelas	With these candles
Arrogamos al Dio	We pray to God
El Dio de muestros padres	The God of our fathers
Avram, Isak i Yakov	Abraham, Isaac and Jacob
Ke muz de vida saludoza	To grant a good, whole life
A todus miz keriduz	To all my dear ones
I al mundo intero	And the whole world

Women's prayer, Spain, 1492

Holy Shekhinah,
as You descend on wings of the Sabbath,
give me the grace
to perceive the living soul
you have placed within me.

May I feel Your love within.

May my loved ones, my community,
and my world know the peace and healing of Your presence.

As You spread your shelter over us,
teach us to spread compassion wherever we go,
knowing that all beings are kindled from Your light.

בְּרוּכָה אַתְּ שְׁכִינָה ☐ beruchah at shekhinah
אֱלֹתֵינוּ רוּחַ הָעוֹלָם eloteinu ruach ha'olam
אֲשֶׁר קִדְּשַׁתְנוּ בְּמִצְוֹתֶיהָ וְצִוַּתְנוּ asher kidshatnu bemitzvoteha vetzivatnu
לְהַדְלִיק נֵר שֶׁל שַׁבָּת. lehadlik ner shel shabbat.

בָּרוּךְ אַתָּה יהוה △ baruch ata adonai
אֱלֹהֵינוּ מֶלֶךְ הָעוֹלָם eloheinu melekh ha'olam
אֲשֶׁר קִדְּשָׁנוּ בְּמִצְוֹתָיו וְצִוָּנוּ asher kidshanu bemitzvotav vetzivanu
לְהַדְלִיק נֵר שֶׁל שַׁבָּת. lehadlik ner shel shabbat.

בְּרוּכֶה אַתֵּה יָה ⊖ berucheh ate yah
אֱלֹהֵינוּ רוּחַ הָעוֹלָם eloheinu ruach ha'olam
אֲשֶׁר קִדְּשֵׁנוּ בְּמִצְוֹתֶה וְצִוֵּנוּ asher kidshenu bemitzvoteh vetzivenu
לְהַדְלִיק נֵר שֶׁל שַׁבָּת. lehadlik ner shel shabbat.

Blessed are You, Indwelling Presence filling and surrounding the world,
who makes us holy with your sacred acts, and commands us to kindle the Sabbath lights.

Sing to Goddess a new song.
Sing to Goddess, all the earth.
Sing to Goddess, bless the Name:
each day, tell of grace.

Tell among nations of the Presence.
Tell among peoples of wonders,
for the Source of Life is vast
and to be deeply honored,

inspiring more awe
that all we call divine—
for the forms and names
we have for deity shift,

but the Source of Life wove the heights.
Glory and beauty walk before Her;
strength and magnificence
dwell in Her shrine.

Surrender, you holy beings!
Surrender to Being's glory and strength!
Open to the One whose name is Presence!
Take up your gift and go on pilgrimage!

Bow down before Mystery
in the beauty of the shrine:
all earth, tremble before the Face!
Say among the peoples:

Divinity has designed
the cosmos will never be shaken,
so let the people preserve it fairly.
Let the skies rejoice! Let the earth be glad!

Let the sea roar, and all its fullness!
Let the fields and their creatures make merry,
and let trees of the forest sing with joy
before Goddess, for oh! She is coming!

coming to know the earth,
to guide the globe rightly
and its peoples faithfully.

The Name of God may be pronounced in many ways but in the transliteration has been rendered as Elah, *Goddess. The word* elilim, *idols, has been changed to* alilim, *crucibles, reminding us that different faces of God, each with flaws and gifts, help us arrive at the oneness of Being.*

PSALM 96 FEMINIZED

shiru la'elah shir hadash
shiru la'elah kol ha'aretz
shiru la'elah barchu shemah
basru miyom leyom yeshuatah

sapru vagoyim kevodah
bechol ha'amim nifloteha
ki gedolah elah
umhulelet me'od

norah hi
al kol elohim
ki kol elohei ha'amim
alilim*

ve'elah shamayim astah
hod vehadar lefaneha
oz vetiferet
bemikdashah

havu la'elah mishpechot ha'amim
havu la'elah kavod va'oz
havu la'elah kavod shmah
se'u minchah uvo'u lechatzroteha

hishtachavu la'elah
behadrat kodesh
chilu mipaneha kol ha'aretz
imru vagoyim

elah malka
af tikon tevel bal timot
tadin amim bemeisharim
yismechu ha'shamayim vatagel ha'aretz

yiram hayam umelo'o
yaaloz sadai vekol asher bo
az yeranenu kol atzei ya'ar
lifnei elah ki va'ah

ki va'ah lishpot ha'aretz
tishpot tevel betzedek
ve'amim be'emunatah

שִׁירוּ לַירהוה* שִׁיר חָדָשׁ
שִׁירוּ לַירהוה כָּל הָאָרֶץ.
שִׁירוּ לַירהוה בָּרְכוּ שְׁמָהּ
בַּשְּׂרוּ מִיּוֹם לְיוֹם יְשׁוּעָתָהּ.

סַפְּרוּ בַגּוֹיִם כְּבוֹדָהּ
בְּכָל הָעַמִּים נִפְלְאוֹתֶיהָ.
כִּי גְדוֹלָה ירהוה
וּמְהֻלֶּלֶת מְאֹד

נוֹרָאָה הִיא
עַל כָּל אֱלֹהִים
כִּי כָּל אֱלֹהֵי הָעַמִּים
עֲלִילִים*

וַירהוה שָׁמַיִם עָשָׂתָה.
הוֹד וְהָדָר לְפָנֶיהָ
עֹז וְתִפְאֶרֶת
בְּמִקְדָּשָׁהּ

הָבוּ לַירהוה מִשְׁפְּחוֹת עַמִּים
הָבוּ לַירהוה כָּבוֹד וָעֹז.
הָבוּ לַירהוה כְּבוֹד שְׁמָהּ
שְׂאוּ מִנְחָה וּבֹאוּ לְחַצְרוֹתֶיהָ

הִשְׁתַּחֲווּ לַירהוה
בְּהַדְרַת קֹדֶשׁ
חִילוּ מִפָּנֶיהָ כָּל הָאָרֶץ
אִמְרוּ בַגּוֹיִם

ירהוה מַלְכָּה
אַף תִּכּוֹן תֵּבֵל בַּל תִּמּוֹט
תָּדִין עַמִּים בְּמֵישָׁרִים.
יִשְׂמְחוּ הַשָּׁמַיִם וְתָגֵל הָאָרֶץ

יִרְעַם הַיָּם וּמְלֹאוֹ.
יַעֲלֹז שָׂדַי וְכָל אֲשֶׁר בּוֹ
אָז יְרַנְּנוּ כָּל עֲצֵי יָעַר
לִפְנֵי ירהוה כִּי בָאָה

כִּי בָאָה לִשְׁפֹּט הָאָרֶץ.
תִּשְׁפֹּט תֵּבֵל בְּצֶדֶק
וְעַמִּים בֶּאֱמוּנָתָהּ.

RECEIVING THE SABBATH

Let the heavens be glad and the earth rejoice
Let the sea and its fullness exult.

Goddess is:
the earth is happy;
each little island is joyful.

Clouds and mist surround Her;
righteousness and justice
stand as Her sentinels.

Fire walks before Her,
consumes all obstacles.
Her lightning lights the earth—

the earth watches and trembles.
Mountains melt like candlewax
before the One who supports the world.

The skies call out about Her;
all that lives perceives Her presence.

Zion hears and is happy.
The daughters of Judah dance with joy
because of all this rightness!

For you, Goddess,
are transcendence
clothed in the real.

How much loftier and deeper you are
than our ideas about You!

Your beloveds turn away from cruelty.
The Guardian of faithful souls
saves them from evildoing.

Light is sown for the righteous;
joy for the openhearted.

O you who seek righteousness, rejoice in Goddess.
Be thankful you have known this holiness.

The Hebrew of this psalm has been feminized and YHWH has been rendered "Shekhinah" in transliteration. One verse has been removed, in order to avoid condemning the deities of other nations. The translation of this psalm was written for and also appears in the Romemu Siddur.

SELECTION FROM PSALM 96

yismechu hashamayim vetagel ha'aretz
yiram hayam umelo'o

יִשְׂמְחוּ הַשָּׁמַיִם וְתָגֵל הָאָרֶץ
יִרְעַם הַיָּם וּמְלֹאוֹ

PSALM 97

shekhinah malka
tagel ha'aretz
yismechu iyim rabim

יהוה מָלְכָה
תָּגֵל הָאָרֶץ
יִשְׂמְחוּ אִיִּים רַבִּים

ana ve'arafel seviveha
tzedek umishpat
mechon kisah

עָנָן וַעֲרָפֶל סְבִיבָיהָ
צֶדֶק וּמִשְׁפָּט
מְכוֹן כִּסְאָהּ

esh lefaneha telech
ut'laheit saviv tzarav
he'iru verakeha tevel

אֵשׁ לְפָנֶיהָ תֵּלֵךְ
וּתְלַהֵט סָבִיב צָרֶיהָ
הֵאִירוּ בְרָקֶיהָ תֵּבֵל

ra'atah vetachel ha'aretz
harim kadonag namasu
milifnei shekhinah milifnei eden kol ha'aretz

רָאֲתָה וַתָּחֵל הָאָרֶץ
הָרִים כַּדּוֹנַג נָמַסּוּ
מִלִּפְנֵי יהוה מִלִּפְנֵי אֲדוֹן כָּל הָאָרֶץ

higidu shamayim tzidkah
vera'u kol ha'amim kevodah

הִגִּידוּ הַשָּׁמַיִם צִדְקָהּ
וְרָאוּ כָל הָעַמִּים כְּבוֹדָהּ

shamah vatismach tzion
vatagelna b'not yehudah
lma'an mishpatayich shekhinah

שָׁמְעָה וַתִּשְׂמַח צִיּוֹן
וַתָּגֵלְנָה בְּנוֹת יְהוּדָה
לְמַעַן מִשְׁפָּטַיִךְ יהוה

ki at
shekhinah elyonah
al kol ha'aretz

כִּי אַתְּ
יהוה עֶלְיוֹנָה
עַל כָּל הָאָרֶץ

me'od na'aleita
al kol elohim

מְאֹד נַעֲלֵית
עַל כָּל אֱלֹהִים.

ohavei shekhinah sinu ra
shomeret nafshot chasidoteha
miyad resha'im tatzilem

אֹהֲבֵי יהוה שִׂנְאוּ רָע
שֹׁמֶרֶת נַפְשׁוֹת חֲסִידוֹתֶיהָ
מִיַּד רְשָׁעִים תַּצִּילֵם

or zarua latzadikah
uleyishrei lev simcha

אוֹר זָרֻעַ לַצַּדִּיקָה
וּלְיִשְׁרֵי לֵב שִׂמְחָה.

simchu tzadikot bashkhinah
vehodu lezecher kodshah

שִׂמְחוּ צַדִּיקוֹת בַּיהוה
וְהוֹדוּ לְזֵכֶר קָדְשָׁהּ.

RECEIVING THE SABBATH 20

SHAM'AH VATISMACH TZION

שָׁמְעָה וַתִּשְׂמַח צִיּוֹן וַתָּגֵלְנָה בְּנוֹת יְהוּדָה
לְמַעַן מִשְׁפָּטַיךְ שְׁכִינָה

shamah vetismach tzion vatagelna b'not yehuda
l'maan mishpatayich shekhinah

Mother Zion hears and delights
and the daughters of Judah are happy
because of your precepts, Everpresent One.

Psalm 97:8

OR ZARUA

אוֹר זָרֻעַ לַצַּדִּיקָה
וּלְיִשְׁרוֹת לֵב שִׂמְחָה

אוֹר זָרֻעַ לַצַּדִּיק
וּלְיִשְׁרֵי לֵב שִׂמְחָה

or zarua latzadikah uleyishrot lev simcha
or zarua latzadik uleyishrei lev simcha

כִּי עִמָּךְ מְקוֹר חַיִּים
בְּאוֹרֵךְ נִרְאֶה אוֹר

כִּי עִמְּךָ מְקוֹר חַיִּים
בְּאוֹרְךָ נִרְאֶה אוֹר

ki eemach m'kor chayyim b'oreich nireh or
ki eemcha m'kor chayyim b'orcha nir'eh or

Plant seeds of light by doing right
Align in joy, polish your heart

For with you is the source of life, in your light we see light.

Psalm 97:11, Psalm 36:10, and Shir Meira Feit

REVELATION

> "I revealed myself to those who didn't ask for me." –*Isaiah 65:1*

> "I Posed in a Bikini in Times Square." –*Cosmopolitan article by Anna O'Brien*

You whisper, grin, push me away, question
whether I'm really there, tell yourself
it doesn't matter

even if I am. Sometimes,
you provoke me to my face.
Usually, though, you keep yourself busy,

eating food that makes you hungry,
worrying about money
and what to do with your body,

eager to pay attention
to anything
but who you are to me. You

are a vigil I keep;
a flock I pasture;
a grape on the vine

still bursting with blessing
even at the end of harvest,
and I'm the light

you're afraid of losing,
the light in which I'm revealing
what it means to be human.

Not an indecipherable mess; not a pot
of meat and feeling,
or a headstone covered in body paint,

or a burning garden, or irony sweating.
A new song
you and I are singing,

me through you and you through me,
about the earth and heaven
and the love

you and I are making.

Joy Ladin

SINGING

> "Sing out O barren one,
> who has not given birth,
> break out into song, shout for joy,
> one who had no labor pains..."
> —*Isaiah 54:1*

> "Why This Woman Is Proud to Be Known as
> 'The Pageant Queen Without a Uterus.'"
> —*Cosmopolitan article by Alex Rees*

Before you were a fetus,
before you were an egg,
you were a song

I was already singing,
a promise
I'd already kept.

I stretch out your curtains,
strengthen your pegs,
make room inside you for the world

I created you to share. You
are my embryo
and I am your womb;

you're my labor pains
and I'm the mother pushing you
to cry, to talk, to stand for something,

to stop being scared
of the joy
rising like waters in the days of Noah,

flooding your foundations,
crowning your head,
answering every question

I created you to ask.
Why you feel incomplete,
like a tiara without a pageant.

Why you mistake affliction for love
and love, my love,
for affliction.

Why you just start crying
when, for a moment, you hear me singing
the secret you forget you're keeping: you

are the child of a queen.
Why it always feels like
the first time to you,
the first shaking of your mountains,

the first bursting into flame,
the very first season
of your first reality show

on which a queen with a whirlwind
where a uterus should be
whose presence fills you with fear

keeps waiting for you
to say "I do"
to the love, my love,

that never stops singing
and follows you
everywhere.

Joy Ladin

Offer this moment up,
images of the divine—

in beauty and strength
invite the presence-name.

Offer this moment up—
a shrine of place and time.

Offer this moment, an ocean—
many waves of being.

A divine voice rides
on these waters.

Hear the power and
beauty of that voice,
cleaving the tree-trunks of our stories,
shaking the mountain forests,
making our shattered fragments dance
and play like lambs and calves.

That voice kindles flame,
awakening the desert within,
bringing wild things to birth,

stirring up the inner forest:
the sacred place where all cries:

This! This!

Above the primordial deep,
above time's spiral,
presence hovers.

To open to this is strength.
To open to this is peace.

PSALM 29

mizmor l'david havu l'adonai b'nei elim	מִזְמוֹר לְדָוִד הָבוּ לַיהוה בְּנֵי אֵלִים
havu ladonai kavod va'oz havu l'adonai kevod shemo	הָבוּ לַיהוה כָּבוֹד וָעֹז הָבוּ לַיהוה כְּבוֹד שְׁמוֹ
hishtachavu l'adonai behadrat kodesh	הִשְׁתַּחֲווּ לַיהוה בְּהַדְרַת קֹדֶשׁ
kol adonai al hamayim el hakavod hirim	קוֹל יהוה עַל הַמָּיִם אֵל הַכָּבוֹד הִרְעִים
adonai al mayim rabim	יהוה עַל מַיִם רַבִּים
kol adonai bakoach kol adonai behadar kol adonai shover arazim vayeshabeir adonai et arzei hal'vanon vayarkideim kemo egel levanon vesirion kemo vein re'eimim	קוֹל יהוה בַּכֹּחַ קוֹל יהוה בֶּהָדָר קוֹל יהוה שֹׁבֵר אֲרָזִים וַיְשַׁבֵּר יהוה אֶת אַרְזֵי הַלְּבָנוֹן וַיַּרְקִידֵם כְּמוֹ עֵגֶל לְבָנוֹן וְשִׂרְיֹן כְּמוֹ בֶן רְאֵמִים
kol adonai chotzev lahavot eish kol adonai yachil midbar yachil adonai midbar kadeish	קוֹל יהוה חֹצֵב לַהֲבוֹת אֵשׁ קוֹל יהוה יָחִיל מִדְבָּר יָחִיל יהוה מִדְבַּר קָדֵשׁ
kol adonai yecholeil ayalot veyechesof ye'arot uv'hechalo	קוֹל יהוה יְחוֹלֵל אַיָּלוֹת וַיֶּחֱשֹׂף יְעָרוֹת וּבְהֵיכָלוֹ
kulo omeir kavod	כֻּלּוֹ אֹמֵר כָּבוֹד
adonai lamabul yashav vayeshev adonai melekh le'olam	יהוה לַמַּבּוּל יָשָׁב וַיֵּשֶׁב יהוה מֶלֶךְ לְעוֹלָם
adonai oz le'amo yiten adonai yevareich et amo vashalom	יהוה עֹז לְעַמּוֹ יִתֵּן יהוה יְבָרֵךְ אֶת עַמּוֹ בַשָּׁלוֹם

ANA B'CHOACH

אָנָא בְּכֹחַ גְּדֻלַת יְמִינְךָ תַּתִּיר צְרוּרָה

ana b'choach g'dulat yemincha tatir tzerurah

Goddess please help us now, with your strength and great knowhow
untie our tangles and set us free

קַבֵּל רִנַּת עַמְּךָ שַׂגְּבֵינוּ טַהֲרֵינוּ נוֹרָא

kabel rinat amcha sagveynu tahareynu norah

Goddess please shelter us make us clear and help us see
Please bless us and how we be

arrangement and English lyrics by Taya Shere

GRACE

How do you sense that someone, from a distance,
is watching you? We each pray to the other, and to
the ghost of the other, and to that third thing
that is watching. We will pray until we pray
love into form. Until love is, and we are in it.
In the bright alive mouth at its center, held
on the lion's tongue. I pray so that
the day it comes, I will be empty. I will be
hungry for it. Sunlit, the way home was, but infinite.

Nina Pick

HERE AND NOW

I live in time
and out of time
by inner experience.
For all of us,
at every instant,
it is possible to do so.
Then, the garden
is Here and Now.

Colette Aboulker-Moscat, from "How to Live"

I REMEMBER (ZACHARTI)

זָכַרְתִּי לָךְ חֶסֶד נְעוּרַיִךְ
אַהֲבַת כְּלוּלֹתָיִךְ

zacharti lach chesed ne'urayich
ahavat kelulotayich

I remember your love
and your kindness
When you walked with me
through desert wildness

I remember (6x)
I remember you

לֶכְתֵּךְ אַחֲרַי בַּמִּדְבָּר
בְּאֶרֶץ לֹא זְרוּעָה

leichteich acharai bamidbar
leichteich acharai b'eretz lo z'rua

How you walked with me
When you were young and free
How you walked with me
Through the sand and sea

I remember (6x)
I remember you

Shoshana Jedwab, based on Jeremiah 2:2

RECEIVING THE SABBATH

COME, BELOVED (L'CHA DODI)

לְכָה דוֹדִי לִקְרַאת כַּלָּה פְּנֵי שַׁבָּת נְקַבְּלָה

l'cha dodi likrat kala, penei shabbat nekabela.

Come, beloved, to greet the Bride, and let us welcome the Sabbath.

שָׁמוֹר וְזָכוֹר בְּדִבּוּר אֶחָד, הִשְׁמִיעָנוּ אֵל הַמְּיֻחָד
יהוה אַחַת וּשְׁמָהּ אֶחָד לְשֵׁם וּלְתִפְאֶרֶת וְלִתְהִלָּה

shamor vezachor bedibur echad, hishmi'anu el ham'yuchad.
havayah achat ushemah echad, lesheim ul'tiferet velit'hila.

The One who weaves all together caused us to hear both "keep" and "remember."
Being is One and Oneness is its name, in beauty and songs of praise.

לִקְרַאת שַׁבָּת לְכוּ וְנֵלְכָה, כִּי הִיא מְקוֹר הַבְּרָכָה
מֵרֹאשׁ מִקֶּדֶם נְסוּכָה, סוֹף מַעֲשֶׂה בְּמַחֲשָׁבָה תְּחִלָּה

likrat shabat lechu venelcha, ki hi mekor habracha.
meirosh mikedem nesucha, sof ma'aseh, bemachshava techila.

Let us go to greet the Sabbath for she is the Wellspring of Blessing,
anointed before creation's dawn; first conceived, last born.

מִקְדַּשׁ מֶלֶךְ עִיר מְלוּכָה, קוּמִי צְאִי מִתּוֹךְ הַהֲפֵכָה
רַב לָךְ שֶׁבֶת בְּעֵמֶק הַבָּכָא, וְהוּא יַחֲמֹל עָלַיִךְ חֶמְלָה

mikdash melech ir meluchah, kumi tze'i mitoch hahafeichah
rav lach shevet be'eimek habacha, vehu yachamol alayich chemlah

Royal Shrine and Regal City, arise from your tumult, for you have been long enough
in the valley of tears, and the Holy One has tenderness for you.

הִתְנַעֲרִי מֵעָפָר קוּמִי, לִבְשִׁי בִּגְדֵי תִפְאַרְתֵּךְ עַמִּי
עַל יַד צְמִיחַת יִשַׁי בֵּית הַלַּחְמִי, קָרְבָה אֶל נַפְשִׁי גְאָלָהּ

hitna'ari me'afar kumi, livshi bigdei tifarteich ami
al yad tzmichat yishai beit halachmi, karvah el nafshi ge'alah

Rise from the earth and become young again. Put on beauty's garments, you who are my
People. Through the Tree of Redemption, the House of Sustenance, let healing come.

הִתְעוֹרְרִי הִתְעוֹרְרִי, כִּי בָא אוֹרֵךְ קוּמִי אוֹרִי
עוּרִי עוּרִי שִׁיר דַּבֵּרִי, כְּבוֹד יהוה עָלַיִךְ נִגְלָה

hitoreri, hitoreri, ki va oreich! kumi, ori,
uri uri, shir dabeiri, kevod shekhinah alayich nigla.

Arise! Arise! Your light has come! Arise, my Light! Awake, sing a song!
The Immanent Glory shines through you!

לֹא תֵבוֹשִׁי וְלֹא תִכָּלְמִי, מַה תִּשְׁתּוֹחֲחִי וּמַה תֶּהֱמִי
בָּךְ יֶחֱסוּ עֲנִיֵּי עַמִּי, וְנִבְנְתָה עִיר עַל תִּלָּהּ

lo teivoshi velo tikalmi, mah tishtochachi umah tehemi
bach yechesu aniyei ami, venivnetah ir al tilah

Do not be shy or ashamed. Why cast yourself down into despair?
In you the poor will shelter, and the City will be built upon her ruins.

וְהָיוּ לִמְשִׁסָּה שֹׁאסָיִךְ, וְרָחֲקוּ כָּל מְבַלְּעָיִךְ
יָשִׂישׂ עָלַיִךְ אֱלֹהָיִךְ כִּמְשׂוֹשׂ אָהוּב וַאֲהוּבָה

vehayu limshisah shosayich, verachaku kol mevalayich
yasis alayich elohayich kimsos ahuv va'ahuvah

The destroyers will be destroyed. The swallowers will be sent away.
Your God will rejoice in you as lovers rejoice with one another.

יָמִין וּשְׂמֹאל תִּפְרוֹצִי וְאֶת יהוה תַּעֲרִיצִי
עַל יַד אֵשׁ בֶּן פַּרְצִי וְנִשְׂמְחָה וְנָגִילָה

yamin usmol tifrotzi ve'et adonai ta'aritzi
al yad eish bein partzi venismecha venagila

You will burst forth to right and left, inspired by Your Beloved,
aided by a redeeming flame that breaks through walls. We will be glad and rejoice!

בּוֹאִי בְשָׁלוֹם עֲטֶרֶת אַהֲבָה, גַּם בְּשִׂמְחָה וּבְצָהֳלָה
תּוֹךְ אֱמוּנֵי עַם סְגֻלָּה, בּוֹאִי כַלָּה, בּוֹאִי כַלָּה

bo'i veshalom, ateret ahavah; gam besimcha uvetsahala
toch emunei am segula. bo'i chalah bo'i chalah!

Come in peace, crown of love, in joy and in merriment
among the faithful of your treasured people. Come, O Beloved! Come, O Bride!

RECEIVING THE SABBATH 30

BOI KALLAH

בּוֹאִי בּוֹאִי בּוֹאִי כַלָּה
שַׁבָּת שַׁבָּת שַׁבָּת הַמַּלְכָּה

boi boi boi chalah
shabbat shabbat shabbat hamalka

Come come come to me
My beloved, my beautiful queen

Yael Schonzeit

MIZMOR SHIR LEYOM HASHABBAT

tov lehodot lashechinah	טוֹב לְהֹדוֹת לַירהוה
ul'zamer lishmeich elyon	וּלְזַמֵּר לְשִׁמְךָ עֶלְיוֹן.
l'hagid baboker chasdayich	לְהַגִּיד בַּבֹּקֶר חַסְדֶּיךָ
ve'emunateich baleylot	וֶאֱמוּנָתְךָ בַּלֵּילוֹת.
alei asor va'alei navel alei higayon vechinor	עֲלֵי עָשׂוֹר וַעֲלֵי נָבֶל עֲלֵי הִגָּיוֹן בְּכִנּוֹר.
ki simechatni yah befo'olayich	כִּי שִׂמַּחְתַּנִי ירהוה בְּפָעֳלֶךָ
bema'asei yadayich aranen	בְּמַעֲשֵׂי יָדֶיךָ אֲרַנֵּן.
mah gadlu ma'asayich lashechinah	מַה גָּדְלוּ מַעֲשֶׂיךָ ירהוה
me'od amku machshevotayich	מְאֹד עָמְקוּ מַחְשְׁבֹתֶיךָ.

You who dwell in forever, holy is your name
We find comfort in your ground, inspiration in your flame
To love, praise and serve you is our delight
We do good work with our day, sing Halleluyah all night!

Arrangement and English lyrics by Taya Shere, from Psalm 92

MEDITATION

Greet the presence of the Beloved as the Beloved appears to you:
friend, lover, child, elder, plant, animal, stone.
Let the Beloved enter, cloaked in the grace of evening.
Reverently receive that Love.

Jill Hammer

TEHOM

תְּהוֹם
אֶל
תְּהוֹם
קוֹרֵא

כֵּן נַפְשִׁי תַעֲרֹג אֵלָיִךְ
צָמְאָה נַפְשִׁי לֵאלֹהִים
כָּל מִשְׁבָּרָיִךְ וְגַלָּיִךְ עָלָי
יְשׁוּעֹת פָּנַי וֵאלֹהָי

tehom el tehom korei
keyn nafshi ta'arog eilayich
tzamah nafshi l'elohim
kol mishbarayich vegalayich alai
yeshuot panai velohai

From the deep I call to you
For you, my soul cries
My soul thirsts for you
You are sweeping me away
You are forever here with me

Arrangement and English lyrics by Taya Shere, based on Psalm 42

TEHOMOT ROLLS

tehomot rolls
all day
all night

bringing it in
bringing it out
bringing it up
bringing it down

all wrong
all right
all dark
all bright

salt on the sand
sand on the foam
foam in the hand
land on the deep

deep on the void
void in the steep
curve of the wave
lift me awake
rock me to sleep

Jill Hammer

MA'ARIVAH
THE EVENING PRAYER

Jewish tradition understands the daily prayers as offerings like those once made on Temple altars. The *maariv* or evening service represents the all-night burning of the ashes of the daily offerings upon the altar. This is a beautiful *kavvanah* (intention): the evening service is a time to offer up the ashes, the remnants, the leftovers of our day. During our *maarivah* (the feminine of *maariv*), we let go of the previous day. If it is Shabbat, we let go of the previous week. We open to the peace of prayer. We enter into the mystery of night, the wisdom of dreamspace, and the healing of rest.

CALL TO PRAYER (BARCHU)

Shekhinah precedes the universe
by myriad myriad years,
and as many years afterward.
The glory of the universe is
above and below, deep and profound.
It is in the east and west, north and south.
It is in all and it is all.
Rise up and give thanksgiving in the heart.

The Book of Raziel

LEADER

בָּרְכוּ אֶת הַבְּרֵכָה הַמְּבֹרֶכֶת

barchu et habereichah hamevorechet

Give blessing to the Pool of Blessing!

PARTICIPANTS

בְּרוּכָה הַבְּרֵכָה הַמְּבֹרֶכֶת לְעוֹלָם וָעֶד

beruchah habereichah hamevorechet le'olam va'ed

Give blessing to the Pool of Blessing from now until the end of time!

LEADER REPEATS

בְּרוּכָה הַבְּרֵכָה הַמְּבֹרֶכֶת לְעוֹלָם וָעֶד

beruchah habereichah hamevorechet le'olam va'ed

Give blessing to the Pool of Blessing from now until the end of time!

BLESSING FOR TIME
(MA'ARIVAH ARAVIM)

beruchah at shekhinah,	בְּרוּכָה אַתְּ שְׁכִינָה
eloheinu ruach ha'olam,	אֱלֹהֵינוּ רוּחַ הָעוֹלָם
asher b'dvarah ma'arivah aravim.	אֲשֶׁר בִּדְבָרָהּ מַעֲרִיבָה עֲרָבִים
bechochmah potachat she'arim	בְּחָכְמָה פּוֹתַחַת שְׁעָרִים
uvitvunah meshanah itim	וּבִתְבוּנָה מְשַׁנָּה עִתִּים
umachalifah et hazmanim	וּמַחֲלִיפָה אֶת הַזְּמַנִּים
umesaderet et hakochavim	וּמְסַדֶּרֶת אֶת הַכּוֹכָבִים
b'mishmeroteihem kirtzonah.	בְּמִשְׁמְרוֹתֵיהֶם בָּרָקִיעַ כִּרְצוֹנָהּ.
boreit yom velailah	בּוֹרֵאת יוֹם וָלַיְלָה
golelet or mipnei choshech	גּוֹלֶלֶת אוֹר מִפְּנֵי חֹשֶׁךְ
vechoshech mipnei or,	וְחֹשֶׁךְ מִפְּנֵי אוֹר
uma'avirah yom umeiviah lailah	וּמַעֲבִירָה יוֹם וּמְבִיאָה לַיְלָה
umavdilah bein yom uvein lailah	וּמַבְדִּילָה בֵּין יוֹם וּבֵין לַיְלָה
yah tzeva'ot sh'mah.	יָהּ צְבָאוֹת שְׁמָהּ
elah chaia vekayemet	אֱלָה חַיָּה וְקַיֶּמֶת
tamid timloch aleinu le'olam va'ed.	תָּמִיד תִּמְלוֹךְ עָלֵינוּ לְעוֹלָם וָעֶד.
beruchah at shekhinah	בְּרוּכָה אַתְּ שְׁכִינָה
hama'arivah aravim.	הַמַּעֲרִיבָה עֲרָבִים.

Blessed are You,
Weaver of the Cosmos,
for Your word spins evening into evening.
In wisdom You open the gates of time,
in understanding you fold
one moment into the next,
and change the seasons,
and order the stars on their paths in the sky,
according to Your design.
Weaving day and night,
winding light away before darkness
and darkness away before light,
you put the day away and bring the night,
dividing day from night,
the Tapestry of All are You.
Ever-living One,
always cause us to know your Presence.
Blessed are You, Infinite,
who makes evening into evening.

מַעֲרִיבָה עֲרָבִים

ma'arivah aravim

You who open up the gates of time

מַעֲרִיבָה עֲרָבִים

ma'arivah aravim

You who flow each moment so sublime

מַעֲרִיבָה עֲרָבִים

ma'arivah aravim

You who cycle forth the seasons

מַעֲרִיבָה עֲרָבִים

ma'arivah aravim

You who give life reason

מַעֲרִיבָה עֲרָבִים

ma'arivah aravim

You who roll the dark and spill the light

מַעֲרִיבָה עֲרָבִים

ma'arivah aravim

You who shine the day and soft the night

מַעֲרִיבָה עֲרָבִים

ma'arivah aravim

Taya Shere

HOLY

Holy Holy Holy Holy
Holy Holy Holy Holy Holy Holy

Holy is the silence and holy is the sound
Holy is each one of us and holy is the ground
Holy is the darkness and holy is the light
Holy is the morning and holy is the night

קָדוֹשׁ קָדוֹשׁ קָדוֹשׁ יהוה צְבָאוֹת
מְלֹא כָל הָאָרֶץ כְּבוֹדוֹ

kadosh kadosh kadosh adonai tzevaot
melo chol ha'aretz kevodo

lyrics and music by Taya Shere, additional verse Jill Hammer

HERE I COME

here i come, all of me: all of my love, passion, anger and desire. all of my wisdom, tenderness and hope. my blood, belly and breasts. my bones, bruises and blessings

here i come through the leaves   rustling and glowing
here i come walking on my feet on my path endurance embodied

here i come, breathing towards you. here i come, steeped in song
carrying nothing except that which carries me

here i come: all of my impatience for myself and the world, all of my longing and laughter soup and celebration, here

here i come all of me welcome me
love me in all of the ways that you know how to love
in all of the ways that you have ever been loved

here i am, all of me. hear me
embrace me, all of me: all song, all whirlwind, all roots

Ilana Streit

BLESSING FOR LOVE
(AHAVAT OLAM)

ahavat olam	אַהֲבַת עוֹלָם
beit yisrael ameich ahavt	בֵּית יִשְׂרָאֵל עַמֵּךְ אָרַבְתָּ
torah umitzvot, chukim umishpatim	תּוֹרָה וּמִצְוֹת חֻקִּים וּמִשְׁפָּטִים
otanu limadt.	אוֹתָנוּ לִמַּדְתְּ
al ken shekhinah eloteinu	עַל כֵּן שְׁכִינָה אֱלֹתֵינוּ
beshachveinu uvekumeinu nasiach bechukayich	בְּשָׁכְבֵנוּ וּבְקוּמֵנוּ נָשִׂיחַ בְּחֻקֶּיךְ
venismach bedivrei torateich	וְנִשְׂמַח בְּדִבְרֵי תוֹרָתֶךְ
uvemitzvotayich leolam vaed	וּבְמִצְוֹתַיִךְ לְעוֹלָם וָעֶד.
ki heim chayeinu veorech yameinu	כִּי הֵם חַיֵּינוּ וְאֹרֶךְ יָמֵינוּ
uvahem nehegeh yomam valailah.	וּבָהֶם נֶהְגֶּה יוֹמָם וָלָיְלָה
veahavateich al tasiri mimenu le'olamim.	וְאַהֲבָתֶךְ אַל תָּסִירִי מִמֶּנּוּ לְעוֹלָמִים.
beruchah at shekhinah	בְּרוּכָה אַתְּ שְׁכִינָה
ohevet amah yisrael.	אוֹהֶבֶת עַמָּהּ יִשְׂרָאֵל.

with worlds of love
have you loved your people
your people who wrestle with You
You have taught us
wisdom and right action,
principles and truths
when we lie down
and when we rise up
we meditate on your paths
we play forever
with the words of Your Torah and mitzvot
they reside in our lives
and our days
we dwell on them as days
and nights go by
let the knowledge of Your love
dwell with us.
blessed are you, Shekhinah
who loves your wrestling people

THE EVENING PRAYER

SH'MA (THE PRAYER FOR ONENESS)

The mystics understood the Shema as a means for bringing what is separate into wholeness. They would recite intentions before the Shema, inviting the Shekhinah to unite with the Holy One of Blessing. We invite you to contemplate one of the following unification prayers, using a variety of languages about the divine, before reciting the Shema.

לְשֵׁם יִחוּד קוּדְשָׁא בְּרִיךְ הוּא וּשְׁכִינְתָּא

l'shem yichud kudsha brich hu ushkhinta

For the sake of the unification of the Holy One and the Shekhinah, God and Goddess.

or

לְשֵׁם יִחוּד אִמָּא עִלָאָה וְאִמָּא תַּתָּאָה

l'shem yichud immah ilaah veimmah tata'ah

For the sake of the unification of Binah and Shekhinah, the Mother and Daugher, Cosmos and Earth.

or

לְשֵׁם יִחוּד אֲרִיךְ אַנְפִּין וְזְעֵיר אַנְפִּין

l'shem yichud arikh anpin uze'ir anpin.

For the sake of the unification of Chochmah and Tiferet, the Lover and the Beloved.

or

לְשֵׁם יִחוּד כָּל פְּנֵי אֱלוֹהוּת

l'shem yichud kol p'nei elohut.

For the sake of the unification of all aspects of deity, all faces of God/dess/exx.

It is customary to cover the eyes when reciting the Shema. As you recite each word, you can use the kabbalistic custom of placing the six words in the six directions as a reminder of the oneness all around. Use whatever name for God calls you. Use whatever name for your people calls you. Multiple options for the Shema are presented here.

שְׁמַע יִשְׂרָאֵל יהוה אֱלֹהֵינוּ יהוה אֶחָד

△ sh'ma yisrael adonai eloheinu adonai echad

שְׁמַע יִשְׂרָאֵל שְׁכִינָה אֱלֹתֵינוּ שְׁכִינָה אַחַת

☐ sh'ma yisrael shekhinah eloheinu shekhinah achat

שִׁמְעָה יִשְׂרָאֵל הֲוָיָה אֱלֹהֵינוּ הֲוָיָה אָחֵד

⊖ shim'eh yisrael havayah eloheinu havayah ached

שִׁמְעִי יִשְׂרָאֵלָה שְׁכִינָה אֱלֹתֵינוּ שְׁכִינָה אַחַת

☐ shimi yisraelah shekhinah eloteinu shekhinah achat

שִׁמְעִי תִּשְׂרָאֵלָה תְּהֹוָה אֱלֹהוֹתֵינוּ תְּהֹוָה אַחַת

☐ shimi tisraelah tehovah elohoteinu tehovah achat

Hear, Godwrestler: The Present One is the Creator, the Present One is One.

RECITE SILENTLY

בָּרוּךְ שֵׁם כְּבוֹד מַלְכוּתָהּ לְעֹלָם וָעֶד

baruch shem kevod malchutah le'olam va'ed

Blessed is the name of the glory of the Shekinah forever.

The final version of SHMA here is from *Toratah: The Regendered Bible* by Yael Kanarek and Tamar Biala.

THE EVENING PRAYER 40

TZIMTZEMAI SH'MA

> The trees of Jerusalem were of cinnamon, and when they were harvested their smell would carry through all the land of Israel. When Jerusalem was destroyed they were hidden away, and only a few remained. They may be found in the treasure house of Queen Tzimtzemai.
>
> *Babylonian Talmud, Shabbat 63a*

This mysterious text suggests that Tzimtzemai is one of the names of Shekhinah. Tzimtzemai means "she who makes herself smaller." This name connects to the kabbalistic process of tzimtzum, in which God has to become smaller in order for there to be space for the universe to grow.

שְׁמַע יִשְׂרָאֵל צִימְצְמַאי אֱלֹהֵינוּ צִימְצְמַאי אַחַת

shema yisrael tzimtzemai eloheinu tzimtzemai achat

Hear, O Israel, the One who Makes Space is Our God, the One who Makes Space is One.

SILENTLY

בָּרוּךְ שֵׁם כְּבוֹד מַלְכוּתָהּ לְעוֹלָם וָעֶד

baruch shem kevod malchutah le'olam va'ed

Blessed is the name of the glory of the Shekinah forever.

ALTERNATE SH'MA FROM THE SONG OF SONGS (5:2, 6:9)

אֲחֹתִי רַעְיָתִי יוֹנָתִי תַמָּתִי אַחַת הִיא

achoti rayati yonati tamati achat hi

My sister, my love, my dove, my pure one, she is one.

SH'MA YISRAEL/LISTEN OH YOU (SHIMI YISRAEL)

sh'ma yisrael	shimi yisraelah	Listen Oh You
adonai eloheinu	shekhinah eloteinu	Who Wrestle With God/dess/exx
adonai echad	shekhinah achat	The Infinite
adonai echad	shekhinah achat	She is One/Zhe is One *Taya Shere*

AND YOU SHALL LOVE (VE'AHAVTA)
PART I: ADAPTED FROM DEUTERONOMY 6:4-9

□ FEMININE

וְאָהַבְתְּ אֵת שְׁכִינָה אֱלֹהַיִךְ בְּכָל לְבָבֵךְ וּבְכָל נַפְשֵׁךְ וּבְכָל מְאֹדֵךְ וְהָיוּ הַדְּבָרִים הָאֵלֶּה אֲשֶׁר אָנֹכִי מְצַוָּתֵךְ הַיּוֹם עַל לְבָבֵךְ. וְשִׁנַּנְתִּם לִבְנוֹתַיִךְ וּלְבָנַיִךְ וְדִבַּרְתְּ בָּם בְּשִׁבְתֵּךְ בְּבֵיתֵךְ וּבְלֶכְתֵּךְ בַּדֶּרֶךְ וּבְשָׁכְבֵּךְ וּבְקוּמֵךְ. וּקְשַׁרְתִּים לְאוֹת עַל יָדֵךְ וְהָיוּ לְטֹטָפֹת בֵּין עֵינָיִךְ וּכְתַבְתִּים עַל מְזֻזֹת בֵּיתֵךְ וּבִשְׁעָרָיִךְ.

ve'ahavt et shekhinah elohayich, bechol levavech, uvechol nafshech, uvechol me'odech. vehayu hadevarim ha'eleh, asher anochi metzavatech hayom al levavech. veshinantim l'vanayich uvnotayich, vedibart bam beshivtech beveitech u'velechtech vaderech, uveshachbech uvekumech. ukshartim le'ot al yadech, vehayu letotafot bein einayich. uchetavtim al mezuzot beitech uvisharayich.

△ MASCULINE

וְאָהַבְתָּ אֵת יהוה אֱלֹהֶיךָ בְּכָל לְבָבְךָ וּבְכָל נַפְשְׁךָ וּבְכָל מְאֹדֶךָ. וְהָיוּ הַדְּבָרִים הָאֵלֶּה אֲשֶׁר אָנֹכִי מְצַוְּךָ הַיּוֹם עַל לְבָבֶךָ. וְשִׁנַּנְתָּם לְבָנֶיךָ וְדִבַּרְתָּ בָּם בְּשִׁבְתְּךָ בְּבֵיתֶךָ וּבְלֶכְתְּךָ בַדֶּרֶךְ וּבְשָׁכְבְּךָ וּבְקוּמֶךָ וּקְשַׁרְתָּם לְאוֹת עַל יָדֶךָ וְהָיוּ לְטֹטָפֹת בֵּין עֵינֶיךָ וּכְתַבְתָּם עַל מְזֻזֹת בֵּיתֶךָ וּבִשְׁעָרֶיךָ.

ve'ahavta et adonai elohecha, bechol levavcha, uvechol nafshecha, uvechol me'odecha. vehayu hadevarim ha'eleh, asher anochi metzavcha hayom al levavcha. veshinantam l'vanecha vedibarta bam beshivtecha be'veitecha, uvelechtecha va'derech, u've'shochbecha u'vekumecha. uk'shartam le'ot al yadecha, vehayu letotafot bein einecha. uch'tavtam al mezzuzot beitecha u'visharecha.

⊖ NONBINARY

וְאָהַבְתֶּה אֵת הֲוָיָה אֱלֹהֶיךֶ בְּכָל לְבָבְךֶ וּבְכָל נַפְשְׁךֶ וּבכל מְאֹדֶךֶ. וְהָיוּ הַדְּבָרִים הָאֵלֶּה אֲשֶׁר אָנֹכִי מְצַוְּתְךֶ הַיּוֹם עַל לְבָבֶךֶ. וְשִׁנַּנְתֶּם לַבָּנֹל בָּךְ וְדִבַּרְתֶּה בָּם בְּשִׁבְתְּךֶ בְּבֵיתְךֶ וּבְלֶכְתְּךֶ בַדֶּרֶךְ וּבְשָׁכְבְּךֶ וּבְעוּרְךֶ. וּקְשַׁרְתֶּם לְאוֹת עַל גּוּפֶךְ וְהָיוּ לְטֹטָפֹת עַל רֹאשֶׁךֶ. וּכְתַבְתֶּם עַל מְזוֹזֹת בֵּיתֶךֶ וּבִשְׁעָרֶיךֶ.

ve'ahavteh et havayah elohecheh, bechol levavcheh, uvechol nafshecheh, uvechol me'odecheh. vehayu hadevarim ha'eleh, asher anochi metzavetcheh hayom al levavcheh. veshinantem labanol bach vedibarteh bam beshivtecheh be'veitecheh, uvelechtecheh va'derech, u've'shochbecheh u'vekumecheh. uk'shartem le'ot al gufecheh, vehayu letotafot al roshecheh. uch'tavtem al mezzuzot beitecheh u'visharecheh.

You shall love Becoming your God with all your heart, with all your life-force, with all your gifts. These words which I tell you this day you shall take into your heart. You shall teach them to your children, and speak of them when you sit in your house and when you walk on the path, when you lie down and when you rise up. Tie them as a sign upon your hand and let them be ornaments between your eyes. Write them on the doorposts of your house and on your gates.

THE EVENING PRAYER 42

SPRING AND AUTUMN RAIN (VE'HAYAH)
PART II: ADAPTED FROM DEUTERONOMY 11:13-21

▫ FEMININE

וְהָיָה אִם שָׁמֹעַ תִּשְׁמַעְנָה אֶל מִצְוֹתַי אֲשֶׁר אָנֹכִי מְצַוָּה אֶתְכֶן הַיּוֹם לְאַהֲבָה אֶת יהוה אֱלֹהֵיכֶן וּלְעָבְדָהּ בְּכָל לְבַבְכֶן וּבְכָל נַפְשְׁכֶן: וְנָתַתִּי מְטַר אַרְצְכֶן בְּעִתּוֹ יוֹרֶה וּמַלְקוֹשׁ וְאָסַפְתְּ דְגָנֵךְ וְתִירֹשֵׁךְ וְיִצְהָרֵךְ: וְנָתַתִּי עֵשֶׂב בְּשָׂדֵךְ לִבְהֶמְתֵּךְ וְאָכַלְתְּ וְשָׂבָעְתְּ: הִשָּׁמְרָנָה לָכֶן פֶּן יִפְתֶּה לְבַבְכֶן וְסַרְתֶּן וַעֲבַדְתֶּן אֱלֹהִים אֲחֵרִים וְהִשְׁתַּחֲוִיתֶן לָהֶם: וְחָרָה אַף שְׁכִינָה בָּכֶן וְעָצְרָה אֶת הַשָּׁמַיִם וְלֹא יִהְיֶה מָטָר וְהָאֲדָמָה לֹא תִתֵּן אֶת יְבוּלָהּ וַאֲבַדְתֶּן מְהֵרָה מֵעַל הָאָרֶץ הַטֹּבָה אֲשֶׁר יהוה נֹתֶנֶת לָכֶן: וְשַׂמְתֶּן אֶת דְּבָרַי אֵלֶּה עַל לְבַבְכֶן וְעַל נַפְשְׁכֶן וּקְשַׁרְתֶּן אֹתָם לְאוֹת עַל יֶדְכֶן וְהָיוּ לְטוֹטָפֹת בֵּין עֵינֵיכֶן: וְלִמַּדְתֶּן אֹתָם אֶת בְּנוֹתֵיכֶן וּבְנֵיכֶן לְדַבֵּר בָּם בְּשִׁבְתֵּךְ בְּבֵיתֵךְ וּבְלֶכְתֵּךְ בַּדֶּרֶךְ וּבְשָׁכְבֵּךְ וּבְקוּמֵךְ: וּכְתַבְתָּם עַל מְזוּזוֹת בֵּיתֵךְ וּבִשְׁעָרֵיךְ: לְמַעַן יִרְבּוּ יְמֵיכֶן וִימֵי בְנוֹתֵיכֶן עַל הָאֲדָמָה אֲשֶׁר נִשְׁבְּעָה שְׁכִינָה לְאִמּוֹתֵיכֶן וְלַאֲבוֹתֵיכֶן לָתֵת לָהֶן כִּימֵי הַשָּׁמַיִם עַל הָאָרֶץ:

vehaya im shamoa tishmanah el mitzvotai asher anochi mitzavah etchen hayom, l'ahava et havaya eloheychen ule'avdah bechol levavchen uv'chol nafshechen. v'natati metar artzechen b'ito yoreh umalkosh v'asaft deganech v'tirshech v'yitzharech. v'natati eisev b'sadech livhemteich v'achalt v'savat. hishamerna lachen pen yifteh l'vavchen vesarten v'avadten elohim acheirim v'hishtachaviten lahem. v'charah af shekhinah bachen v'atzar et hashamayim velo yihyeh matar veha'adamah lo titein et yevulah va'avadten meheira me'al ha'aretz hatova asher havayah notenet lachem. v'samten et dvarai eileh al levavchen v'al nafshechen uksharten otam l'ot al yed'chen, v'hayu l'totafot bein eineichen. v'limadten otam et b'neichen uv'noteichen l'dabeir bam, b'shivteich b'veiteich uv'lechteich baderech uveshachbeich uvekumeich. uchtavtim al mezuzot beiteich uvish'arayich. lma'an yirbu y'meichen vimei b'noteichen al ha'adamah asher nishbe'ah shekhinah l'imoteichen v'la'avoteichen lateit lahen kimei hashamayim al ha'aretz:

△ MASCULINE

וְהָיָה אִם שָׁמֹעַ תִּשְׁמְעוּ אֶל מִצְוֹתַי אֲשֶׁר אָנֹכִי מְצַוֶּה אֶתְכֶם הַיּוֹם לְאַהֲבָה אֶת יהוה אֱלֹהֵיכֶם וּלְעָבְדוֹ בְּכָל לְבַבְכֶם וּבְכָל נַפְשְׁכֶם: וְנָתַתִּי מְטַר אַרְצְכֶם בְּעִתּוֹ יוֹרֶה וּמַלְקוֹשׁ וְאָסַפְתָּ דְגָנֶךָ וְתִירֹשְׁךָ וְיִצְהָרֶךָ: וְנָתַתִּי עֵשֶׂב בְּשָׂדְךָ לִבְהֶמְתֶּךָ וְאָכַלְתָּ וְשָׂבָעְתָּ: הִשָּׁמְרוּ לָכֶם פֶּן יִפְתֶּה לְבַבְכֶם וְסַרְתֶּם וַעֲבַדְתֶּם אֱלֹהִים אֲחֵרִים וְהִשְׁתַּחֲוִיתֶם לָהֶם: וְחָרָה אַף יהוה בָּכֶם וְעָצַר אֶת הַשָּׁמַיִם וְלֹא יִהְיֶה מָטָר וְהָאֲדָמָה לֹא תִתֵּן אֶת יְבוּלָהּ וַאֲבַדְתֶּם מְהֵרָה מֵעַל הָאָרֶץ הַטֹּבָה אֲשֶׁר יהוה נֹתֵן לָכֶם: וְשַׂמְתֶּם אֶת דְּבָרַי אֵלֶּה עַל לְבַבְכֶם וְעַל נַפְשְׁכֶם וּקְשַׁרְתֶּם אֹתָם לְאוֹת עַל יֶדְכֶם וְהָיוּ לְטוֹטָפֹת בֵּין עֵינֵיכֶם: וְלִמַּדְתֶּם אֹתָם אֶת בְּנֵיכֶם וּבְנוֹתֵיכֶם לְדַבֵּר בָּם בְּשִׁבְתְּךָ בְּבֵיתֶךָ וּבְלֶכְתְּךָ בַדֶּרֶךְ וּבְשָׁכְבְּךָ וּבְקוּמֶךָ: וּכְתַבְתָּם עַל מְזוּזוֹת בֵּיתֶךָ וּבִשְׁעָרֶיךָ: לְמַעַן יִרְבּוּ יְמֵיכֶם וִימֵי בְנֵיכֶם וּבְנוֹתֵיכֶם עַל הָאֲדָמָה אֲשֶׁר נִשְׁבַּע יהוה לַאֲבֹתֵיכֶם וּלְאִמּוֹתֵיכֶם לָתֵת לָהֶם כִּימֵי הַשָּׁמַיִם עַל הָאָרֶץ:

△ MASCULINE CONTINUED

vehaya im shamoa tishme'u el mitzvotai asher anochi metzaveh etchem hayom le'ahavah et havayah eloheichem ul'avdo bechol l'vavchem uvechol nafesheichem. venatati m'tar artzechem be'ito yoreh umalkosh ve'asafta d'ganecha vetiroshecha veyitzharecha. venatati eisev besadecha uvhemtecha ve'achalta vesavata. hishamru lachem pen yifteh levavchem vesartem va'avadtem elohim acherim vehishtachavitem lachem. vechara af havaya bachem ve'atzar et hashamayim velo yihiyeh matar veha'adamah lo titen et yevulah va'avadtem meheirah me'al ha'aretz hatovah asher havayah noten lachem. vesamtem et devarai eileh al levachem ve'al nafsheichem ukshartem otam le'ot al yadchem vehayu letotafot bein eineichem. velimadtem otam el beneichem uvnoteichem ledaber bam beshivtecha beveitecha uvlechtecha vaderech uveshachbecha uvekumecha uktavtem al mezuzot beitecha uvishe'arecha. lma'an yirbu yemeichem viymei vnoteichem uvneichem al ha'adamah asher nishba havayah l'imoteichem vela'avoteichem latet lahem kiymei shamayim al ha'aretz.

Spring and autumn rain
corn and wine and oil you shall have
if only you will love
Becoming itself
and sit with it at home
and walk with it on your journeys
and lie down with it in your dreams
and rise up with it in your hopes
you will eat and be satisfied
and if you will close your heart
and turn away
from your nefesh-wisdom
and your communion with the world
and serve gods that are Other than Becoming
the earth will not yield her fruit
and the skies will shut their doors
and you will be lost from the good land
that Becoming gives you
yet if you will love Becoming
with heart, body, and soul
and weave it into the thoughts of your mind
and the works of your hands
and teach it to your children
and tell it in your stories
then your days will be long and whole
as the days of the sky above the earth

THE EVENING PRAYER 44

FRINGES (VA'YOMER)
PART III: ADAPTED FROM NUMBERS 13:37-41

▢ FEMININE

וַיֹּאמֶר יהוה אֶל מִרְיָם וּמֹשֶׁה לֵּאמֹר: דַּבְּרִי אֶל בְּנוֹת וּבְנֵי יִשְׂרָאֵל וְאָמַרְתְּ אֲלֵהֶן: וְעָשׂוּ לָהֶן צִיצִת עַל כַּנְפֵי בִגְדֵיהֶן לְדֹרֹתָן וְנָתְנוּ עַל צִיצִת הַכָּנָף פְּתִיל תְּכֵלֶת: וְהָיָה לָכֶן לְצִיצִת וּרְאִיתֶן אֹתוֹ וּזְכַרְתֶּן אֶת כָּל מִצְוֹת יהוה וַעֲשִׂיתֶן אֹתָן וְלֹא תְתוּרֵינָה מֵאַחֲרֵי לְבַבְכֶן וְאַחֲרֵי עֵינֵיכֶן אֲשֶׁר אַתֶּן זָנוֹת מֵהֶן: לְמַעַן תִּזְכֹּרְנָה וַעֲשִׂיתֶן אֶת כָּל מִצְוֹתַי וִהְיִיתֶן קְדֹשׁוֹת לֶאֱלָתְכֶן אֲנִי יהוה אֱלָתְכֶן אֲשֶׁר הוֹצֵאתִי אֶתְכֶן מֵאֶרֶץ מִצְרַיִם לִהְיוֹת לָכֶן לְאֵלָה אֲנִי יהוה אֱלָתְכֶן:

vayomer havayah el miryam lemor: dabri el b'not uvnei yisrael ve'amart aleihen ve'asu lahen tzitzit al kanfei bigdeihen ledorotan venatnu al tzitzit hakanaf ptil tcheilet. vehaya lahen letzitzit ure'iten oto uzecharten et kol mitzvot havayah velo teturenah me'acharei levavchen ve'acharei eineihen asher aten zanot meihen. lema'an tizkornah va'asiten et kol mitzvotai, vihyiten kedoshot le'elatchen. ani havayah eletchen, asher hotzeiti etchen me'eretz mitzrayim lihiyot lachen l'elah. ani havayah elatchen.

△ MASCULINE

וַיֹּאמֶר יהוה אֶל מֹשֶׁה וּמִרְיָם לֵאמֹר: דַּבֵּר אֶל בְּנוֹת וּבְנֵי יִשְׂרָאֵל וְאָמַרְתָּ אֲלֵהֶם: וְעָשׂוּ לָהֶם צִיצִת עַל כַּנְפֵי בִגְדֵיהֶם לְדֹרֹתָם וְנָתְנוּ עַל צִיצִת הַכָּנָף פְּתִיל תְּכֵלֶת: וְהָיָה לָכֶם לְצִיצִת וּרְאִיתֶם אֹתוֹ וּזְכַרְתֶּם אֶת כָּל מִצְוֹת יהוה וַעֲשִׂיתֶם אֹתָן וְלֹא תָתֻרוּ מֵאַחֲרֵי לְבַבְכֶם וְאַחֲרֵי עֵינֵיכֶם אֲשֶׁר אַתֶּם זֹנִים מֵהֶם: לְמַעַן תִּזְכְּרוּ וַעֲשִׂיתֶם אֶת כָּל מִצְוֹתָי וִהְיִיתֶם קְדֹשִׁים לֵאלֹהֵיכֶם אֲנִי יהוה אֱלֹהֵיכֶם אֲשֶׁר הוֹצֵאתִי אֶתְכֶם מֵאֶרֶץ מִצְרַיִם לִהְיוֹת לָכֶם לֵאלֹהִים אֲנִי יהוה אֱלֹהֵיכֶם:

vayomer havayah el moshe umiriyam lemor: daber el bnot uvnei yisrael va'amarta aleihem ve'asu lahem tzitzit al kanfei bigdeihem ledorotam venatnu al tzitzit hakanaf ptil tcheilet. vehaya lahem letzitzit ure'item oto uzechartem et kol mitzvot havayah velo taturu acharei levavchem ve'acharei eineichem asher atem zanim meihem. lema'an tizkeru va'asitem et kol mitzvotai, vihyiten kedoshim lelohechem. ani havayah eloheichem, asher hotzeiti etchem me'eretz mitzrayim lihiyot lachem leilohim. ani havayah eloheichem.

God said to Miriam and Moshe: Speak to the children of Israel and say to them that they should make fringes on the corners (wings) of their garments throughout their generations, and they should put upon the fringe of the corner a thread of blue. They will be fringes for you, and you will look at them and remember the desires of the Eternal your God, and you will not turn aside from the knowing of your hearts or the understanding your eyes by which you nourish yourselves. Thus shall you remember my desires and be holy to the Infinite. I, Havayah, am the Infinite who led you out of Egypt to be infinite to you. I, the Infinite, am your God.

In the above section, the God-name usually pronounced as ADONAI has been rendered as YHWH (the Tetragrammaton) with the pronunciation HAVAYAH (Havayah means Being, and a permutation of the name YHWH). This name has been translated Becoming (another possible translation of YHWH), or simply as Havayah. This is with the understanding that individuals will use the God-name that is right for them.

There has been a change from the original Torah text in the third section, in the biblical passage regarding fringes. The original passage says: "do not wander after your hearts or your eyes, after which you stray (act like a whore)." In the interests of promoting the intuition of the heart, and removing the prostitute imagery, the passage has been rendered: 'do not wander away from your heart and your eyes, which nourish you." (The words "to lust" and "to feed or nourish" are similar.)

While according to the Torah, the texts of these passages were given to Moshe (Moses) and not to Miriam, we include the priestess and prophetess Miriam's name as a reminder that inspiration was also received by prophetesses and priestesses. In this siddur, we include that wisdom in what we hold sacred.

1. BLESSING FOR REDEMPTION (MI CHAMOCHA)

umalchuto veratzon kiblu aleihem
moshe umiriam uvnei yisrael
lecha anu shirah besimcha rabah veamru chulam

וּמַלְכוּתוֹ בְּרָצוֹן קִבְּלוּ עֲלֵיהֶם
מֹשֶׁה וּמִרְיָם וּבְנֵי יִשְׂרָאֵל
לְךָ עָנוּ שִׁירָה בְּשִׂמְחָה רַבָּה וְאָמְרוּ כֻלָּם

mi chamocha ba'elim adonai
mi kamocha nedar bakodesh
norah tehilot oseh feleh

מִי כָמֹכָה בָּאֵלִים יהוה
מִי כָּמֹכָה נֶאְדָּר בַּקֹּדֶשׁ
נוֹרָא תְהִלֹּת עֹשֵׂה פֶלֶא

malchutcha ra'u vanecha
bokea yam lifnei moshe umiryam
zeh eli anu ve'amru:
havayah yimloch le'olam va'ed

מַלְכוּתְךָ רָאוּ בָנֶיךָ
בּוֹקֵעַ יָם לִפְנֵי מֹשֶׁה וּמִרְיָם
זֶה אֵלִי עָנוּ וְאָמְרוּ
יהוה יִמְלֹךְ לְעֹלָם וָעֶד

☐ vene'emar ki fadah havayah et yaakov
uge'alo miyad chazak mimenu.

☐ וְנֶאֱמַר: כִּי פָדָה יהוה אֶת יַעֲקֹב
וּגְאָלוֹ מִיַּד חָזָק מִמֶּנּוּ.

△ vene'emar ki fadetah havayah et hagar
uge'altah miyad hazakah mimenah.

△ וְנֶאֱמַר: כִּי פָדְתָה הוִיה אֶת הָגָר
וּגְאָלְתָה מִיַּד חֲזָקָה מִמֶּנָּה.

beruchah at shekhinah, ga'alah yisrael.

בְּרוּכָה אַתְּ שְׁכִינָה גָּאֲלָה יִשְׂרָאֵל.

Your children acclaimed your sovereignty, Moses and Miriam and the Israelites sang:
Who is like you, Adonai, among all powers of the world?
Who is like you, glorious in holiness, Awesome in praises, doing wonders?
You redeem the one who wrestles, and make us whole
in the face of of what overwhelms us.
Blessed is Shekhinah, the Redeemer of Israel.

2. SPIRIT IS FLOWING

מִי כָמֹכָה בָּאֵלִים יהוה
מִי כָּמֹכָה נֶאְדָּר בַּקֹּדֶשׁ
נוֹרָאָה תְהִלֹּת עֹשֵׂה פֶלֶא

mi chamocha ba'elim adonai
mi kamocha nedar bakodesh
nora'ah tehilot oseh feleh

The Spirit is flowing, flowing and growing
The Spirit is flowing, through you and me
HaShem guide me, be faithfully beside me
HaShem guide me, and bless how I be
The Spirit is flowing, flowing and growing
The Spirit is flowing, through you and me
Shechinah, reside in me, your wisdom lives inside of me
Shechinah, reside in me, oh Holy of Holies!

Taya Shere, adaptation of traditional circle song

3. GROVE SONG

מִי כָמוֹהָ בָּאֵילִים שָׁדַי
מִי כָּמוֹהָ הָדָר בַּקֹּדֶשׁ
נוֹרָאָה תְהִלֹּת עֹשָׂה פֶלֶא

mi chamoha ba'eylim shaddai
mi kamoha hadar bakodesh
nora'ah tehilot osah feleh

Who is like Her, the Nourishing One, in all the groves?
Who is like her, the glory in the sanctuary,
mysterious in praises, doing wondrously?

Jill Hammer

4. VATIKACH MIRIAM

vatikach miriam haneviah
achot aharon et hatof beyada
vatetzena khol hanashim achareha

וַתִּקַּח מִרְיָם הַנְּבִיאָה
אֲחוֹת אַהֲרֹן אֶת הַתֹּף בְּיָדָהּ
וַתֵּצֶאןָ כָל הַנָּשִׁים אַחֲרֶיהָ

And Miriam the prophetess sister of Aharon took a drum in her hand
and all the women went out after her.

Exodus 15:20, melody by Tziona Achishena

WE ARE WRITING

We are writing each other's freedom stories,
Riding the waves toward true selves
We are writing each other's freedom stories,
Planting the seeds of holiness.

We are, we are seeking wholeness.
We are, we are breaking hearts.
We are, we are shards of lightness.
We are, we are sacred dark.

We are writing each other's healing stories:
Cresting the waves of sovereignty.
We are writing each other's resistance stories:
Tending the trees of divinity.

We are, we are seeking wholeness.
We are, we are breaking hearts.
We are, we are shards of lightness.
We are, we are sacred dark.

Harriette Wimms

JOURNEY

between
a pillar of cloud
and a pillar of fire
the sea yawns
birth canal
labyrinth
blood-painted door

we enter joyful
that the future is just ahead

we enter afraid
of what pursues us

we enter
present with not knowing

we have escaped slavery
just barely
someone bought our freedom
we're not sure who
ancestors
children
prophets
the all-weaver
the angel of death

to either side
the water is mirrors
is windows
is a view of the deep

just ahead
is darkness
is a light shining
is the sound of singing
and the pounding of feet

Jill Hammer

BLESSING FOR PROTECTION
(HASHKIVINU)

hashkivinu shekhinah eloteinu leshalom	הַשְׁכִּיבֵינוּ שְׁכִינָה אֱלֹתֵינוּ לְשָׁלוֹם
veha'amidinu sukkateinu lechayyim.	וְהַעֲמִידֵנוּ סֻכָּתֵנוּ לְחַיִּים
ufrosi aleinu sukkat shelomeich	וּפְרְשִׂי עָלֵינוּ סֻכַּת שְׁלוֹמֵךְ
vetakninu be'etzah tovah milifanayich	וְתַקְּנֵנוּ בְּעֵצָה טוֹבָה מִלְּפָנָיִךְ
vehoshi'inu lemaan shmech vehagani ba'adeinu	וְהוֹשִׁיעֵנוּ לְמַעַן שְׁמֵךְ וְהָגֵנִּי בַּעֲדֵנוּ
vehaseri me'aleinu oyev dever vecherev	וְהָסִירִי מֵעָלֵינוּ אוֹיֵב דֶּבֶר וְחֶרֶב
veraav veyagon vehaseiri satan	וְרָעָב וְיָגוֹן וְהָסִירִי שָׂטָן
milifaneinu umeachareinu	מִלְּפָנֵינוּ וּמֵאַחֲרֵנוּ
uvetzel kenafayich tastirinu.	וּבְצֵל כְּנָפַיִךְ תַּסְתִּירֵנוּ
ki elah shomarteinu umatzilateinu at	כִּי אֵלָה שׁוֹמַרְתֵּינוּ וּמַצִּילָתֵינוּ אָתְּ
ki elah chanunah urchumah at	כִּי אֵלָה חֲנוּנָה וְרְחוּמָה אָתְּ
veshimri tzeiteinu uvo'einu	וְשִׁמְרִי צֵאתֵנוּ וּבוֹאֵנוּ
lechayim uleshalom me'ata ve'ad olam	לְחַיִּים וּלְשָׁלוֹם מֵעַתָּה וְעַד עוֹלָם
ufrosi aleinu sukat shelomeich.	וּפְרְשִׂי עָלֵינוּ סֻכַּת שְׁלוֹמֵךְ.
beruchah at shekhinah	בְּרוּכָה אַתְּ שְׁכִינָה
haporeset sukkat shalom aleinu	הַפּוֹרֶשֶׂת סֻכַּת שָׁלוֹם עָלֵינוּ
veal kol amo yisrael ve'al yerushalayim	וְעַל כָּל יִשְׂרָאֵל וְעַל יְרוּשָׁלַיִם
ve'al ha'olam.	וְעַל הָעוֹלָם.
ON WEEKDAYS END:	ימי חול
beruchah at shekhinah	בְּרוּכָה אַתְּ שְׁכִינָה
shomeret amah yisrael le'ad.	שׁוֹמֶרֶת עַמָּהּ יִשְׂרָאֵל לָעַד.

Cause us to lie down, Indwelling Presence, in peace,
and cause us to awaken, our Sukkah, to life.
Spread over us the sukkah of your peace.
Help us repair ourselves and the world with your good advice.
Protect us from violence, disease, and our own impulses.
Shelter us in the shadow of your wings,
For you are guardian and rescuer,
Grace and womb of mercy
Guard our coming and our going,
For life and for peace, now and always.
Spread over us the sukkah of your peace.
Blessed are You, Presence, who spreads a sukkah of peace
over us, over the Godwrestling people, over Jerusalem, over the world.

THE SUKKAH OF SHEKHINAH

We ask the sukkah to spread itself over us and rest upon us and protect us as a mother protects her children, so that we will feel safe on every side. When Israel... welcomes this sukkah of peace to their homes as a holy guest, the holy Divine presence comes down and spreads Her wings over the people Israel like a mother embracing her children. This sukkah of peace grants new souls to Her children, for all souls have their home in her.

Zohar I, 48a

ANU MATZANU

אָנוּ מָצָאנוּ מְנוּחָה
מִתַּחַת כַּנְפֵי הַשְּׁכִינָה

anu matzanu menucha
mitachat kanfei hashekhinah

We have found rest beneath Shekhinah's wings.

Penina Adelman

EL SHADDAI

In the Light and in the Darkness, if I fly or if I fall
Shekhinah, El Shaddai, I am not alone at all

Ruach-El Rachel Rose Reid

SHEKHINAH SPREADS HER WINGS

Shekhinah, ya dai dai dai, ya dai dai dai dai
Spreads Her wings, ya dai dai dai, ya dai dai dai dai
We come home, ya dai dai dai, ya dai dai dai dai
To receive Her love, ya dai dai dai, ya dai dai dai dai (x3)

Jo Kent Katz

HATZI KADDISH

תִּתְגַּדַּל וְתִתְקַדַּשׁ שְׁמָהּ רַבָּא

בְּעָלְמָא דִּי בְרָאת כִּרְעוּתָהּ וְתַמְלִיךְ מַלְכוּתָהּ
בְּחַיֵּיכוֹן וּבְיוֹמֵיכוֹן וּבְחַיֵּי דְכָל בֵּית יִשְׂרָאֵל
בַּעֲגָלָא וּבִזְמַן קָרִיב וְאִמְרוּ אָמֵן

יְהֵא שְׁמָהּ רַבָּא מְבָוָרךְ לְעָלַם וּלְעָלְמֵי עָלְמַיָּא

תִּתְבָּרַךְ וְתִשְׁתַּבַּח וְתִתְפָּאַר וְתִתְרוֹמַם וְתִתְנַשֵּׂא
וְתִתְהַדָּר וְתִתְעַלֶּה וְתִתְהַלָּל
שְׁמָהּ דְּקֻדְשָׁתָא בְּרִיכָה הִיא

לְעֵלָּא מִן כָּל בִּרְכָתָא וְשִׁירָתָא
תֻּשְׁבְּחָתָא וְנֶחֱמָתָא דַּאֲמִירָן בְּעָלְמָא
וְאִמְרוּ אָמֵן

titgadal vetitkadash shemah rabbah

be'alma di vrat kirutah vetamlich malchutah
bechayeichon uveyomeichon uvechayei d'chol beit yisrael
ba'agalah uvizman kariv ve'imru amen.

yehei shmah rabbah mevorach le'alam ul'almei almaya

titbarach vetitkadash tetitpa'ar vetitromam vetitnasei
vetithadar vetitaleh vetitalal shemah d'kudsha brichah hi

le'ela min kol birchata veshirata
tushbechata venechemata da'amiran be'alma ve'imru amein.

Holy and growing is God's great name in the world
which She has created according to Her desire.
May She establish Her Shekhinah
in our lifetime and our days
and in the lifetimes of all the House of the Godwrestlers quickly,
and say: Amen.
May Her great name be blessed in this world and all the worlds.
Blessed and praised, beautified and exalted,
raised up and glorified, elevated and extolled be the Name of the Holiness,
blessed be She, beyond all the blessings and hymns,
praises and consolations that are spoken in the world; and say:
Amen.

GOD IS ALL

God is all. God is an apple orchard. God is a beggar. God is the beginning. God is a breastfeeding mother. God is breath. God is concealed and totally unknown. God is clouds. God is crowns. God is the days of Creation. God is death. God is desire. God is an eagle. God is the earth. God is eyes. God is faces. God is fear. God is purple silk. God is fire. God is a flowing gushing stream. God is the Garden of Eden. God is gateways. God is a gazelle. God is holiday guests. God is the Holidays. God is Jerusalem. God is a lion. God is love. God is matzah. God is a menorah. God is mirrors. God is the moon. God is a mountain of darkness. God is night. God is North, South, East, West. God is nothing. God is a nursing child. God is olive oil. God is the oldest of the old. God is a palace. God is peace. God is prayer. God is a rainbow. God is rivers of balsam. God is a rose. God is shadow. God is a shofar. God is a silkworm. God is silk. God is silver. God is skies. God is a snake. God is Song. God is the soul of the soul. God is sparks. God is the sun. God is a tent. God is time. God is the Torah. God is the Tree of Life. God is voices. God is wine. God is wind. God is words.

Justin Lewis (all images are from mystical Jewish literature)

RUACH ASSIYAH
SPIRIT OF THE WORLD

Shekhinah, foundation of the world,
How glorious is your name throughout the earth.
You who say:
Mine is the world and all it holds—
its myrtles, palms, and cedar trees,
green grass and dust and stone
blood and flesh and bone.
Shekhinah, show us the seeds that wait
in stillness and frozen earth.
Send forth your strength—
We invoke you and call you
to help us find our place
in the great cycle of life and death and transformation.
Bend over each of us, like blades of grass,
and whisper, grow, grow!

Melissa Weintraub

VESHAMRU

וְשָׁמְרוּ בָתֵּי יִשְׂרָאֵל אֶת הַשַּׁבָּת לַעֲשׂוֹת אֶת הַשַּׁבָּת לְדֹרֹתָם בְּרִית עוֹלָם: בֵּינִי וּבֵין בָּתֵּי יִשְׂרָאֵל אוֹת הִוא לְעֹלָם כִּי שֵׁשֶׁת יָמִים עָשְׂתָה ירהורה אֶת הַשָּׁמַיִם וְאֶת הָאָרֶץ וּבַיּוֹם הַשְּׁבִיעִי שָׁבְתָה וַתִּנָּפַשׁ:

veshamru vatei yisrael et hashabbat la'asot et hashabbat ledorotam berit olam.
beini u'vein vatei yisrael ot hi le'olam ki sheishet yamim asta adonai
et hashamayim ve'et ha'aretz uvayom hashevi'i shavtah vatinafash.

The Jewish people shall keep Shabbat, to make Shabbat throughout the generations as a covenant for always. It is a sign forever between Spirit and the people, that in six cycles Spirit created sky and earth, and on the seventh day, the day of completion, Spirit rested.

after Exodus 31:16-17

AMIDAH

When praying the Amidah,
one should direct one's heart to the Holy of Holies.

Mishnah Berachot 4:5

The Amidah is the central prayer of the three daily services. If prayer is a shrine, the Amidah is the Holy of Holies. It is customary to stand during the Amidah, but the Kohenet community has evolved the custom for some to lie on the ground during the Amidah in order to receive the shefa (divine energy) of the earth, and/or in order to engage in spirit journey (meditative visualization).

DOORWAYS INTO THE AMIDAH

You will find, here and elsewhere in the siddur, a variety of traditional and creative options for entering the Amidah Prayer, to be used by themselves or in combination.

Amidah I   Seven Breath Meditation, page 55
Amidah II   Shabbat Amidah with Feminine God-Language, page 56
Amidah III Alternate Amidah: The Dream, page 62
Amidah IV   Traditional Weekday Amidah with Feminine God-language, page 64
Amidah V   Traditional Festival Amidah with Feminine God-language, page 76

OTHER OPTIONS

Seven Blessings: An Amidah of Guided Meditation, page 166
Shrine Meditation, page 164
Elemental Amidah, page 167
Circle of Life Amidah, page 168
Nineteen Blessings: Earth-Based Meditations for the Weekday Amidah, page 171

PRAYER BEFORE THE AMIDAH

אֲדֹנָי שְׂפָתַי תִּפְתָּח וּפִי יַגִּיד תְּהִלָּתֶךָ
שְׁכִינָה שְׂפָתַי תִּפְתְּחִי וּפִי יַגִּיד תְּהִלָּתֵךְ

adonai s'fatai tiftakh, ufi yagid t'hilatekha
shekhinah s'fatai tiftekhi ufi yagid t'hilateich

Open up my lips Oh G!d and I will sing your praise

ANCESTOR CHANT

We are the old people, we are the new people
We are the same people, stronger than before

You bless us Elohei Sarah
You bless us Elohei Rivka
You bless us Elohei Rachel
You bless us Elohei Leah
You bless us Elohei Avraham
You bless us Elohei Yitzhak
You bless us Elohei Yaakov
You bless us Elohei Yisrael

"We are an Old People" chorus by morning feather / Will Shepardson, adaptation Taya Shere

AMIDAH I. SEVEN BREATH MEDITATION

Breathing in, I take breath into myself.
Breathing out, I join the web of being.
Breathing in, I rest in the present.
Breathing out, I am part of past and future.
Breathing in, I honor the shrine of my body.
Breathing out, I honor the shrine of the cosmos.
Breathing in, Presence fills me.
Breathing out, Presence enfolds me.
Breathing in, I witness what is broken.
Breathing out, I bow to what is perfect.
Breathing in, I offer gratitude for what is.
Breathing out, I accept that all changes.
Breathing in, I pray for peace for myself.
Breathing out, I pray for peace for all beings.

Jill Hammer

II. SHABBAT AMIDAH WITH FEMININE GOD-LANGUAGE

1. BLESSING FOR ANCESTORS (IMAHOT, AVOT, DOROT)

beruchah at shekhinah eloteinu veilohei	בְּרוּכָה אַתְּ שְׁכִינָה אֱלֹתֵינוּ וֵאלֹהֵי
imoteinu va'avoteinu vedoroteinu	אִמּוֹתֵנוּ וַאֲבוֹתֵינוּ וְדוֹרוֹתֵינוּ
elohei sarah, elohei rivka,	אֱלֹהֵי שָׂרָה אֱלֹהֵי רִבְקָה
elohei rachel, veilohei leah	אֱלֹהֵי רָחֵל וֵאלֹהֵי לֵאָה
(veilohei vilhah, veilohei zilpah)	וֵאלֹהֵי בִלְהָה וֵאלֹהֵי זִלְפָּה
elohei avraham elohei yitzchak veilohei yaakov	אֱלֹהֵי אַבְרָהָם אֱלֹהֵי יִצְחָק וֵאלֹהֵי יַעֲקֹב
ha'elah hagedolah hagiborah vehanora'ah	הָאֵלָה הַגְּדוֹלָה הַגִּבּוֹרָה וְהַנּוֹרָאָה
elah ilaah	אֵלָה עִלָּאָה
gomelet chasadim tovim	גּוֹמֶלֶת חֲסָדִים טוֹבִים
vekonah hakol vezocheret chasdei avot ve'imahot	וְקוֹנָה הַכֹּל וְזוֹכֶרֶת חַסְדֵי אָבוֹת וְאִמָּהוֹת
umeviah goelet livnot benoteihen	וּמְבִיאָה גּוֹאֶלֶת לִבְנוֹת בְּנוֹתֵיהֶן
(velivnei v'neihem)	וְלִבְנֵי בְנֵיהֶם
lma'an shmah be'ahavah.	לְמַעַן שְׁמָהּ בְּאַהֲבָה

BETWEEN ROSH HASHANAH AND YOM KIPPUR   בעשרת ימי תשובה

zochrinu lechayim ruach chafetzah vachayim	זָכְרִינוּ לְחַיִּים רוּחַ חֲפֵצָה בַחַיִּים
vechotvinu lesefer hachayyim	וְכָתְבִינוּ בְּסֵפֶר הַחַיִּים
lema'anech ma'yan chayim.	לְמַעֲנֵךְ מַעְיָן חַיִּים

malka ozeret u'moshiah u'mayan.	מַלְכָּה עוֹזֶרֶת וּמוֹשִׁיעָה וּמַעְיָן.
beruchah at shekhinah,	בְּרוּכָה אַתְּ שְׁכִינָה
ma'yan avraham ve'ezrat sarah.	מַעְיַן אַבְרָהָם וְעֶזְרַת שָׂרָה.

Blessed are You, Shekhinah, our Source and Source of our parents:
Life-force of Sarah, Rebekah, Rachel, Leah, Bilhah, and Zilpah,
of Abraham, Isaac and Jacob.
Great Goddess, strong, revered, exalted,
pouring out Your abundant kindness on all beings,
forming the All and all things in it,
weaving a web of connection for our ancestors,
bringing wholeness to all generations
for the sake of your Name that dwells with us in love.

BETWEEN ROSH HASHANAH AND YOM KIPPUR
Remember us for life, Spirit who desires life
and write us in the book of life, for your sake, Source of Life.

Ruler of the cosmos and its servant,
aiding us in our brokenness and bringing us to wholeness:
Blessed are You, wellspring of Abraham, helper of Sarah.

2. BLESSING FOR THE CIRCLE OF LIFE (GEVUROT)

at gebirah le'olam shadai	אַתְּ גְּבִירָה לְעוֹלָם שַׁדַּי
mechayah meitim at rav lehoshiah	מְחַיָּה מֵתִים אַתְּ רַב לְהוֹשִׁיעָה

BETWEEN SHEMINI ATZERET AND PASSOVER — בין ש״א ופסח

meishivah haruach umoridah hagashem — מַשִּׁיבָה הָרוּחַ וּמוֹרִידָה הַגֶּשֶׁם

mechalkelet chayim bechesed	מְכַלְכֶּלֶת חַיִּים בְּחֶסֶד
mechayah meitim berachamim rabim	מְחַיָּה מֵתִימוֹת בְּרַחֲמִים רַבִּים
somechet noflot verofeit cholim	סוֹמֶכֶת נוֹפְלוֹת וְרוֹפֵאת חוֹלִימוֹת
umatirah asurot	וּמַתִּירָה אֲסוּרוֹת
umekayemet emunatah lisheinot afar	וּמְקַיֶּמֶת אֱמוּנָתָהּ לִישֵׁנוֹת עָפָר
mi chamoch gevirat gevurot	מִי כָמוֹךְ גְּבִירַת גְּבוּרוֹת
umi domah lach	וּמִי דוֹמָה לָךְ
malkah memitah umechayah	מַלְכָּה מְמִיתָה וּמְחַיָּה
umatzmichah yeshuah	וּמַצְמִיחָה יְשׁוּעָה

BETWEEN ROSH HASHANAH AND YOM KIPPUR — בעשרת ימי תשובה

mi chamoch eim harachamim	מִי כָמוֹךְ אֵם הָרַחֲמִים
zocheret yetzureha lechayyim berachamim	זוֹכֶרֶת יְצוּרֶיהָ לְחַיִּים בְּרַחֲמִים

vene'emenet at lehachayot meitim	וְנֶאֱמֶנֶת אַתְּ לְהַחֲיוֹת מֵתִים.
beruchah at shekhinah,	בְּרוּכָה אַתְּ שְׁכִינָה
mechayah hameitim	מְחַיָּה הַמֵּתִים.

You are eternally gatekeeper and nurturer
turning life to death and death to life,
rescuing us from the void, sustaining life in love,
enlivening what dies in your great womb,
making what falls rise again
healing the hurt, freeing the enslaved, weaving all that sleeps in earth
into the bond of life.
Who could be like you, most potent
Queen who turns the wheel of death and life and makes redemption flower.

BETWEEN ROSH HASHANAH AND YOM KIPPUR

Who is like you, mother of mercy,
transforming your creatures in Your womb of compassion?

Faithful are you in turning the wheel from death to life.
Blessed are You, Presence who turns the wheel
from death to life.

3. BLESSING FOR HOLINESS (KEDUSHAH)

at kedoshah ushmeich kadosh
ukedoshot bechol yom tehaleluch selah.
beruchah at shekhinah
ha'elah hakedoshah

אַתְּ קְדוֹשָׁה וּשְׁמֵךְ קָדוֹשׁ
וּקְדוֹשׁוֹת בְּכָל יוֹם תְּהַלְלוּךְ סֶלָה.
בְּרוּכָה אַתְּ שְׁכִינָה
הָאֵלָה הַקְּדוֹשָׁה.

You are holy, Your Name is holy,
and those committed to holiness praise You at every moment.
Blessed are You, holy Goddess.

4. BLESSING FOR THE SABBATH (KEDUSHAT HASHABBAT)

at kidasht et yom hashvi'i lishmeich
tachlit ma'aseh shamayim va'aretz
uverchato mikol hayamim
vekidshato mikol hazmanim
vechen katuv betoratech
vat'chulu hashamayim veha'aretz vechol tzeva'am
vatechal elohim bayom hashevi'i
mikol melechtah asher astah
vatishbot bayom hashevi'i
mikol melachtah asher astah
vatevarech elohim et yom hashevi'i
vatekadesh oto
ki vo shavtah mikol melachtah
asher bar'ah elohim la'asot.

אַתְּ קִדַּשְׁתְּ אֶת יוֹם הַשְּׁבִיעִי לִישְׁמֵךְ
תַּכְלִית מַעֲשֵׂה שָׁמַיִם וָאָרֶץ
וּבֵרַכְתּוֹ מִכָּל הַיָּמִים
וְקִדַּשְׁתּוֹ מִכָּל הַזְּמַנִּים
וְכֵן כָּתוּב בְּתוֹרָתֵךְ
וַיְכֻלּוּ הַשָּׁמַיִם וְהָאָרֶץ וְכָל צְבָאָם
וַתְּכַל אֱלֹהִים בַּיּוֹם הַשְּׁבִיעִי
מְלַאכְתָּהּ אֲשֶׁר עָשְׂתָה
וַתִּשְׁבֹּת בַּיּוֹם הַשְּׁבִיעִי
מִכָּל מְלַאכְתָּהּ אֲשֶׁר עָשְׂתָה
וַתְּבָרֶךְ אֱלֹהִים אֶת יוֹם הַשְּׁבִיעִי
וַתְּקַדֵּשׁ אֹתוֹ
כִּי בוֹ שָׁבְתָה מִכָּל מְלַאכְתָּהּ
אֲשֶׁר בָּרְאָה אֱלֹהִים לַעֲשׂוֹת:

You, Divine One, made the seventh day holy to Your presence, a completion of sky and earth, and you blessed it above all days and seasons, as it is written in the Torah:
And there was evening and there was morning, the sixth day. Heaven, earth, and all their hosts were finished. God/dess completed on the seventh day all the work that had been done, and ceased upon the seventh day from all the work that had been done. God/dess blessed the seventh day and made it holy, for on it God/dess ceased from all the work that God/dess had created to do.

adapted from Genesis 1:31-2:3

eloheinu ve'elohei horeinu	אֱלֹהֵינוּ וֵאלֹהֵי הוֹרֵינוּ
retzi na vimnuchateinu	רְצִי נָא בִמְנוּחָתֵנוּ
kadshinu bemitzvotayich	קַדְּשֵׁנוּ בְּמִצְוֹתַיִךְ
utni chelkeinu betorateich	וּתְנִי חֶלְקֵנוּ בְּתוֹרָתֵךְ
sabinu mituvech vesamchinu biyeshuatech	שַׂבְּעֵנוּ מִטּוּבֵךְ וְשַׂמְּחֵנוּ בִּישׁוּעָתֵךְ
vetahari libeinu le'avdech be'emet	וְטַהֲרִי לִבֵּנוּ לְעָבְדֵךְ בֶּאֱמֶת
vehanchilinu havayah eloheinu	וְהַנְחִילֵנוּ הוֹיָה אֱלֹהֵינוּ
be'ahavah uveratzon shabbat kodshech	בְּאַהֲבָה וּבְרָצוֹן שַׁבַּת קָדְשֵׁךְ
veyanuchu vo yisrael mekadshei shmech.	וְיָנוּחוּ בָהּ כָּל יִשְׂרָאֵל מְקַדְּשֵׁי שְׁמֵךְ.
beruchah at shekhinah	בְּרוּכָה אַתְּ שְׁכִינָה
mekadeshet hashabbat.	מְקַדֶּשֶׁת הַשַּׁבָּת.

O Holiness, revered of our ancestors, delight in our rest. Make us holy through engaging us with mitzvot, and may your teachings be the earth we cultivate. Satisfy us with your abundance and awaken us to the ever-unfolding spiral of life's journey. Clarify our hearts that we may serve the world through truth, and allow us to inherit the love that is Shabbat. May all who wrestle with the Divine and with the holy come to find rest on this day. Blessed is the Holy, that sanctifies Shabbat.

SHABBAT MEDITATION

Shekhinah, you dwell in place, time, and soul. In the dimension of place, you are the Cosmos itself, a home for all that is. In the dimension of time, you are the Sabbath, the new moons and the sacred occasions, reminding us of the possibility of transformation. In the dimension of the soul, you are the Great Soul, bringing into being the many facets of our consciousness. On this Sabbath, as we stand before You in this place, at this time, with the soul you have given, reveal to us the mysteries of becoming. Be our Peacemaker as we meet the conflicts within and without. Be our Unweaver as we untie the tangles of our lives. Be our Lover as we learn the lessons of love again and again. May this Sabbath be a sanctuary of rest and healing, so that we may be healers of the world.

↵

AMIDAH 60

5. BLESSING FOR PRAYER (R'TZI)

retzi shekhinah eloteinu	רְצִי שְׁכִינָה אֱלֹתֵינוּ
bedorot yisrael uvitefilatan	בְּדוֹרוֹת יִשְׂרָאֵל וּבִתְפִלָּתָן
vehashivi et ha'avodah lidvir beiteich	וְהָשִׁיבִי אֶת הָעֲבוֹדָה לִדְבִיר בֵּיתֵךְ
ve'ishei yisrael utefilatan be'ahavah	וְאִשֵׁי יִשְׂרָאֵל וּתְפִלָּתָן בְּאַהֲבָה
tekabli beratzon utehi leratzon tamid	תְּקַבְּלִי בְּרָצוֹן וּתְהִי לְרָצוֹן תָּמִיד
avodat yisrael ameich	עֲבוֹדַת יִשְׂרָאֵל עַמֵּךְ
vetechezena eineinu	וְתֶחֱזֶינָה עֵינֵינוּ
beshuvech letzion berachamim.	בְּשׁוּבֵךְ לְצִיּוֹן בְּרַחֲמִים.
beruchah at shekhinah	בְּרוּכָה אַתְּ שְׁכִינָה
hamachazirah shekhinatah letzion.	הַמַּחֲזִירָה שְׁכִינָתָהּ לְצִיּוֹן.

Be glad, Shekhinah, in the generations of our tribe and their prayers, and return the rituals to your holy shrine, the earth. Accept the offerings of the people and their prayers in love, and may our ceremonies always rise to join with your desire. May our eyes see your return to the land in compassion. Blessed are You, Shekhinah returning to Zion and to all sacred earth.

6. BLESSING FOR GRATITUDE (MODIM)

modim anachnu lach she'at hi	מוֹדִים אֲנַחְנוּ לָךְ שֶׁאַתְּ הִיא
havayah eloheinu ve'elohei avoteinu ve'imoteinu	הֲוָיָה אֱלֹהֵינוּ וֵאלֹהֵי אֲבוֹתֵינוּ
leolam va'ed tzur chayeinu	וְאִמּוֹתֵינוּ לְעוֹלָם וָעֶד צוּר חַיֵּינוּ
magein yisheinu at hi ledor vador	מָגֵן יִשְׁעֵנוּ אַתְּ הִיא לְדוֹר וָדוֹר
nodeh lach unesaper tehilatech	נוֹדֶה לָךְ וּנְסַפֵּר תְּהִלָּתֵךְ
al chayeinu hamesurim beyadech	עַל חַיֵּינוּ הַמְּסוּרִים בְּיָדֵךְ
ve'al nishmoteinu hapekudot lach	וְעַל נִשְׁמוֹתֵינוּ הַפְּקוּדוֹת לָךְ
ve'al niseich shebechol yom imanu	וְעַל נִסֵּיךְ שֶׁבְּכָל יוֹם עִמָּנוּ
ve'al niflotayich vetovotayich shebechol eit	וְעַל נִפְלְאוֹתַיִךְ וְטוֹבוֹתַיִךְ שֶׁבְּכָל עֵת
erev vavoker vetzaharayim	עֶרֶב וָבֹקֶר וְצָהֳרָיִם
hatov ki lo chalu rachamayich	הַטּוֹב כִּי לֹא כָלוּ רַחֲמַיִךְ
vehamerachemet shelo tamu chasadayich	וְהַמְרַחֶמֶת כִּי לֹא תַמּוּ חֲסָדַיִךְ
me'olam kivinu lach	מֵעוֹלָם קִוִּינוּ לָךְ

We give thanks to You, Being and Becoming, Strength of our ancestors, Rock on which our lives evolve, our protecting Shell within which we transform. You are That, for all generations, and we are grateful. You hold our bodies in your hands and keep the archive of our spirits. We thank You, for You are daily miracles, those of morning, noon, and night. You are the abundance of creation, in which compassion and creativity are endless. We have hoped in You since the beginning of the world.

ON CHANUKAH AND PURIM / בחנוכה ופורים

al hanisim ve'al hapurkan
ve'al hag'vurot ve'al hatshuot
ve'al hatekufot sheasit ledoroteinu
bayamim haheim bazman hazeh.

עַל הַנִסִּים וְעַל הַפֻּרְקָן
וְעַל הַגְּבוּרוֹת וְעַל הַתְּשׁוּעוֹת
וְעַל הַתְּקוּפוֹת שֶׁעָשִׂיתָ לְדוֹרוֹתֵינוּ
בַּיָּמִים הָהֵם בַּזְּמַן הַזֶּה

For the miracles and changes and triumphs worked in the world
for our ancestors and us, we are grateful.

ve'al kulam yitbarach sh'meich
rucheinu tamid le'olam va'ed.

וְעַל כֻּלָּם יִתְבָּרַךְ וְיִתְרוֹמַם שְׁמֵךְ
רוּחֵנוּ תָּמִיד לְעוֹלָם וָעֶד

And for all these things, many-named one, we are grateful.

ON THE TEN DAYS OF REPENTANCE / בעשרת ימי תשובה

uchitvi lechayyim tovim kol b'nei briteich

וּכְתְבִי לְחַיִּים טוֹבִים כָּל בְּנֵי בְּרִיתֵךְ

Scribe of Life, inscribe for abundant life all who are children of your web of life.

vekol hachayim yoduch selah
vihallelu et sh'meich be'emet
ha'el yeshuateinu ve'ezrateinu selah.
beruchah at shekhinah
hatov sh'meich velach naeh lehodot.

וְכֹל הַחַיִּים יוֹדוּךְ סֶּלָה
וִיהַלְלוּ אֶת שְׁמֵךְ בֶּאֱמֶת
הָאֵל יְשׁוּעָתֵנוּ וְעֶזְרָתֵנוּ סֶּלָה.
בְּרוּכָה אַתְּ שְׁכִינָה
הַטּוֹב שְׁמֵךְ וְלָךְ נָאֶה לְהוֹדוֹת.

All life sings to the essence of life, the Changer who changes us. Blessed are You who hold the many names and the abundant voices calling out in praise.

7. BLESSING FOR PEACE (SHALOM RAV)

shalom rav al yisrael amech tasimi le'olam
ki at hi malka eden lekhol hashalom
vetov be'eynech levarekh et amekh yisrael
bechol eit uvechol sha'ah bishlomech.
berucha at shechina
hamvorechet et amah yisrael
ve'kol yoshvei tevel bashalom.

שָׁלוֹם רָב עַל יִשְׂרָאֵל עַמֵּךְ תָּשִׂימִי לְעוֹלָם
כִּי אַתְּ הִיא מַלְכָּה אֶדֶן לְכָל הַשָּׁלוֹם
וְטוֹב בְּעֵינַיִךְ לְבָרֵךְ אֶת עַמֵּךְ יִשְׂרָאֵל
בְּכָל עֵת וּבְכָל שָׁעָה בִּשְׁלוֹמֵךְ.
בְּרוּכָה אַתְּ שְׁכִינָה
הַמְבָרֶכֶת אֶת עַמָּהּ יִשְׂרָאֵל
וְכָל יוֹשְׁבֵי תֵבֵל בַּשָּׁלוֹם

May peace, abundance, blessing, grace, compassion
come to us and all Israel and all the world.
Bless us, mothersource of being, as one in the light of your presence,
for in the light of your many faces you have given us a path of life,
loving kindness and justice and blessing and mercy and life and peace.
May our eyes be your eyes,
shining and blessing your people everywhere with peace.

Blessed are You, Yah-Shekhinah,
who blesses her people Israel and all those who dwell on earth with peace.

III. ALTERNATE AMIDAH: THE DREAM

I had and am the dream
in the dream I touched the pulse of the all that is
fringes made of milk and honey
ancient stories
imprints of love
seamlessly weaving
always completing
And as I stood
my arms became doorposts
my legs like gates

And it was there and then that my heart burst forth with love
overflowing into the valleys running up the mountains
and down the hills
out of me came the letters
the letters became words
and the words became fire
like flecks of gold riding on the wind
looking for places to bring the light in
My body mind surrendered and the joy spilled over
With my sight I heard a thousand dreams being born
Each one a different shape a different color
different size
no dream the same
no dream too wrong
no words frozen in time
This my dream that I am living out
the day the Torah could no longer be contained on paper
but an in-habitation of the heart
all the words were alive
And oh how I love the goddess, in her I am inscribed

To elevate and praise
to finally be reunited with all the pieces of yourself you sent into exile
the lands and the dimensions rise up and call you blessed

For the pain of your disbelonging has come to an end
How the stories of the past, the places of our greatest pain
then become the markers of the places we have been
To elevate and praise
to embrace
to for-give without diminishing what once was the site of pain.

Oh where your journey will take you
you just never know
that following your neshama just may save us all
oh praise be.
That the neglected
the rejected
the return, the turn
the indwelling of the inscription–you be-long

and how you have long to be
be-coming, coming to be
what has never been lost
hidden in plain sight
what only your third eye can perceive-that you are no longer "the children"
you have become the cultivator of a living dream
Oh praise and exaltation to the holy and sacred process of learning to live
not in regret of your story
but in celebration because that story brought you here
You didn't know of what's to come
and we cannot live afraid- for it is in this season
in this lifetime we've come to put a famine to end

The silent tears and whispered pillow prayers when will G!d be a she, he, they and them
You/we/me are the living answers of clamoring prayers
And when your work is complete
it will have been your journey that fed our deepest longings
And so you see/be and innerstand
you are the dream

Angelique Rivera

SHE WHO MAKES PEACE (OSAH SHALOM)

עוֹשָׂה שָׁלוֹם בִּמְרוֹמֶיהָ
הִיא תַעֲשֶׂה שָׁלוֹם עָלֵינוּ

osah shalom bimromeha
hi ta'aseh shalom aleynu

May She Who Makes Peace
Shine Peace Upon All of Us

Taya Shere, adaptation of Bhajamana Ma / traditional Devi Kirtan melody

IV. TRADITIONAL WEEKDAY AMIDAH FEMININE GOD-LANGUAGE

1. BLESSING FOR ANCESTORS (IMAHOT, AVOT, DOROT

beruchah at shekhinah eloheinu ve'elohei	בְּרוּכָה אַתְּ שְׁכִינָה אֱלֹהֵינוּ וֵאלֹהֵי
imoteinu va'avoteinu vedoroteinu	אִמּוֹתֵנוּ וַאֲבוֹתֵינוּ וְדוֹרוֹתֵינוּ
elohei sarah, elohei rivka,	אֱלֹהֵי שָׂרָה אֱלֹהֵי רִבְקָה
elohei rachel, ve'elohei leah	אֱלֹהֵי רָחֵל וֵאלֹהֵי לֵאָה
(ve'elohei bilhah ve'elohei zilpah)	וֵאלֹהֵי בִּלְהָה וֵאלֹהֵי זִלְפָּה
elohei avraham elohei yitzchak ve'elohei yaakov	אֱלֹהֵי אַבְרָהָם אֱלֹהֵי יִצְחָק וֵאלֹהֵי יַעֲקֹב
ha'elah hagedolah hagiborah vehanora'ah	הָאֵלָה הַגְּדוֹלָה הַגִּבּוֹרָה וְהַנּוֹרָאָה
elah ilaah	אֵלָה עִלָּאָה
gomelet chasadim tovim	גּוֹמֶלֶת חֲסָדִים טוֹבִים
vekonah hakol vezocheret chasdei avot ve'imahot	וְקוֹנָה הַכֹּל וְזוֹכֶרֶת חַסְדֵי אָבוֹת וְאִמָּהוֹת
umeviah goelet livnot venoteihen	וּמְבִיאָה גּוֹאֶלֶת לִבְנוֹת בְּנוֹתֵיהֶן
(velivnei v'neihem)	וְלִבְנֵי בְּנֵיהֶם
lma'an shmah be'ahavah.	לְמַעַן שְׁמָהּ בְּאַהֲבָה.

BETWEEN ROSH HASHANAH AND YOM KIPPUR	בעשרת ימי תשובה
zochrinu lechayim ruach chafetzet bachayim	זָכְרִינוּ לְחַיִּים רוּחַ חֲפֵצֶת בַּחַיִּים
vekitvinu lesefer hachayyim	וְכִתְבִינוּ בְּסֵפֶר הַחַיִּים
lema'anech ma'yan chayim.	לְמַעֲנֵךְ מַעְיָן חַיִּים

malka ozeret u'moshiah u'mayan.	מַלְכָּה עוֹזֶרֶת וּמוֹשִׁיעָה וּמָעְיָן.
beruchah at shekhinah	בְּרוּכָה אַתְּ שְׁכִינָה
magen avraham ve'ezrat sarah.	מָגֵן אַבְרָהָם וְעֶזְרַת שָׂרָה.

Blessed are You, Shekhinah, our Source and Source of our parents:
Life-force of Sarah, Rebekah, Rachel, Leah, Bilhah, and Zilpah,
of Abraham, Isaac and Jacob.
Great Goddess, strong, revered, exalted,
pouring out Your abundant kindness on all beings,
forming the All and all things in it,
weaving a web of kindness for our ancestors,
bringing wholeness to all generations
for the sake of your Name that dwells with us in love.

BETWEEN ROSH HASHANAH AND YOM KIPPUR
Remember us for life, Spirit who desires life
and write us in the book of life, for your sake, Source of Life.

Ruler of the cosmos and its servant,
aiding us in our brokenness and bringing us to wholeness:
Blessed are You, shield of Abraham, helper of Sarah.

2. BLESSING FOR THE CIRCLE OF LIFE (GEVUROT)

at gevirah le'olam shadai אַתְּ גְּבִירָה לְעוֹלָם שָׁדַי
mechayah meitim at rav lehoshia מְחַיָּה מֵתִים אַתְּ רַב לְהוֹשִׁיעַ

BETWEEN SHEMINI ATZERET AND PASSOVER בין ש"א ופסח
meishivah haruach umoridah hagashem מַשִּׁיבָה הָרוּחַ וּמוֹרִידָה הַגֶּשֶׁם

mechalkelet chayim bechesed מְכַלְכֶּלֶת חַיִּים בְּחֶסֶד
mechayah meitim berachamim rabim מְחַיָּה מֵתִים בְּרַחֲמִים רַבִּים
somechet noflot verofeit cholim סוֹמֶכֶת נוֹפְלוֹת וְרוֹפֵאת חוֹלִים
umatirah asurot וּמַתִּירָה אֲסוּרוֹת
umekayemet emunatah lishnot afar וּמְקַיֶּמֶת אֱמוּנָתָהּ לִישֵׁנוֹת עָפָר
mi chamoch gevirat gevurot מִי כָמוֹךְ גְּבִירַת גְּבוּרוֹת
umi domah lach וּמִי דוֹמָה לָךְ
malkah meimitah umechayah מַלְכָּה מְמִיתָה וּמְחַיָּה
umatzmichat yeshuah וּמַצְמִיחַת יְשׁוּעָה

BETWEEN ROSH HASHANAH AND YOM KIPPUR בעשרת ימי תשובה
mi chamoch eim harachamim מִי כָמוֹךְ אֵם הָרַחֲמִים
zocheret yetzureha lechayyim berachamim זוֹכֶרֶת יְצוּרֶיהָ לְחַיִּים בְּרַחֲמִים

vene'emanah at lehachayot meitim. וְנֶאֱמָנָה אַתְּ לְהַחֲיוֹת מֵתִים.
beruchah at shekhinah בְּרוּכָה אַתְּ שְׁכִינָה
mechayah hameitim. מְחַיָּה הַמֵּתִים.

You are eternally gatekeeper and nurturer
turning life to death and death to life,
rescuing us from the void, sustaining life in love,
enlivening what dies in your great womb,
making what falls rise again
healing the hurt, freeing the enslaved, weaving all that sleeps in earth
into the bond of life.
Who could be like you, most potent
Queen who turns the wheel of death and life
and makes redemption flower.

BETWEEN ROSH HASHANAH AND YOM KIPPUR
Who is like you, mother of mercy,
remembering your creatures in Your womb of compassion?

Faithful are you in turning the wheel from death to life.
Blessed are You, Presence
who turns the wheel from death to life.

3. BLESSING FOR HOLINESS (KEDUSHAH)

אַתְּ קְדוֹשָׁה וּשְׁמֵךְ קָדוֹשׁ וּקְדוֹשׁוֹת בְּכָל יוֹם תְּהַלְלוּךְ סֶלָה.
בְּרוּכָה אַתְּ שְׁכִינָה הָאֵלָה הַקְּדוֹשָׁה.

at kedoshah ushimeich kadosh ukedoshot bechol yom tehalelookh selah. beruchah at shekhinah, ha'elah hakedoshah

You are holy, Your Name is holy, and those committed to holiness praise You at every moment. Blessed are You, holy Goddess.

4. BLESSING FOR WISDOM (DA'AT)

אַתְּ חוֹנֶנֶת לְאִשָּׁה דַּעַת וּמְלַמֶּדֶת לֶאֱנוֹשׁ בִּינָה. חָנֵּנוּ מֵאִתֵּךְ דֵּעָה בִּינָה וְהַשְׂכֵּל.
בְּרוּכָה אַתְּ שְׁכִינָה חוֹנֶנֶת הַדָּעַת.

at chonenet l'isha da'at umelamedet le'enosh binah. chaninu me'iteich de'ah binah vehaskel. beruchah at shekhinah, chonenet hada'at.

You grant knowledge to the earthling and teach wisdom to mortals. May we receive sense, discernment, and knowledge from You.
Blessed are You, who graces us with knowledge.

5. BLESSING FOR TURNING (TESHUVAH)

הֲשִׁיבֵנוּ אִמֵּינוּ לְתוֹרָתֵךְ וְקָרְבִינוּ מוֹרָתֵנוּ לַעֲבוֹדָתֵךְ וְהַחֲזִירִינוּ בִּתְשׁוּבָה שְׁלֵמָה לְפָנָיִךְ.
בְּרוּכָה אַתְּ שְׁכִינָה הָרוֹצָה בִּתְשׁוּבָה.

hashivinu imeinu letoratech vekarvinu morateinu la'avodateich vehachazirinu biteshuvah shleimah lefanayich. beruchah at shekhinah, harotzah biteshuvah.

Return us, our Source, to your ways, and draw us close, our Teacher, to your work.
Return us in a complete returning to you.
Blessed are You, who desires the circle of return.

6. BLESSING FOR FORGIVENESS (SELICHAH)

סִלְחִי לָנוּ אִמֵּינוּ כִּי חָטָאנוּ מַחֲלִי לָנוּ רוּחֵנוּ כִּי פָשַׁעְנוּ כִּי מוֹחֶלֶת וְסוֹלַחַת אָתְּ.
בְּרוּכָה אַתְּ שְׁכִינָה חַנוּנָה הַמַּרְבָּה לִסְלֹחַ.

silchi lanu imeinu ki chatanu machli lanu rucheinu ki fashanu ki mochelet ve solachat at. beruchah at shekhinah, chanunah hamarbah lisloach.

Forgive us, our Source, for we have lost ourselves. Be tender toward us, our guide, for we have made mistakes. You are a forgiver and a consoler.
Blessed are You, who is gracious in forgiveness.

7. BLESSING FOR REDEMPTION (GE'ULAH)

רְאִי בְעָנְיֵנוּ וְרִיבִי רִיבֵנוּ וּגְאָלֵינוּ מְהֵרָה לְמַעַן שְׁמֵךְ כִּי גּוֹאֶלֶת חֲזָקָה אָתְּ.
בְּרוּכָה אַתְּ שְׁכִינָה גּוֹאֶלֶת יִשְׂרָאֵל.

re'i ve'anyeinu verivi riveinu uge'alinu meheirah lemaan shmeich ki go'elet chazakah at. beruchah at shekhinah, goelet yisrael.

See our suffering, and care for us! Re-weave us into your web of abundant destiny, for the sake of your name, for you are a powerful re-maker.
Blessed are You, re-maker of those who wrestle with You.

8. BLESSING FOR HEALING (REFUAH)

רְפָאֵנוּ יהוה וְנֵרָפֵא הוֹשִׁיעֵנוּ וְנִוָּשֵׁעָה כִּי תְהִלָּתֵנוּ אָתְּ וְהַעֲלִי רְפוּאָה שְׁלֵמָה לְכָל מַכּוֹתֵינוּ.
כִּי אֱלָה רוּחַ רוֹפֵאת נֶאֱמָנָה וְרַחֲמָנָה אָתְּ. בְּרוּכָה אַתְּ שְׁכִינָה רוֹפֵאת חוֹלֵי עַמָהּ יִשְׂרָאֵל.

rifa'inu havayah venerapei hoshi'inu venivashea ki tehilateinu at veha'ali refuah sheleimah l'chol makoteinu. ki elah ruach rofei neemanah verachamanah at. beruchah at shekhinah, rofeit cholei amah yisrael.

Heal us, and we shall be healed, for You are the healing within. Raise up a full healing for all our hurts, for You are faithful and compassionate.
Blessed are You, healer of all who wrestle with the life-force.

9. BLESSING FOR ABUNDANCE (TOVAH)

בָּרְכִי עָלֵינוּ יָהּ אֱלֹהֵינוּ אֶת הַשָּׁנָה הַזֹּאת וְאֶת כָּל מִינֵי תְבוּאָתָהּ לְטוֹבָה בקיץ וְתֵן בְּרָכָה
בחרף וְתֵן טַל וּמָטָר לִבְרָכָה עַל פְּנֵי הָאֲדָמָה וְשַׂבְּעֵנוּ מִטּוּבֵךְ וּבָרְכִי שְׁנָתֵנוּ כַּשָּׁנִים הַטּוֹבוֹת.
בְּרוּכָה אַתְּ שְׁכִינָה מְבָרֶכֶת הַשָּׁנִים.

barchi aleinu yah eloheinu et hashanah hazot ve'et kol minei tevuatah letovah.
IN WINTER: vetein berachah. IN SUMMER: vetein tal umatar livrachah
al pnei ha'adamah vesabinu mituveich uvarchi shnateinu kashanim hatovot.
beruchah at shekhinah, mevarechet hashanim

Bless us with a good year, and may all the year's produce be for good. Grant blessing (dew and rain to bless) to the face of the earth, and sustain us with your abundance.
O bless the transformations of this year, as You bless all good years.
Blessed are You, who blesses the changing years.

10. BLESSING FOR INGATHERING (KIBBUTZ)

תִּקְעִי בְּשׁוֹפָר גָּדוֹל לְחֵרוּתֵנוּ וְשִׂאִי נֵס לְקַבֵּץ גָּלֻיּוֹתֵינוּ וְקַבְּצִנוּ יַחַד מֵאַרְבַּע כַּנְפוֹת הָאָרֶץ. בְּרוּכָה אַתְּ שְׁכִינָה מְקַבֶּצֶת נִדְחֵי עַמָּהּ יִשְׂרָאֵל.

tiki bashofar gadol lecheiruteinu u'se'i nes lekabeitz galuyoteinu vekabtzinu yachad me'arba kanfot ha'aretz. beruchah at shekhinah, mekabetzet nidchei amah yisrael.

Blow on the great ram's horn to summon freedom! Lift up the miracles that will gather in the exiles! Gather us together from the four corners of the earth. Blessed are You, who gathers in the wanderers who have wrestled with the Divine.

11. BLESSING FOR JUSTICE (MISHPAT)

הָשִׁיבִי שׁוֹפְטֵינוּ וְשָׂרוֹתֵינוּ כְּבָרִאשׁוֹנָה וְיוֹעֲצֵינוּ כְּבַתְּחִלָּה וְהָסֵרִי מִמֶּנּוּ יָגוֹן וַאֲנָחָה וּמִלְכִי עָלֵינוּ אַתְּ יָהּ לְבַד בְּחֶסֶד וּבְרַחֲמִים, וְצַדְּקִינוּ בַּמִּשְׁפָּט. בְּרוּכָה אַתְּ שְׁכִינָה מַרְאָה אוֹהֶבֶת צְדָקָה וּמִשְׁפָּט.

hashivi shofteinu vesaroteinu kevarishonah veyoatzeinu kevatechilah, vehaseiri mimenu yagon va'anachah umilchi aleinu at yah l'vad bechesed uverachamim vetzadkinu bamishpat. beruchah at shekhinah, marah ohevet tzedakah umishpat.

Restore our leaders to us as it was in the very beginning, and our advisors, as it was at first, and keep far from us plague and persecution, and you alone rule through us in love and compassion, and teach us righteous justice. Blessed are You, Mirror who loves righteousness and justice.

12. BLESSING FOR PROTECTION (SHEMIRAH)

וְלַמַּלְשִׁינִים אַל תְּהִי תִקְוָה וְכָל הָרִשְׁעָה כְּרֶגַע תֹּאבֵד וְכָל אוֹיְבַיִךְ מְהֵרָה יִכָּרֵתוּ וְהַזֵּדִים מְהֵרָה תְעַקְּרִי וּתְשַׁבְּרִי וּתְמַגְּרִי וְתַכְנִיעָה בִּמְהֵרָה בְיָמֵינוּ. בְּרוּכָה אַתְּ שְׁכִינָה שׁוֹבֶרֶת אֹיְבִים וּמַכְנִיעָה זֵדִים.

velamalshinim al tehi tikvah vechol harishah karega toveid vechol oyvayich meheirah yikareitu vehazeidim meheirah te'akri uteshabri utmageri vetachni'ah bimheirah veyameinu. beruchah at shekhinah, shoveret oyvim umachnia zeidim.

Do not be a support to those who hurt others for their own gain! Let wickedness disappear like a passing moment. May those who act as enemies quickly be cut off from their enmity, and may hatred be uprooted and broken quickly, in our own days. Blessed are You, who breaks down hatred and enmity.

13. BLESSING FOR THE RIGHTEOUS (TZADIKIM)

עַל הַצַדִּיקִים וְעַל הַחֲסִידוֹת וְעַל זִקְנוֹת עַמֵּךְ בֵּית יִשְׂרָאֵל וְעַל פְּלֵיטַת סוֹפְרֵיהֶן וְעַל גֵּרֵי הַצֶּדֶק וְעָלֵינוּ יֶהֱמוּ נָא רַחֲמַיִךְ שְׁכִינָה אֱלֹהֵינוּ וּתְנִי שָׂכָר טוֹב לְכָל הַבּוֹטְחוֹת בְּשְׁמֵךְ בֶּאֱמֶת וְשִׂימִי חֶלְקֵנוּ עִמָּהֶן לְעוֹלָם וְלֹא נֵבוֹשׁ כִּי בָךְ בָּטָחְנוּ. בְּרוּכָה אַתְּ שְׁכִינָה מִשְׁעָן וּמִבְטָח לַצַדִּיקוֹת.

al hatzadikim ve'al hachasidot ve'al ziknot ameich beit yisrael ve'al peleitat sofreihen ve'al gerei hatzedek ve'aleinu ychcmu na rachamayich shekhinah eloheinu uteni sachar tov lechol habotchot bishmeich be'emet vesimi chelkeinu imahen le'olam velo neivosh ki vach batachnu. beruchah at shekhinah, mishan umivtach latzadikot.

Upon the righteous and the kind, and on the elders of the house of Israel, upon the remnant of its scholars, upon all who have chosen to cling to the Tree of Life, upon all beings, and upon us, may Your compassionate womb be moved, Shekhinah, and may you give a good reward to all who trust in your name. Make our destiny like our righteous ancestors, so that we may not be shamed, for we trust in you.
Blessed are You, staff and shelter to the righteous.

14. BLESSING FOR SACRED SPACE (YERUSHALAYIM)

וְלִירוּשָׁלַיִם עִירָהּ בְּרַחֲמִים תָּשׁוּבִי וְתִשְׁכּוֹן בְּתוֹכָהּ כַּאֲשֶׁר דִּבֵּרָה וּבְנִי אוֹתָהּ בְּקָרוֹב בְּיָמֵינוּ בִּנְיַן עוֹלָם וְאֶבֶן שְׁתִיָּה מְהֵרָה לְתוֹכָהּ תָּכִינִי. בְּרוּכָה אַתְּ שְׁכִינָה בּוֹנָה יְרוּשָׁלַיִם.

veliyerushalayim irah berachamim tashuvi vetishkon betochah ka'asher diberah uvni otah bekarov beyameinu binyan olam ve'even shetiyah meheirah letochah tachin. beruchah at shekhinah, bonah yerushalayim.

May She return in compassion to Jerusalem her city, and dwell in her midst as she promised. O build her quickly into an eternal home for all seekers! Establish the foundation stone in her midst. Blessed are You, Builder of the city of peace.

15. BLESSING FOR THE FUTURE (YESHUAH)

אֶת צֶמַח דָּוִד עַבְדֵּךְ מְהֵרָה תַצְמִיחִי וְקֶרֶן רוּת תָּרוּמִי בִּישׁוּעָתֵךְ כִּי לִישׁוּעָתֵךְ קִוִּינוּ כָּל הַיּוֹם. בְּרוּכָה אַתְּ שְׁכִינָה מַצְמִיחָה קֶרֶן יְשׁוּעָה.

et tzemach david avdeich meheirah tatzmichi vekeren rut tarumi biyeshuatech ki liyeshuateich kivinu kol hayom. beruchah at shekhinah, matzmichah keren yeshuah.

May the sprout of David grow, and may Ruth's horn sound the redeeming power of change, for every day we wait for transformation. Blessed are You, who sounds the horn of change.

16. BLESSING FOR PRAYER (TEFILAH)

שְׁמְעִי קוֹלֵנוּ ירוה אֱלֹהֵינוּ חוּסִי וְרַחֲמִי עָלֵינוּ וְקַבְּלִי בְּרַחֲמִים וּבְרָצוֹן אֶת תְּפִלָּתֵנוּ כִּי אֵלָה שׁוֹמַעַת תְּפִלּוֹת וְתַחֲנוּנִים אָתְּ וּמִלְּפָנַיִךְ מְקוֹרֵנוּ רֵיקָם אַל תְּשִׁיבֵנוּ כִּי אַתְּ שׁוֹמַעַת תְּפִלַּת עַמֵּךְ יִשְׂרָאֵל בְּרַחֲמִים. בְּרוּכָה אַתְּ שְׁכִינָה שׁוֹמַעַת תְּפִלָּה.

shema koleinu shekhinah eloheinu chusi verachami aleinu, vekabli berachamim uvratzon et tefilateinu ki elah shoma'at tefilot vetachanunim at umilifanayich mekoreinu al teshivinu ki at shoma'at tefilat ameich yisrael berachamim. beruchah at shekhinah, shoma'at tefilah.

Hear our prayer, Eternal, and have compassion on us. With desire and compassion receive our prayer, for You are the one who hears prayer and petition. Do not turn us away empty, for You are one who hears the prayers of the people with kindness. Blessed are You, hearer of prayer.

17. BLESSING FOR PRESENCE (SHEKHINAH)

רְצִי שְׁכִינָה אֱלֹהֵינוּ בְּדוֹרוֹת יִשְׂרָאֵל וּבִתְפִלָּתָן וְהָשִׁיבִי אֶת הָעֲבוֹדָה לִדְבִיר בֵּיתֵךְ וְאִשֵּׁי יִשְׂרָאֵל וּתְפִלָּתָן בְּאַהֲבָה תְקַבְּלִי בְרָצוֹן וּתְהִי לְרָצוֹן תָּמִיד עֲבוֹדַת יִשְׂרָאֵל עַמֵּךְ. וְתֶחֱזֶינָה עֵינֵינוּ בְּשׁוּבֵךְ לְצִיּוֹן בְּרַחֲמִים. בְּרוּכָה אַתְּ שְׁכִינָה הַמַּחֲזִירָה שְׁכִינָתָהּ לְצִיּוֹן.

retzi shekhinah eloheinu bedorot yisrael uvitefilatan vehashivi ha'avodah lidvir beiteich ve'ishei yisrael utefilatan be'ahavah tekabli veratzon tamid avodat yisrael ameich. vetechezena eineinu beshuvech letzion berachamim.
bruchah at shekhinah, hamachazirah shechinatah letzion.

Be glad, Shekhinah, in the generations of our tribe and their prayers, and return the ancient rituals to your holy shrine, the earth. Accept the offerings of the people and their prayers in love, and may our ceremonies always join with your desire. May our eyes see your return to the land in compassion. Blessed are You, Shekhinah returning to sacred earth, in Zion and everywhere.

18. BLESSING FOR GRATITUDE (MODIM)

modim anachnu lach she'at hi havayah	מוֹדִים אֲנַחְנוּ לָךְ שֶׁאַתְּ הִיא הֲוָיָה
eloheinu ve'elohei avoteinu ve'imoteinu	אֱלֹהֵינוּ וֵאלֹהֵי אֲבוֹתֵינוּ וְאִמּוֹתֵינוּ
leolam va'ed tzur chayeinu	לְעוֹלָם וָעֶד צוּר חַיֵּינוּ
magein yisheinu at hi ledor vador	מָגֵן יִשְׁעֵנוּ אַתְּ הִיא לְדוֹר וָדוֹר
nodeh lach unesaper tehilatech	נוֹדֶה לָּךְ וּנְסַפֵּר תְּהִלָּתֵךְ
al chayeinu hamesurim beyadech	עַל חַיֵּינוּ הַמְּסוּרִים בְּיָדֵךְ
ve'al nishmoteinu hapekudot lach	וְעַל נִשְׁמוֹתֵינוּ הַפְּקוּדוֹת לָךְ
ve'al niseich shebechol yom imanu	וְעַל נִסֵּיךְ שֶׁבְּכָל יוֹם עִמָּנוּ
ve'al niflotayich vetovotayich shebechol eit	וְעַל נִפְלְאוֹתַיִךְ וְטוֹבוֹתַיִךְ שֶׁבְּכָל עֵת
erev vavoker vetzaharayim	עֶרֶב וָבֹקֶר וְצָהֳרָיִם
hatov ki lo chalu rachamayich	הַטּוֹב כִּי לֹא כָלוּ רַחֲמֶיךָ
vehamerachemet ki lo tamu chasadayich	וְהַמְרַחֶמֶת כִּי לֹא תַמּוּ חֲסָדַיִךְ
me'olam kivinu lach	מֵעוֹלָם קִוִּינוּ לָךְ

We give thanks to You, Being and Becoming, Strength of our ancestors, Rock on which our lives evolve, our protecting Shell within which we transform. You are That, for all generations, and we are grateful. You hold our bodies in your hands and keep the archive of our spirits. We thank You, for You are daily miracles, those of morning, noon, and night. You are the abundance of creation, in which compassion and creativity are endless. We have hoped in You since the beginning of the world.

ON CHANUKAH AND PURIM	בחנוכה ופורים
al hanisim ve'al hapurkan ve'al hag'vurot	עַל הַנִּסִּים וְעַל הַפֻּרְקָן וְעַל הַגְּבוּרוֹת
ve'al hatshuot ve'al hatekufot sheasit ledoroteinu	וְעַל הַתְּשׁוּעוֹת וְעַל הַתְּקוּפוֹת שֶׁעָשִׂית לְדוֹרוֹתֵינוּ
bayamim haheim bazman hazeh.	בַּיָּמִים הָהֵם בַּזְּמַן הַזֶּה

For the miracles and changes and triumphs worked in the world
for our ancestors and us, we are grateful.

ve'al kulam yitbarach sh'meich	וְעַל כֻּלָּם יִתְבָּרַךְ וְיִתְרוֹמַם שְׁמֵךְ
rucheinu tamid le'olam va'ed.	רוּחֵנוּ תָּמִיד לְעוֹלָם וָעֶד

And for all these things, many-named one, we are grateful.

ON THE TEN DAYS OF REPENTANCE	בעשרת ימי תשובה
uchitvi lechayyim tovim kol b'nei vriteich	וּכְתְבִי לְחַיִּים טוֹבִים כָּל בְּנֵי בְרִיתֵךְ

Scribe of Life, inscribe for abundant life all who are children of your web of life.

vekol hachayim yoduch selah	וְכֹל הַחַיִּים יוֹדוּךְ סֶּלָה
vihallelu et shmeich be'emet	וִיהַלְלוּ אֶת שְׁמֵךְ בֶּאֱמֶת
ha'el yeshuateinu ve'ezrateinu selah.	הָאֵל יְשׁוּעָתֵנוּ וְעֶזְרָתֵנוּ סֶּלָה.
beruchah at shekhinah	בְּרוּכָה אַתְּ שְׁכִינָה
hatov shimech velach naeh lehodot.	הַטּוֹב שִׁמֵךְ וְלָךְ נָאֶה לְהוֹדוֹת.

All life sings to the essence of life, the Changer who changes us. Blessed are You who hold the many names and the abundant voices calling out in praise.

AT NIGHT, CONTINUE BELOW;
BY DAY, CONTINUE ON THE FOLLOWING PAGE.

19. BLESSING FOR PEACE (SHALOM RAV)

shalom rav al yisrael amech tasimi le'olam	שָׁלוֹם רָב עַל יִשְׂרָאֵל עַמֵּךְ תָּשִׂימִי לְעוֹלָם
ki at hi malka eden lekhol hashalom	כִּי אַתְּ הִיא מַלְכָּה אֶדֶן לְכָל הַשָּׁלוֹם
vetov be'eynayich levarekh et amekh yisrael	וְטוֹב בְּעֵינַיִךְ לְבָרֵךְ אֶת עַמֵּךְ יִשְׂרָאֵל
bechol eit uvechol sha'ah bishlomech	בְּכָל עֵת וּבְכָל שָׁעָה בִּשְׁלוֹמֵךְ
berucha at yah-shechina	בְּרוּכָה אַתְּ יָהּ שְׁכִינָה
hamvorechet et amah yisrael	הַמְבֹרֶכֶת אֶת עַמָּהּ יִשְׂרָאֵל
ve'kol yoshvei tevel bashalom.	וְכָל יוֹשְׁבֵי תֵבֵל בַּשָּׁלוֹם.

May peace, abundance, blessing, grace, compassion come to us and all Israel and all the world. Bless us, mothersource of being, as one in the light of your presence, for in the light of your many faces you have given us a path of life, loving kindness and justice and blessing and mercy and life and peace. May our eyes be your eyes, shining and blessing your people everywhere with peace. Blessed are You, Yah-Shekhinah, who blesses her people Israel and all those who dwell on earth with peace.

BY DAY, CONTINUE HERE

PRIESTEXXLY BLESSING

תְּבָרְכֵךְ שַׁדַּי וְתִשְׁמְרֵךְ □ tevarcheich shadai vetishmereich
תָּאֵר שַׁדַּי פָּנֶיהָ אֵלַיִךְ וּתְחֻנֵּךְ   ta'er shadai paneha elayich ut'chuneich
תִּשָּׂא שַׁדַּי פָּנֶיהָ אֵלַיִךְ   tisa shadai paneha elayich
וְתָשֵׂם לָךְ שָׁלוֹם   vetasem lach shalom

יְבָרֶכְךָ יהוה וְיִשְׁמְרֶךָ △ yevarechecha adonai veyishmerecha
יָאֵר יהוה פָּנָיו אֵלֶיךָ וִיחֻנֶּךָּ   ya'er adonai panav elecha viychuneka
יִשָּׂא יהוה פָּנָיו אֵלֶיךָ   yisa adonai panav eilecha
וְיָשֵׂם לְךָ שָׁלוֹם   veyasem lecha shalom

יְבָרְכֹךְ הֲוָיָה וְיִשְׁמְרֹךְ ⊖ yevarchocheh havayah vishmerocheh
יָאֱרֶה הֲוָיָה פָּנֶהֶ אֵילֶיחֶ וִיחֳנֹחֶ   yaeyreh havayah paneheh eilecheh viychonocheh
יִשְׂאֶה הֲוָיָה פָּנֶהֶ אֵילֶיחֶ   yiseh havayah paneheh eilecheh
וְיָשֵׂמֶה לֶחֶ שָׁלוֹם   veyaseymeh leche shalom

May the One of Being bless you and keep you.
May the One Who Is shine the Divine faces on you and show you grace.
May the Who Is Becoming lift up the Divine faces to you,
and grant you wholeness and peace.

PRIESTESS BLESSING

May She bless you and May She keep you

As She shines Her face

May you embody grace

May Zhe bless you and may Zhe keep you

As Zhe brings release

May you embody peace (alt: May you give birth to peace)

Taya Shere

↵

19. BLESSING FOR PEACE (SIM SHALOM)

simi shalom tovah uvrachah
chein vachesed verachamim aleinu ve al ameich.
barcheinu imeinu kulanu ke'echad be'or panayich
ki ve'or panayich natat lanu shaddai eloteinu
torat chayim ve'ahavat chesed utzdakah uvrachah
verachamim vechayim veshalom.
vetov be'eineich levarech
et umotayich yisrael vekol umotayich
bechol eit uvechol sha'ah bishlomeich.

שִׂימִי שָׁלוֹם טוֹבָה וּבְרָכָה
חֵן וָחֶסֶד וְרַחֲמִים עָלֵינוּ וְעַל כָּל עַמֵּךְ
בָּרְכֵנוּ אִמֵּנוּ כֻּלָּנוּ כְּאֶחָד בְּאוֹר פָּנָיִךְ
כִּי בְאוֹר פָּנַיִךְ נָתַתְּ לָנוּ שַׁדַּי אֱלֹתֵינוּ
תּוֹרַת חַיִּים וְאַהֲבַת חֶסֶד וּצְדָקָה וּבְרָכָה
וְרַחֲמִים וְחַיִּים וְשָׁלוֹם
וְטוֹב בְּעֵינַיִךְ לְבָרֵךְ
אֶת אֻמּוֹתַיִךְ יִשְׂרָאֵל
בְּכָל עֵת וּבְכָל שָׁעָה בִּשְׁלוֹמֵךְ.

Plant peace,
abundance,
blessing,
grace,
love,
compassion
in us and all Your people.

Bless us, our Mother, one and all, with the light of Your Faces,
for by that light you have given us life-wisdom and a love of love itself,
and justice and blessing and compassion and life and peace.

For it is good in your eyes to bless this Godwrestling people,
and all peoples, at all times, with Your peace.

brucha at yah shechina
hamevorechet et amah yisrael
ve'et kol yoshvei tevel bashalom.

בְּרוּכָה אַתְּ יָהּ שְׁכִינָה
הַמְבָרֶכֶת אֶת עַמָּהּ יִשְׂרָאֵל
וְאֶת כָּל יוֹשְׁבֵי תֵבֵל בַּשָּׁלוֹם.

Blessed are You, Yah-Shekhinah,
who blesses her people Israel
and all those who dwell on earth with peace.

SHE WHO MAKES PEACE (OSAH SHALOM)

עוֹשָׂה שָׁלוֹם בִּמְרוֹמֶיהָ
הִיא תַּעֲשֶׂה שָׁלוֹם עָלֵינוּ

osah shalom bimromeha
hi ta'aseh shalom aleynu

May She Who Makes Peace
Shine Peace Upon All of Us

Taya Shere, adaptation of Bhajamana Ma / traditional Devi Kirtan melody

SISTER

אֲחֹתֵנוּ אַתְּ הֲיִי לְאַלְפֵי רְבָבָה

achoteynu at hayi l'alfei r'vava

Sister may you know
Her myriad faces within you
Sister may you grow
Her myriad faces, She is you

Sibling may you know
The myriad faces within you
Sibling may you grow
The myriad faces, Zhe is you

Taya Shere, from Genesis 24:60 (the Hebrew of this chant is the blessing received by Rivka the matriarch as she embarks on her journey. This English adaptation blesses generativity, creativity and becoming of many kinds.)

V. TRADITIONAL FESTIVAL AMIDAH, GENDER-BALANCED

1. BLESSING FOR ANCESTORS (IMAHOT, AVOT, DOROT)

beruchah at shekhinah eloheinu	בְּרוּכָה אַתְּ שְׁכִינָה אֱלֹהֵינוּ
ve'elohei imoteinu va'avoteinu vedoroteinu	וֵאלֹהֵי אִמוֹתֵנוּ וַאֲבוֹתֵינוּ וְדוֹרוֹתֵינוּ
elohei sarah, elohei rivka,	אֱלֹהֵי שָׂרָה אֱלֹהֵי רִבְקָה
elohei rachel, ve'elohei leah	אֱלֹהֵי רָחֵל וֵאלֹהֵי לֵאָה
(ve'elohei bilhah ve'elohei zilpah)	וֵאלֹהֵי בִּלְהָה וֵאלֹהֵי זִלְפָּה
elohei avraham elohei yitzchak ve'elohei yaakov	אֱלֹהֵי אַבְרָהָם אֱלֹהֵי יִצְחָק וֵאלֹהֵי יַעֲקֹב
ha'elah hagedolah hagiborah vehanora'ah	הָאֵלָה הַגְּדוֹלָה הַגִּבּוֹרָה וְהַנּוֹרָאָה
elah ilaah	אֵלָה עִלָּאָה
gomelet chasadim tovim	גּוֹמֶלֶת חֲסָדִים טוֹבִים
vekonah hakol vezocheret chasdei avot ve'imahot	וְקוֹנָה הַכֹּל וְזוֹכֶרֶת חַסְדֵי אָבוֹת וְאִמָּהוֹת
umeviah goelet livnot venoteihen	וּמְבִיאָה גּוֹאֶלֶת לִבְנוֹת בְּנוֹתֵיהֶן
(velivnei v'neihem)	וְלִבְנֵי בְּנֵיהֶם
lma'an shmah be'ahavah.	לְמַעַן שְׁמָהּ בְּאַהֲבָה
malka ozeret u'moshiah u'mayan.	מַלְכָּה עוֹזֶרֶת וּמוֹשִׁיעָה וּמַעְיָן.
beruchah at shekhinah,	בְּרוּכָה אַתְּ שְׁכִינָה
magen avraham ve'ezrat sarah.	מָגֵן אַבְרָהָם וְעֶזְרַת שָׂרָה.

Blessed are You, Shekhinah, our Source and Source of our parents
Life-force of Sarah, Rebekah, Rachel, Leah, Bilhah, and Zilpah,
of Abraham, Isaac and Jacob.
Great Goddess, strong, revered, exalted,
pouring out Your abundant kindness on all beings,
forming the All and all things in it,
weaving a web of kindness for our ancestors,
bringing wholeness to all generations
for the sake of your Name that dwells with us in love.
Ruler of the cosmos and its servant,
seeing us in our brokenness and bringing us to wholeness.

2. BLESSING FOR THE CIRCLE OF LIFE (GEVUROT)

at gebirah le'olam shadai
mechayah meitim at rav lehoshiah

   BETWEEN SHEMINI ATZERET AND PASSOVER
   meishivah haruach umoridah hagashem

mechalkelet chayim bechesed
mechayah meitim berachamim rabim
somechet noflot verofeit cholim
umatirah asurot
umekayemet emunatah lisheinot afar
mi chamoch gevirat gevurot
umi domah lach
malkah memitah umechayah
umatzmichah yeshuah

   BETWEEN ROSH HASHANAH AND YOM KIPPUR
   mi chamoch eim harachamim
   zocheret yetzureha lechayyim berachamim

vene'emenet at lehachayot meitim
beruchah at shekhinah,
mechayah hameitim

אַתְּ גְּבִירָה לְעוֹלָם שַׁדַּי
מְחַיָּה מֵתִים אַתְּ רַב לְהוֹשִׁיעָה

   בין ש״א ופסח
   מַשִּׁיבָה הָרוּחַ וּמוֹרִידָה הַגֶּשֶׁם

מְכַלְכֶּלֶת חַיִּים בְּחֶסֶד
מְחַיָּה מֵתִימוֹת בְּרַחֲמִים רַבִּים
סוֹמֶכֶת נוֹפְלוֹת וְרוֹפֵאת חוֹלִימוֹת
וּמַתִּירָה אֲסוּרוֹת
וּמְקַיֶּמֶת אֱמוּנָתָהּ לִישֵׁנוֹת עָפָר
מִי כָמוֹךְ גְּבִירַת גְּבוּרוֹת
וּמִי דוֹמָה לָךְ
מַלְכָּה מְמִיתָה וּמְחַיָּה
וּמַצְמִיחָה יְשׁוּעָה

   בעשרת ימי תשובה
   מִי כָמוֹךְ אֵם הָרַחֲמִים
   זוֹכֶרֶת יְצוּרֶיהָ לְחַיִּים בְּרַחֲמִים

וְנֶאֱמֶנֶת אַתְּ לְהַחֲיוֹת מֵתִים.
בְּרוּכָה אַתְּ שְׁכִינָה
מְחַיָּה הַמֵּתִים.

   You are eternally gatekeeper and nurturer
     turning life to death and death to life,
   rescuing us from the void, sustaining life in love,
     enlivening what dies in your great womb,
       making what falls rise again
  healing the hurt, freeing the enslaved, weaving all that sleeps in earth
         into the bond of life.
       Who could be like you, most potent
Queen who turns the wheel of death and life and makes redemption flower.

   BETWEEN ROSH HASHANAH AND YOM KIPPUR
     Who is like you, mother of mercy,
  transforming your creatures in Your womb of compassion?

Faithful are you in turning the wheel from death to life.
   Blessed are You, Presence who turns the wheel
      from death to life.

AMIDAH 78

3. BLESSING FOR HOLINESS (KEDUSHAH)

אַתְּ קְדוֹשָׁה וּשְׁמֵךְ קָדוֹשׁ וּקְדוֹשׁוֹת בְּכָל יוֹם תְּהַלְלוּךְ סֶלָה.
בְּרוּכָה אַתְּ שְׁכִינָה, הָאֵלָה הַקְּדוֹשָׁה.

at kedoshah ushmeich kadosh ukedoshot bechol yom tehaleluch selah.
beruchah at shekhinah, ha'elah hakedoshah

You are holy, Your Name is holy, and those committed to holiness
praise You at every moment. Blessed are You, holy Goddess.

4. BLESSING FOR THE FESTIVAL (KEDUSHAT HAYOM)

אַתְּ בְּחַרְתָּנוּ עִם כָּל הָעַמִּים אָהַבְתְּ אוֹתָנוּ וְרָצִית בָּנוּ וְרוֹמַמְתָּנוּ עִם כָּל הַלְּשׁוֹנוֹת וְקִדַּשְׁתָּנוּ בְּמִצְוֹתַיִךְ וְקֵרַבְתָּנוּ שְׁכִינָה לַעֲבוֹדָתֵךְ וּשְׁמֵךְ הַגָּדוֹל וְהַקָּדוֹשׁ עָלֵינוּ קָרָאת וַתִּתְּנִי לָנוּ שְׁכִינָה אֱלֹהֵינוּ בְּאַהֲבָה (שַׁבָּתוֹת לִמְנוּחָה וּ) מוֹעֲדִים לְשִׂמְחָה חַגִּים וּזְמַנִּים לְשָׂשׂוֹן אֶת יוֹם (הַשַּׁבָּת הַזֶּה וְאֶת יוֹם)

לְפֶסַח	לְשָׁבֻעוֹת	לְסֻכּוֹת	לִשְׁמִינִי עֲצֶרֶת וְשִׂמְחַת תּוֹרָה
חַג הַמַּצּוֹת הַזֶּה.	חַג הַשָּׁבֻעוֹת הַזֶּה.	חַג הַסֻּכּוֹת הַזֶּה.	שְׁמִינִי חַג הָעֲצֶרֶת הַזֶּה. זְמַן שִׂמְחָתֵנוּ.
זְמַן חֵרוּתֵנוּ	זְמַן מַתַּן תּוֹרָתֵנוּ	זְמַן שִׂמְחָתֵנוּ	זְמַן צֵאת הַשָּׁנָה
זְמַן קְצִירָתֵנוּ	זְמַן בִּכּוּרֵנוּ	זְמַן אֲסִיפֵנוּ	

(בְּאַהֲבָה) מִקְרָא קֹדֶשׁ, זֵכֶר לִיצִיאַת מִצְרָיִם.

אֱלֹהֵינוּ וֵאלֹהֵי אֲבוֹתֵינוּ וְאִמּוֹתֵינוּ יַעֲלֶה וְיָבֹא וְיַגִּיעַ וְיֵרָאֶה וְיֵרָצֶה וְיִשָּׁמַע וְיִפָּקֵד וְיִזָּכֵר זִכְרוֹנֵנוּ וּפִקְדוֹנֵנוּ וְזִכְרוֹן אִמּוֹתֵינוּ וְזִכְרוֹן מָשִׁיחַ בֶּן דָּוִד עַבְדֵּךְ/בַּת רוּת אֲמָתֵךְ וְזִכְרוֹן יְרוּשָׁלַיִם עִיר קָדְשֵׁךְ וְזִכְרוֹן כָּל עַמֵּךְ בֵּית יִשְׂרָאֵל לְפָנֶיךְ לִפְלֵיטָה לְטוֹבָה לְחֵן וּלְחֶסֶד וּלְרַחֲמִים לְחַיִּים וּלְשָׁלוֹם בְּיוֹם

לְפֶסַח	לְשָׁבֻעוֹת	לְסֻכּוֹת	לִשְׁמִינִי עֲצֶרֶת וְשִׂמְחַת תּוֹרָה
חַג הַמַּצּוֹת הַזֶּה	חַג הַשָּׁבֻעוֹת הַזֶּה	חַג הַסֻּכּוֹת הַזֶּה	שְׁמִינִי חַג הָעֲצֶרֶת הַזֶּה

at bechartinu im kol ha'amim ahavt otanu veratzit banu veromamtinu im kol haleshonot vekidashtinu bemitzvotayich vekeravtinu shekhinah la'avodateich ushmeich hagadol vehakadosh aleinu karat vetitni lanu shekhinah eloteinu be'ahavah (shabbatot limenucha u)moadim lesimcha chagim uzmanim lesasson et yom (hashabbat hazeh ve'et yom):

ON PASSOVER	chag hamatzot hazeh	zman cheruteinu	zman ketzirateinu
ON SHAVUOT	chag hashavuot hazeh	zman matan torateinu	zman bikkureinu
ON SUKKOT	chag hasukkot hazeh	zman simchateinu	zman asifeinu

ON SHMINI ATZERET AND SIMCHAT TORAH shemini chag ha'atzeret hazeh, zman simchateinu, zman tzeit hashanah

(be'ahavah) mikra kodesh zecher letziat mitzrayim.

THE BLESSING CONTINUES IN THE MASCULINE

eloheinu ve'elohei avoteinu ve'imoteinu yaaleh veyavo veyagia ve'yeira'eh veyeiratzeh veyishama veyipaked veyizacher zichroneinu ufikdoneinu vezichron imoteinu ve'avoteinu vezichron mashiach ben david avdecha/bat rut amateich vezichron yerushalayim ir kodshecha vezichron kol amcha beit yisrael lifanecha lifleita letovah lechen ulechesed ulerachamim lechayim uleshalom beyom:

chag hamatzot hazeh/chag hashavuot hazeh/chag hasukkot hazeh/shemini chag ha'atzeret hazeh

You have ripened us along with all other peoples into a unique nation, and have loved us and delighted in us, and have raised us up among all peoples, and have sanctified us through Your mitzvot, and have drawn us close to you, Shekhinah, to do Your work, and have whispered within us Your name. May we be granted festivals, seasons and celebrations (and Sabbaths) at their proper times in love and joy:

this Passover, season of our freedom, season of spring renewal;	this Shavuot, season of the giving of the Torah, season of first fruits;	this Sukkot, season of our joy, season of full harvest;	this Shemini Atzeret/ Simchat Torah, season of our joy, of autumn rain;

as a holy gathering and a reminder of the wonders of creation.

God of our ancestors, may our prayer come before you on this Passover/Shavuot/Sukkot/Shemini Atzeret/Simchat Torah.

AMIDAH 80

זָכְרֵנוּ יהוה אֱלֹהֵינוּ בּוֹ לְטוֹבָה וּפָקְדֵנוּ בּוֹ לִבְרָכָה וְהוֹשִׁיעֵנוּ בּוֹ לְחַיִּים וּבִדְבַר יְשׁוּעָה וְרַחֲמִים חוּסִי וְחָנֵּנוּ וְרַחֲמִי עָלֵינוּ וְהוֹשִׁיעֵנוּ כִּי אֵלַיִךְ עֵינֵינוּ כִּי אֵלָה מַלְכָּה חֲנוּנָה וּרְחוּמָה אָתְּ.

וְהַשִּׂיאֵנוּ יהוה אֱלֹהֵינוּ אֶת בִּרְכַּת מוֹעֲדֶיךָ לְחַיִּים וּלְשָׁלוֹם לְשִׂמְחָה וּלְשָׂשׂוֹן כַּאֲשֶׁר רָצִיתָ וְאָמַרְתָּ לְבָרְכֵנוּ (אֱלֹהֵינוּ וֵאלֹהֵי דוֹרוֹתֵינוּ רְצֵה בִמְנוּחָתֵנוּ) קַדְּשֵׁנוּ בְּמִצְוֹתֶיךָ וְתֵן חֶלְקֵנוּ בְּתוֹרָתֶךָ שַׂבְּעֵנוּ מִטּוּבֶךָ וְשַׂמְּחֵנוּ בִּישׁוּעָתֶךָ וְטַהֵר לִבֵּנוּ לְעָבְדְּךָ בֶּאֱמֶת וְהַנְחִילֵנוּ יהוה אֱלֹהֵינוּ (בְּאַהֲבָה וּבְרָצוֹן) בְּשִׂמְחָה וּבְשָׂשׂוֹן (שַׁבָּת וּ) מוֹעֲדֵי קָדְשֶׁךָ וְיִשְׂמְחוּ בָךְ יִשְׂרָאֵל מְקַדְּשֵׁי שְׁמֶךָ.

בְּרוּכָה אַתְּ שְׁכִינָה מְקַדֶּשֶׁת (הַשַּׁבָּת וְ) יִשְׂרָאֵל וְהַזְּמַנִּים.

zochrinu havayah eloheinu bo letovah ufokdinu bo livrachah vehoshi'inu bo lechayim uvidvar yeshuah verachamim chusi vechaninu verachmi aleinu vehoshi'inu ki eilayich einenu ki elah malkah chanunah urchumah at.

vehasi'einu yah eloheinu et birkat moadecha lechayyim uleshalom lesimcha ulesasson ka'asher ratzita ve'amarta lvarcheinu (eloheinu velohei doroteinu r'tzei vimenuchateinu) kadsheinu bemitzvotecha veten chelkeinu betoratecha sab'einu mituvecha vesamcheinu biyeshuatecha vetaher libeinu le'avdecha be'emet. vehanchileinu yah eloheinu be'ahavah uveratzon besimcha uvessason (shabbat u) moadei kodshecha veyosmechu v'cha yisrael mekadshei shmecha.

BLESSING RETURNS TO THE FEMININE

berucha at shechinah mekadeshet (hashabbat ve) yisrael vehazemanim.

Remember our ancestors who stood before you, remember the Anointed One [son of David/daughter of Ruth], remember Jerusalem, remember the house of Israel for grace, love, compassion, life, and peace.

Grant us the blessing of the festivals with life and joy, for blessing is the desire of the universe. (O Holiness, revered of our ancestors, delight in our rest.) Make us holy through engaging us with wisdom, and may your teachings be the earth we cultivate. Satisfy us with our abundance and awaken us to the ever-unfolding spiral of life's journey. Clarify our hearts that we may serve the world through truth, and allow us to inherit the love that is Shabbat. May all who wrestle with the Divine and with the holy come to find rest on this day.

Blessed is the Holy, that sanctifies (Shabbat) and the festivals.

CONCLUDE THE FESTIVAL AMIDAH WITH
"BLESSING FOR PRAYER (RETZI)" ON PAGE 160

SHNIRELE PERELE

shnirele perele gilderne fon
meshiekh ben dovid zist oybn on
halt a bekher in der rekhter hant
makht a brokhe afn gantsn land
oy, omeyn v'omeyn dos iz vor
meshiekh vet kumen hayntiks yor

Ribbons and pearls in a web of golden thread
The mother of mothers sits overhead
As she weaves her magic unfurls
She casts her blessings over the whole world
Amen ve'amen this we know
A better world will grow from the seeds that we sow

And as she speaks
She gives blessing to this week
She casts off our fears
And weaves wonder through our years
And if we ground her in our hearts
The healing of this world will start

Yiddish: Traditional, English: Annabel Gottfried Cohen

MOON MOTHER

On the occasion of my first Kiddush Levana

Mmm? It does not sit well with me:
the moon at her vanity, pouting and
powdering her round face. Counter-
offered prizes piling up because she is not
pulled by Apollo across the sky.

Moon as jilted lover? Diminished in the
patriarchy's midrash:
She blows a whistle, points out duplicity
and is silenced by spiritual consolation
acquiescence:
Rosh Chodesh.

This is not My Mother Moon, the one
who guides my way through the delicious
dark.

Might the Moon, noting two lights, have
decided to be ever changing?
Choosing ebb and flow with the tides,
with the winds, with the rhythm of all
life?

Maybe the Moon peeked the pricelessness
of becoming and becoming and becoming
. . .
to be in process, in motion, in opposition
to the constant rise and set of the sun.

Maybe the Moon moves with Tzimtzemai
. . . the cyclical dance of shifting
dimensions.
Relational illusions of largesse and
smallness twirl around the truth:
She is whole no matter what is visible to
the eye.

My Moon is shadow casting: luscious,
deep, sweet.

Maybe the Moon realized witnessing . . .
holding reflection . . .
is a gift to the speaker and the listener.
To the beholder and the beheld.

Maybe the Moon is the beloved of
The Divine: the Duo wrapped in an
undulating embrace.
Moon is then set free to rule the night:
to frolic with the foxes, to travel
adventurous throughout time and space.
Enveloped in the ever-unfolding potential
of that which is not yet what it is meant to
be.

Free.

Mother Moon, in her consistent
inconsistency, embodies the Divinity of
Change.
Diminishment is just a trick of mirrors
and smoke.

Our Moon is unbound longing, reaching,
stretching, leaning, loving, jumping
toward the heavens: climbing outside of
and falling into our stardust sovereign
selves.

Mother Moon: My Muse.

Full.

Harriette Wimms

Note: This poem is a response to the talmudic midrash (Chullin 60b) in which the moon complains that she should be bigger than the sun, and God therefore makes her smaller. The moon protests, and God apologizes but still leaves the moon smaller. In Wimms' poem, this myth is revised and reversed.

MASTER KEY

In the queen's palace there are many gates and doors,
leading to many halls and chambers.

The palace-keepers have great rings holding many keys,
each of which opens a different door.

But there is one key that fits all the locks,
a master key that opens all the doors.

וְאִם רָץ לִבְּךָ לְהַרְהֵר שׁוּב לַמָּקוֹם

ve'im ratz libcha l'harheir shuv lamakom

if the heart runs return to the place

Every key unlocks another door in our souls,
brings us to another chamber

But there is one key that unlocks all the doors,
that master key is a broken heart.

וְאִם רָץ לִבְּךָ לְהַרְהֵר שׁוּב לַמָּקוֹם

ve'im ratz libcha l'harheir shuv lamakom

if the heart runs return to the place

The master key it is a broken heart.

רָצוֹא וָשׁוֹב

ratzoh vashov

קָרוֹב יְיָ לְנִשְׁבְּרֵי לֵב

karov adonai lenishberei lev

G-d is close to the broken hearted.

Avra Shapiro

BUILDING THE ALTAR

Put something on it for life,

something for death. Something red
for a fierceness felt in body,
heart, spine, feet moving
in protest or prayer.

Something round and silver
for the well,
and a shard
for the long broken thirst.

Something green
for the earth—
a handful of leaves, perhaps,
real and green and disappearing.

A cord
we can follow to find each other.

A pillow
for sleeping children,
a stone for dreaming

a ram's horn
for we who must awaken

but nothing for hatred.
Let it creep away from the holes it makes in us.

A coin
to pay the gatekeeper
because it costs to be here

oh how it costs
to be here

and an empty hand
for grace, because
this is grace,
all of it.

Jill Hammer

GROUNDING PRAYERS AND FUTURE HOPES

ALEINU means "it is upon us" or "we are responsible." The traditional Aleinu prayer is a prayer of hope and responsibility for a redemptive future. These creative Aleinu prayers express a vision for a future in which we enter into deep relationship with ourselves, one another, and the earth.

AND WE WILL SEE SHEKHINAH

יִהְיֶה יהוה אֶחָד וּשְׁמוֹ אֶחָד
יִהְיֶה הוֹיָה אַחַת וְרוּחָהּ אַחַת

yihiyeh adonai echad

ushemo echad (x3)

tihiyeh havaya achat

verucha achat (x3)

And we will see Shekhinah in the wind across the land
we are a circle within her circle

And we will be Shekhinah in the work of our hearts and our hands
She is a circle within our circle

Taya Shere, adaptation of "We Are A Circle" by Rick Hamouris ("v'rucha achat" lyric by Jill Hammer)

VEHASHEIVOTA

△ וַהֲשֵׁבֹתָ אֶל לְבָבֶךָ כִּי יהוה הוּא הָאֱלֹהִים
□ וַהֲשֵׁבֹת אֶל לְבָבֵךְ כִּי שְׁכִינָה הִיא הָאֱלֹהִים
⊖ וַהֲשֵׁבֹתֶה אֶל לְבָבֶךֶ כִּי הֲיוֹה הֶא הָאֱלֹהִים

△ vehasheivota el levavecha ki adonai hu ha'elohim

□ vehasheivot el levaveich ki shekhinah hi ha'elohim

⊖ vehasheivoteh el levavecheh ki havayah heh ha'elohim

Keep telling your heart: the Source of Life, that is what we call divine.

Shir Meira Feit based on Deuteronomy 4:39

THE WIND THAT BLOWS THROUGH ME

I feel the hand of God inside my hand
when I write said the old woman
it blows me away like a hat
I'll swear God's needy hand is inside every atom
waving at us hoping we'll wave back

Sometimes I feel the presence
of the goddess inside me said the dark red tulip
and sometimes I see her
waltzing in the world around me
skirts flying though everything looks still

It doesn't matter whether you call the thing
God or goddess those are only words
said the dog panting after a run through the park
and a sprint after a squirrel
theology is bunk but the springtime wind is real

Alicia Ostriker, from The Old Woman, the Tulip, and the Dog

STRETCHING OUR HANDS TO THE WORK

כֵּיצַד בָּרָא הַקָדוֹשׁ בָּרוּךְ הוּא אֶת עוֹלָמוֹ
פְּשׁוֹט יָדְךָ לְמִזְרָח וּלְמַעֲרָב לְצָפוֹן וּלְדָרוֹם
כָּךְ הָיָה הַמַּעֲשֶׂה לִפְנֵי הַקָדוֹשׁ בָּרוּךְ הוּא
כָּךְ הַמַּעֲשֶׂה לְפָנֵינוּ

keitzad bara hakadosh baruch hu et olamo?
pshot yadcha l'mizrach ulemaarav ltzafon uldarom.
kach haya hamaaseh lifnei hakadosh baruch hu.
kach hamaaseh lifaneinu.

"How did the Holy One of Blessing create the world?
Stretch out your hand to east, west, north, and south.
Even so was the work of Creation before the Holy One."
Even so is the work before us.

After Genesis Rabbah 10:3

ANGEL SONG

בְּשֵׁם יהוה אֱלֹהֵי יִשְׂרָאֵל
מִימִינִי מִיכָאֵל וּמִשְּׂמֹאלִי גַבְרִיאֵל
וּמִלְּפָנַי אוּרִיאֵל וּמֵאֲחוֹרַי רְפָאֵל
וְעַל רֹאשִׁי וְעַל רֹאשִׁי שְׁכִינַת אֵל

b'shem hashem elohei yisrael
miymini michael umismoli gavriel
umilfanai uriel umeacharai refael
ve'al roshi, ve'al roshi shekhinat el

I am surrounded by the angels of peace
I am connected, I am safe at ease
And you are surrounded by the angels of peace
you are connected, you are safe at ease

With lovingkindness to the right
And to the left a great shield of might
And before your eyes that guiding light
And the flow of healing from behind
And up above, the Holy One holds us in Her presence
And down below the Earth turns slow
Rocking us like a cradle

And we are surrounded by the angels of peace
we are connected, we are safe at ease

Elana Brody

A PROTEST PRAYER

Beloved siblings striving for justice,
Shma!
Listen. Closely. At all times.
My prayer for you
is that you remember protest
is a sacred act.
Just as the Mourner's Kaddish
helps souls ascend to God,
May our cries soothe those
whose lives were prematurely extinguished.
And rattle the bones and stones
of leaders and institutions.
Leaving no question about the fact
that things are never going back, only forward.
For more of us are clear
that "We have nothing to lose but our chains."
We affirm we are a multiracial people,
and we will stand strong, humble, and proud
as we follow and work in partnership
with black leaders, taking steady strides
in the direction of collective liberation.

April N. Baskin, originally created for @modern_ritual

MAALAH MATA

מַעֲלָה מַטָּה maalah mata
מִזְרָח מַעֲרָב mizrach maarav
עוֹלָם וְשָׁנָה olam veshanah
חוֹזְרוֹת חָלִילָה chozrot chalila
שְׁעָרִים שְׁעָרִים she'arim she'arim
רוּחַ אֱלֹהִים חַיִּים ruach elohim chayim

ya la la la la, above and below

ya la la la, everywhere everywhen

ya la la la, we turn and return

ya la la la la, the world starts again

Jill Hammer

4. THE THREE MOTHERS

שְׁלוֹשׁ אִמּוֹת אֲוִיר מַיִם אֵשׁ

אֵשׁ לְמַעְלָה
וּמַיִם לְמָטָה
וַאֲוִיר רוּחַ חוֹק מַכְרִיעַ בֵּינְתָיִם

מ דוֹמֶמֶת שׁ שׁוֹרֶקֶת
אֲוִיר רוּחַ
חוֹק מַכְרִיעַ בֵּינְתָיִם

shlosh imot avir mayim eish

eish lemaalah umayim lematah
va'avir ruach chok machria beintayim

mem domemet shin shoreket
avir ruach chok machria beintayim

The three mothers
are air, water, fire.

Fire is above, water below,
and air, breath, balances between them.

Water hums, fire hisses
and air, breath
balances between them.

Sefer Yetzirah

MOURNER'S KADDISH

The Kaddish, composed in Aramaic, is a prayer of mourning and of remembering our ancestors and our beloved dead. It is also a prayer of praise for all that is.

1. TRADITIONAL ARAMAIC

yitgadal veyitkadash shemeh rabbah	יִתְגַּדַּל וְיִתְקַדַּשׁ שְׁמֵהּ רַבָּא.
be'almah di vra chirutei	בְּעָלְמָא דִּי בְרָא כִרְעוּתֵיהּ
veyamlich malchutei	וְיַמְלִיךְ מַלְכוּתֵיהּ
bechayeichon uveyomeichon	בְּחַיֵּיכוֹן וּבְיוֹמֵיכוֹן
uvechayei dechol beit yisrael	וּבְחַיֵּי דְכָל בֵּית יִשְׂרָאֵל.
ba'agalah uvizman kariv ve'imru amein.	בַּעֲגָלָא וּבִזְמַן קָרִיב וְאִמְרוּ אָמֵן:
yehei shmei rabbah mevorach	יְהֵא שְׁמֵהּ רַבָּא מְבָרַךְ
le'alam ulalmei almaya.	לְעָלַם וּלְעָלְמֵי עָלְמַיָּא:
yitbarach veyishtabach	יִתְבָּרַךְ וְיִשְׁתַּבַּח
veyitpaar veyitromam veyitnasei	וְיִתְפָּאַר וְיִתְרוֹמַם וְיִתְנַשֵּׂא
veyithadar veyitaleh veyithalal	וְיִתְהַדָּר וְיִתְעַלֶּה וְיִתְהַלָּל
shemei dekudsha brich hu	שְׁמֵהּ דְּקֻדְשָׁא בְּרִיךְ הוּא
le'eilah min kol birchata veshirata	לְעֵלָּא (בעשי״ת וּלְעֵלָּא מִכָּל) מִן כָּל בִּרְכָתָא וְשִׁירָתָא
tushbechata venechemata	תֻּשְׁבְּחָתָא וְנֶחֱמָתָא
da'amiran be'alma ve'imru amen.	דַּאֲמִירָן בְּעָלְמָא וְאִמְרוּ אָמֵן.
yehei shlamah rabbah min sh'maya	יְהֵא שְׁלָמָא רַבָּא מִן שְׁמַיָּא
vechayyim aleinu ve'al kol yisrael	וְחַיִּים עָלֵינוּ וְעַל כָּל יִשְׂרָאֵל
ve'al kol yoshvei tevel ve'imru amen.	וְעַל כָּל יוֹשְׁבֵי תֵבֵל וְאִמְרוּ אָמֵן.
osah shalom bimromeha	עֹשָׂה שָׁלוֹם בִּמְרוֹמֶיהָ
hi taaseh shalom	הִיא תַעֲשֶׂה שָׁלוֹם
aleinu ve'al kol yisrael	עָלֵינוּ וְעַל כָּל יִשְׂרָאֵל
ve'al kol yoshvei tevel ve'imru amen.	וְעַל כָּל יוֹשְׁבֵי תֵבֵל וְאִמְרוּ אָמֵן

Blessed and praised, beautified and exalted, raised up and glorified,
elevated and extolled be the Name of the Holiness, blessed be She,
beyond all the blessings and hymns, praises and consolations
that are spoken in the world; and say, Amen.
May there be much peace from Heaven and Earth
and life for us and all Israel and all the world, and say Amen.
May She who makes peace in Her shrines
make peace for us and all the people Israel and all the world, and let us say Amen.

2. WE ARE A SPIRAL (KI AFAR AT)

כִּי עָפָר אַתְּ וְאֶל עָפָר תָּשׁוּבִי

ki afar at ve'el afar tashuvi

Earth we are and earth we will be
We are a spiral coming home

Taya Shere

3. KADDISH CHANT

יְהֵא שְׁלָמָא רַבָּא מִן שְׁמַיָּא
וְחַיִּים עָלֵינוּ וְעַל כָּל יִשְׂרָאֵל

yehei shelama raba min shemaya
vechayyim aleinu ve'al kol yisrael

May the name
which is all names
that have been
and will be
be blessed
in this here world
and all the worlds
forever

Rakia Shemaya

4. THE WHOLE WIDE WORLD
WEAVER'S SONG (SHIRAT HAPAROCHET)

The whole wide world is a very narrow bridge
Don't be afraid of it
The whole wide world is a very narrow bridge

The whole wide world is a very narrow thread
I think i'll follow it
The whole wide world is a very narrow thread

The whole wide world is abundant colored string
Scarlet, purple, blue & green
The whole wide world is abundant colored string

The whole wide world is in the weaver's hand
Fire, water, air & land
The whole wide world is in the weaver's hand

The whole wide world is the sacred work of love
Earth & heaven, moon & sun
The whole wide world is the sacred work of love

The whole wide world is many strands in one
Those who've come & those who've gone
The whole wide world is many strands in one

The whole wide world is a very narrow bridge
Don't be afraid of it
The whole wide world is a very narrow bridge

Very narrow bridge, very narrow thread, abundant colored string
in the weaver's hand, the sacred work of love, many strands in one

The whole wide world is a very narrow bridge

Based on a teaching by Rebbe Nachman of Breslov; Music and lyrics by Shoshana Jedwab

SHACHARIT
THE DAWNING PRAYER

Shacharit, or the dawn-offering, recalls the morning offering once made in the Temple. It consists of four parts.

The first is *Birchot haShachar*: dawn blessings, or blessings over the actions and sensations of waking. The Kohenet siddur also includes in this section prayers and songs for creating sacred space, and for acknowledging the sacred elements of our world. This section of the prayer corresponds to the world and the body, the kabbalistic realm of *Assiyah*. Its elemental association is earth.

The second section is *Pesukei deZimra* or Verses of Song. These psalms and prayers are designed to open us to joy and gratitude and awaken the heart. This section of the prayer corresponds to the heart and the emotions, the kabbalistic realm of *Yetzirah*. Its elemental association is water.

The third section is *Kriat Sh'ma uVirchoteha*: The Calling of the *Sh'ma* and Her Blessings. This section of the prayer centers on the *Sh'ma*, and also contains blessings over light, love, and redemption (integration. This section of the prayer is meant to open the mind and stimulate the creative forces, and corresponds to the kabbalistic realm of *Briyah*. Its elemental association is air.

The fourth section is the *Amidah* or standing prayer, also known as the Shemoneh Esrei or Eighteen Benedictions (though actually there are nineteen in the weekday Amidah and seven in the Shabbat Amidah). The heart of this prayer is silent communion with the Divine. It corresponds to the world of the soul and the kabbalistic realm of *Atzilut*. Its elemental association is fire. While many communities recite some or all of this prayer out loud before or after individuals recite it silently, the Kohenet community tends to focus on the silent intention of this prayer.

On Monday, Thursday, and Shabbat, a *Torah Service* may also be included. On new moons and holidays, it is customary to hold a Torah service and also recite the *Hallel* or praise-offering.

The morning prayers end with prayers of hope, memory, grounding and sealing: *Aleinu, Kaddish*, and other songs and readings.

WEAVING THE CIRCLE (ARIGAT HAMA'AGAL)

*Everything in the sky has its counterpart on earth,
and everything on earth has its counterpart in the sea,
and yet all form a unity.*

Zohar II, 20a

לִשְׁמָהּ

לִשְׁמוֹ

לִשֵׁם עָלְמַיָּא

אַרְעָה יַמָּא וּשְׁמַיָּא

אֲנוּ עֹשִׂין עִיגוּל נַפְשַׁיָּא

lishmah lishmo leshem almaya
ar'ah, yama, ushamaya
anu osin igul nafshaya
we are the earth, wind, water and fire

lishmah lishmo leshem almaya
ar'ah, yama, ushamaya
anu osin igul nafshaya
may our souls circle deeper and higher

*In Her name, in His name, in the Name of the worlds,
earth, sea, and sky
we make a circle of our souls.*

Jill Hammer & Taya Shere

PRESENCE IN THE BODY

I AM GRATEFUL (MODAH/MODEH/MODET ANI)

◻ FEMININE

מוֹדָה אֲנִי לְפָנַיִךְ רוּחַ חָיָה וְקַיֶּמֶת
שֶׁהֶחֱזַרְתְּ בִּי נִשְׁמָתִי בְּחֶמְלָה רַבָּה אֱמוּנָתֵךְ

modah ani lefanayich ruach chaya vekayamet
shehechezart bi nishmati bechemlah raba emunateich

△ MASCULINE

מוֹדֶה אֲנִי לְפָנֶיךָ רוּחַ חַי וְקַיָּם
שֶׁהֶחֱזַרְתָּ בִּי נִשְׁמָתִי בְּחֶמְלָה רַבָּה אֱמוּנָתֶךָ

modeh ani lefanecha ruach chai vekayam
shehechezartah bi nishmati bechemlah raba emunatecha

⊖ NONBINARY

מוֹדֶת אֲנִי לְפָנֶיךְ רוּחַ חַיֶת וְקַיֶמֶה
שֶׁהֶחֱזַרְתֶּה בִּי נִשְׁמָתִי בְּחֶמְלָה רַבָּה אֱמוּנָתֶכֶרה

modet ani lefanecheh ruach chayet vekayemeh
shehechezarteh bi nishmati bechemlah raba emunateche

oh I am grateful, oh I am grateful,
in the face of the One, in the face of the One

I am grateful before you, spirit-wind circulating within my body,
for you have returned my breath to me in kindness. Great is your faithfulness.

Traditional morning liturgy, English chant by Taya Shere

ROIZA'S NIGGUN

מוֹדָה אֲנִי לְפָנַיִךְ
שֶׁהֶחֱזַרְתְּ בִּי נִשְׁמָתִי בְּחֶמְלָה רַבָּה אֱמוּנָתֵךְ

modah ani lifanayich (x2)
shehechezart bi nishmati bechemlah raba emunateich

I wake with thanks upon my lips
for you have returned my soul to me
In love and trust I wake from sleep

Shoshana Jedwab

SHEKHINAH THANK YOU FOR BLESSING THIS DAY

Shekhinah thank you for blessing this day (x2)
Shekhinah thank you for blessing all we do and all we say
Thank you for blessing this day

Shekhinah thank you for blessing this day (x2)
Shekhinah thank you for blessing how we be and how we pray
Thank you for blessing this day

Shekhinah thank you for blessing this day (x2)
Shekhinah thank you for blessing where we go and where we stay
Thank you for blessing this day

Taya Shere

MAMA TOVU

מַמַמַמַמַמָּה טֹבוּ	mamamamamamamatovu
אֹהָלַיִךְ חַוָּה טֹבוּ	ohalayich chava tovu
אֹהָלַיִךְ נַעֲמָה טֹבוּ	ohalayich naamah tovu
אֹהָלַיִךְ שָׂרָה	ohalayich sarah
מַמַמַמַמָּה טֹבוּ	mamamamamamatovu
אֹהָלַיִךְ רִבְקָה טֹבוּ	ohalayich rivka tovu
אֹהָלַיִךְ רָחֵל טֹבוּ	ohalayich rachel tovu
אֹהָלַיִךְ לֵאָה	ohalayich leah
מַמַמַמַמָּה טֹבוּ	mamamamamamatovu
אֹהָלַיִךְ בִּלְהָה טֹבוּ	ohaylaich bilhah tovu
אֹהָלַיִךְ זִלְפָּה טֹבוּ	ohalayich zilpah tovu
אֹהָלַיִךְ דִּינָה	ohalayich dina

How good are your tents, Mama! How good are your tents, our ancestors Sarah, Rivka, Rachel, Leah, Binah, Zilpah, and Dinah!
(add whichever matriarchs you like, and/or names of worshippers...)

וַאֲנִי בְּרֹב חַסְדֵּךְ אָבוֹא בֵיתֵךְ
אֶשְׁתַּחֲוֶה אֶל הֵיכַל קָדְשֵׁךְ בְּיִרְאָתֵךְ

va'ani b'rov hasdeich avo veiteich
eshtachaveh el heichal kodsheich b'yirateich

MamaMamaMama your ground is our home
We live revering each tree river and stone
Your are in our blood flesh and bone

Mamamamamamama ma ma ma ma ma!

שְׁכִינָה אָהַבְתִּי מְעוֹן בֵּיתֵךְ
וּמְקוֹם מִשְׁכַּן כְּבוֹדֵךְ
עֲנֵינִי בֶּאֱמֶת יִשְׁעֵךְ

shekhinah ahavti me'on beiteich
um'kom mishkan k'vodeich,
aneini b'emet yisheich

MamaMamaMa You who dwell in each soul
You who give us our rock and our roll
You who make us increasingly whole

Mamamamamamama ma ma ma ma ma!

Taya Shere

OPENINGS

I bless Shechinah for creating my body
I bless Shechinah for my beautiful form
With passageways and organs working together
Chambers of wonder that open and close

I bless Shechinah for the wisdom inside me
I bless Shechinah for my skin, flesh and bone
I'm an animal creature of hunger and kindness
A puzzle of pieces, fragile and strong

But if one of them should fail, I cannot stand before You
Shechinah You're my healer, the Life Force that I know
In my heart beating, lungs breathing, muscles reaching,
excreting, pleasure seeking, deep feeling
body in rhythm, singing Your song

Openings, chalulim, boundaries, nnnnn'kavim
Openings, chalulim, boundaries, mmmmmysteries

I bless Shechinah for the touch of another
I bless Shechinah for the power we hold
And the love that we bring through our beautiful bodies
The games that we play, and the lives that we grow

And when I'm at the end, when my breath will release then
I will shed my skin, I will join with the whole
But for now, I will sing with my beautiful body
Shechinah has made for my journeying soul

בְּרוּכָה אֲשֶׁר יָצְרָה אֶת הָאָדָם בְּחָכְמָה
וּבָרְאָה בוֹ נְקָבִים נְקָבִים נְקָבִים
וּבָרְאָה בוֹ חֲלוּלִים חֲלוּלִים חֲלוּלִים

brucha asher yatzra et ha'adam b'chochmah (x2)
uvara vo nkavim nkavim nkavim
uvara vo chalulim chalulim chalulim

בְּרוּכָה אַתְּ שְׁכִינָה רוֹפֵאת כֹּל בָּשָׂר וּמַפְלִיאָה לַעֲשׂוֹת

brucha aht shechinah rofeit kol basar umafliah laasot

Blessed are You Shechinah, healer of all flesh, sustaining our bodies in wondrous ways.

Shoshana Jedwab

THE DAWNING PRAYER **100**

HOW GOOD (MAH TOVU)

mah tovu ohalayich leah	מַה טֹּבוּ אֹהָלַיִךְ לֵאָה
mishkenotayich rachel.	מִשְׁכְּנֹתַיִךְ רָחֵל.
va'ani berov chasdeich avo veiteich.	וַאֲנִי בְּרֹב חַסְדֵּךְ אָבוֹא בֵיתֵךְ
eshtachaveh el heichal kodsheich beyirateich.	אֶשְׁתַּחֲוֶה אֶל הֵיכַל קָדְשֵׁךְ בְּיִרְאָתֵךְ.
shekhinah ahavti me'on beiteich	שְׁכִינָה אָהַבְתִּי מְעוֹן בֵּיתֵךְ
umakom mishkan kevodeich	וּמְקוֹם מִשְׁכַּן כְּבוֹדֵךְ.
va'ani eshtachaveh ve'echra'ah	וַאֲנִי אֶשְׁתַּחֲוֶה וְאֶכְרָעָה
evrechah lifnei elah osati.	אֶבְרְכָה לִפְנֵי אֵלָה עֹשָׂתִי
va'ani tefilati lach rachamana eit ratzon.	וַאֲנִי תְפִלָּתִי לָךְ רַחֲמָנָה עֵת רָצוֹן
elah berov chasdech aneini be'emet yishech.	אֵלָה בְּרָב חַסְדֵּךְ עֲנֵנִי בֶּאֱמֶת יִשְׁעֵךְ

How abundant are your tents, o Leah, your shrines, o Rachel! I, in your lovingkindness, will come to your house; I will bend to the earth in your sacred shrine, in reverence to You. Shekhinah, One who Dwells, I love the dwelling of Your house, and the place of the shrine of Your presence. I bow to the earth and bless my creator. My prayer is to You, merciful one. Divine deity, in your great love, answer me with Your unfolding truth.

PUTTING ON THE TALLIT

The tallit is a four-corned fringed garment that many Jews wear during morning prayer, in fulfillment of a biblical commandment to wear fringes on one's clothing. We see this four-cornered garment as a representation of the four directions, which in turn represent the sacred whole, the holy cosmos. The fringes of the tallit, when brought together, remind us of the many and the one.

beruchah at shekhinah	בְּרוּכָה אַתְּ שְׁכִינָה
eloteinu ruach ha'olam	אֱלֹתֵינוּ רוּחַ הָעוֹלָם
asher kidshatnu bemitzvoteha	אֲשֶׁר קִדְּשָׁתְנוּ בְּמִצְוֹתֶיהָ
vetzivatnu lehitatef batzitzit.	וְצִוַּתְנוּ לְהִתְעַטֵּף בַּצִּיצִת.

Blessed are You, Divine Weaver and Spirit of the world, who has made us holy through Your desires and has desired us to perform the ritual of tzitzit.

MEDITATION ON THE TALLIT

barchi nafshi et elah,	בָּרְכִי נַפְשִׁי אֶת אֱלָה
shadai elotai gadalt m'od.	שָׁדַי אֱלֹתַי גָּדַלְתְּ מְאֹד
hod vehadar lavasht	הוֹד וְהָדָר לָבָשְׁתְּ
otah or kesalma	עֹטָה אוֹר כַּשַּׂלְמָה
notah shamayim kayiriyah.	נוֹטָה שָׁמַיִם כַּיְרִיעָה.
mah yakar chasdeich shekhinah	מַה יָּקָר חַסְדֵּךְ שְׁכִינָה
vedorot chava b'tzel k'nafayich yechesayoon.	וְדוֹרוֹת חָוָה בְּצֵל כְּנָפַיִךְ יֶחֱסָיוּן
yirveyoon mideshen beiteich	יִרְוְיֻן מִדֶּשֶׁן בֵּיתֵךְ
venachal adanayich tashkem.	וְנַחַל עֲדָנַיִךְ תַשְׁקֵם.
ki imach makor hachayim,	כִּי עִמָּךְ מְקוֹר חַיִּים,
be'oreich nireh or.	בְּאוֹרֵךְ נִרְאֶה אוֹר.

O my life-spirit, bless Elah! Shadai, my maker, you are vast! You have clothed yourself in beauty and splendor. You spread out light like a robe. You stretch out heaven like a tapestry. How precious is your love, Shekhinah, and the generations of Eve shelter under Your wings. They are nourished from the abundance of your house, this earth, and the river of your pleasure waters them. Within You is the source of life, and in your light we see light.

THE SELF GIVES THANKS

the world wears light like a robe

above the earth, the sky is spread like a canopy

in the shadow of these wings

we feast on the abundance of the trees

and bathe in the coral fountains of the deep

we see ourselves by all this radiance

Jill Hammer

BLESSING FOR TEFILLIN

Tefillin are boxes with sacred text inside them, attached to leather straps, ritually worn by Jews during weekday morning prayer. One way to think of tefillin is as a divine umbilical cord attaching the worshipper to the Source of Life—this ancient idea appears in the Talmud.

ON YOUR HAND

beruchah at shekhinah בְּרוּכָה אַתְּ שְׁכִינָה
eloteinu ruach ha'olam אֱלֹתֵינוּ רוּחַ הָעוֹלָם
asher kidshatnu bemitzvoteha אֲשֶׁר קִדְּשָׁתְנוּ בְּמִצְוֹתֶיהָ
vetzivatnu lehaniach tefillin. וְצִוְּתָנוּ לְהָנִיחַ תְּפִלִּין

Blessed are You, Shekhinah, Divine-Weaver and Spirit of the world, who has made us holy through Your desires and has desired us to perform the ritual of tefillin.

ON YOUR HEAD

beruchah at shekhinah eloteinu בְּרוּכָה אַתְּ שְׁכִינָה
ruach ha'olam אֱלֹתֵינוּ רוּחַ הָעוֹלָם
asher kidshatnu bemitzvoteha אֲשֶׁר קִדְּשָׁתְנוּ בְּמִצְוֹתֶיהָ
vetzivatnu al mitzvat tefillin. וְצִוְּתָנוּ עַל מִצְוַת תְּפִלִּין

Blessed are You, Shekhinah, Divine-Weaver and Spirit of the world, who has made us holy through Your desires and has desired us to perform the mitzvah of tefillin.

baruch shem kevod shekhinatah le'olam vaed. בָּרוּךְ שֵׁם כְּבוֹד שְׁכִינָתָהּ לְעוֹלָם וָעֶד

Blessed is the name of Her glorious presence throughout time and space.

UPON WINDING AROUND THE FINGER, CHOOSE ONE OF THE FOLLOWING

ve'eyrastich li le'olam, וְאֵרַשְׂתִּיךְ לִי לְעוֹלָם
ve'eyrastich li betzedek uvemishpat וְאֵרַשְׂתִּיךְ לִי בְּצֶדֶק וּבְמִשְׁפָּט
uvechesed uverachamim וּבְחֶסֶד וּבְרַחֲמִים
ve'eyrastich li be'emunah, veyadat et shekhinah. וְאֵרַשְׂתִּיךְ לִי בֶּאֱמוּנָה וְיָדַעַתְּ אֶת שְׁכִינָה

I will betroth you to Me forever, I will betroth You to Me with righteousness and justice and love and compassion, and I will betroth you to me in faithfulness, and you shall know the Presence. *Hosea 2:21-22*

כִּי אֶל אֲשֶׁר תֵּלְכִי אֵלֵךְ וּבַאֲשֶׁר תָּלִינִי אָלִין עַמֵּךְ עַמִּי וֵאלֹהַיִךְ אֱלֹהָי

ki el asher telchi elech, uvaasher talini alin amech ami...

Where you go, I will go; where you lodge, I will lodge;
your people shall be my people and your divinity shall be mine. *Ruth 1:15*

WHAT IS IN THE GODDESS'S TEFILLIN?

a tendril from a grapevine
one grape clinging like a jewel
a stone from a funeral
hide from a tambourine
the bag of a weary midwife
wicks of Sabbath candles
ink of burst berries
ground antlers
floodwater from a submerged city
seed from a barley harvest
emptiness of famine
sugarcane quartz crystal sun
a parchment
who is like your people
one nation in all the earth
or
nothing
no words
nothing
blackness
blackness
stars
who is like you
o my people
who bind your stories to your arms
I too
tie my story to the parabolic curves of my body
my physics like an alphabet
you must recover me
from the tar pits of the years
bind me as a sign upon your hand
let me be an ornament
between your eyes
my temple
is in the glands and synapses of your body
remember

Jill Hammer

BLESSING OVER TORAH STUDY

בְּרוּכָה אַתְּ שְׁכִינָה אֱלֹתֵינוּ רוּחַ הָעוֹלָם אֲשֶׁר קִדְּשַׁתְנוּ בְּמִצְוֹתֶיהָ וְצִוְּתָנוּ לַעֲסוֹק בְּדִבְרֵי תּוֹרָה

beruchah at shekhinah eloteinu ruach ha'olam asher kidshatnu bemitzvoteha vetzivatnu la'asok bedivrei torah.

Blessed are You, Shekhinah, Divine-Weaver and Spirit of the world, who has made us holy through Your desires and has desired us to cultivate words of Torah.

GODDESS, MY SOUL (ELOTAI NESHAMAH)

אֱלֹתַי נְשָׁמָה שֶׁנָּתַתְּ בִּי טְהוֹרָה הִיא. אַתְּ בְּרָאתְ אַתְּ יְצַרְתְּ אַתְּ נְפַחְתְּ בִּי וְאַתְּ מְשַׁמֶּרֶת אוֹתָהּ בְּקִרְבִּי וְאַתְּ עָתִיד לִטְלָה מִמֶּנִּי, וּלְהַחֲזִירָהּ בִּי לְעָתִיד לָבוֹא. כָּל זְמַן שֶׁהַנְּשָׁמָה בְקִרְבִּי מוֹדָה אֲנִי לְפָנַיִךְ אֵלָה אֱלֹתַי וֵאלֹתֵי אִמּוֹתַי רִמּוֹן הַמַּעֲשִׂים עֵדֶן כָּל הַנְּשָׁמוֹת. בְּרוּכָה אַתְּ שְׁכִינָה הַמַּחֲזִירָה נְשָׁמוֹת לִפְגָרִים מֵתִים.

elotai neshamah shenatat bi tehorah hi. at barat, at yetzart, at nefacht bi,
ve'at meshameret ota bekirbi, ve'at atid litlah mimemi ulehahazirah bi le'atid lavo.
kol zman shehaneshamah bekirbi, modah ani lefanayich,
elah elotai ve'elotei imotai, rimon kol hama'asim, eden kol haneshamot.
beruchah at shekhinah, hamachazirah neshamot lifgarim meitim.

Goddess, the soul you gave me is timeless. You birthed her, You shaped her, You breathed her into me, and You guard her within me, and in the fullness of time You will take her from me and return her to me again as the future unfolds. All the time that my soul is in me, I will be grateful before You, Goddess of my self and of my mothers, as full of happenings as a pomegranate, fountain of all soul-streams. Blessed are You, Shekhinah, who joins the soul with the body.

SHEKHINAH EL SHADDAI

שְׁכִינָה אֵל שַׁדָּי
אִמָּא עִלָּאָה צִמְצְמַי

shekhinah el shaddai

immah ila'ah tzimtzemai

Summoning, embodying, sacred She who dwells within
We celebrate, we co-create, Me and the Goddess, we are kin

Taya Shere

ELOHAI NESHAMA (SHE IS FREE)

אֱלֹהַי נְשָׁמָה שֶׁנָּתַתָּ בִּי טְהוֹרָה הִיא

אֱלֹתַי נְשָׁמָה שֶׁנָּתַתְּ בִּי טְהוֹרָה הִיא

elohai neshama shenatata bi tehorah hi
elotai neshama shenatat bi tehorah hi

My God the soul you place inside of me
She is clear, she is whole and she is free!
Goddess the Soul You Place inside of me
She is clear, she is whole and she is free!

Taya Shere

MAH NORAH

מַה נוֹרָא הַמָּקוֹם הַזֶּה

mah norah hamakom hazeh

How awesome is this body
How awesome is this place
How awesome is this journey
Through time and space.

Genesis 28:17, English lyrics, Taya Shere, melody inspired by Jaquelyn Westhead

BIRCHOT HASHACHAR
MORNING BLESSINGS

These blessings praise the Source of Life for each action and experience as we wake up in the morning. In our liturgy, the first blessing in each category uses feminine God-language; the second blessing in each category uses masculine God-language. Verbs and nouns used with reference to people are given in the feminine/masculine.

1. AWAKENING

בְּרוּכָה אַתְּ שְׁכִינָה אֱלֹתֵינוּ רוּחַ הָעוֹלָם אֲשֶׁר נָתְנָה לַשֶּׂכְוִי בִינָה לְהַבְחִין בֵּין יוֹם וּבֵין לָיְלָה.

beruchah at shekhinah eloteinu ruach ha'olam asher natnah lasechvi vinah lehavchin bein yom uvein lailah.

Blessed are You, Present One, spirit of the world, who gives the rooster wisdom to discern between day and night.

2. SELFHOOD

בְּרוּכָה אַתְּ שְׁכִינָה אֱלֹתֵינוּ רוּחַ הָעוֹלָם שֶׁעָשְׂתָנִי/עָשַׂנִי עִבְרִיָּה/עִבְרִי/עִבְרִיֶּה.

beruchah at shekhinah eloteinu ruach ha'olam she'astani/asani ivriyah/ivri/ivriyeh.

Blessed are You, Present One, spirit of the world, who made me one who crosses over.

3. FREEDOM

בְּרוּכָה אַתְּ שְׁכִינָה אֱלֹתֵינוּ רוּחַ הָעוֹלָם שֶׁעָשְׂתָנִי/עָשַׂנִי בַּת/בֶּן/מִבֵּית חוֹרִין.

beruchah at shekhinah eloteinu ruach ha'olam she'astani/asani bat/ben/mibeit chorin.

Blessed are You, Present One, spirit of the world, who made me a child of freedom.

4. DIVINE IMAGE

בְּרוּכָה אַתְּ שְׁכִינָה אֱלֹתֵינוּ רוּחַ הָעוֹלָם שֶׁעָשְׂתָנִי/עָשַׂנִי בְּצַלְמָהּ.

beruchah at shekhinah eloteinu ruach ha'olam she'astani betzalmah.

Blessed are You, Present One, spirit of the world, who has made me in Her image.

5. VISION

בְּרוּכָה אַתְּ שְׁכִינָה אֱלֹתֵינוּ רוּחַ הָעוֹלָם פּוֹקַחַת עִוְרִים.

beruchah at shekhinah eloteinu ruach ha'olam pokachat ivrim.

Blessed are You, Present One, spirit of the world, who opens the eyes.

6. GARMENTING

בְּרוּכָה אַתְּ שְׁכִינָה אֱלֹתֵינוּ רוּחַ הָעוֹלָם מַלְבִּישָׁה עֲרֻמִּים.

beruchah at shekhinah eloteinu ruach ha'olam malbishah arumim.

Blessed are You, Present One, spirit of the world, who clothes the naked.

7. UNBINDING

בְּרוּכָה אַתְּ שְׁכִינָה אֱלֹתֵינוּ רוּחַ הָעוֹלָם מַתִּירָה אֲסוּרִים.

beruchah at shekhinah eloteinu ruach ha'olam matirah asurim.

Blessed are You, Present One, spirit of the world, who frees the bound.

8. UNTWISTING

בְּרוּכָה אַתְּ שְׁכִינָה אֱלֹתֵינוּ רוּחַ הָעוֹלָם זוֹקֶפֶת כְּפוּפִים.

beruchah at shekhinah eloteinu ruach ha'olam zokefet kefufim.

Blessed are You, Present One, spirit of the world, who straightens what is bent.

9. GROUNDING

בְּרוּכָה אַתְּ שְׁכִינָה אֱלֹתֵינוּ רוּחַ הָעוֹלָם רוֹקַעַת הָאָרֶץ עַל הַמָּיִם.

beruchah at shekhinah eloteinu ruach ha'olam roka'at ha'aretz al hamayim.

Blessed are You, Present One, spirit of the world, who spreads earth upon the water.

10. SUSTENANCE

בְּרוּכָה אַתְּ שְׁכִינָה אֱלֹתֵינוּ רוּחַ הָעוֹלָם שֶׁעָשְׂתָה לִי כָּל צָרְכִּי.

beruchah at shekhinah eloteinu ruach ha'olam she'astah li kol tzarki.

Blessed are You, Present One, spirit of the world, who has made for me all that I need.

11. GUIDANCE

בְּרוּכָה אַתְּ שְׁכִינָה אֱלֹתֵינוּ רוּחַ הָעוֹלָם הַמֵּכִינָה מִצְעֲדֵי אִשָּׁה/גֶּבֶר/אֱנוֹשׁ.

beruchah at shekhinah eloteinu ruach ha'olam hameichinah mitzadei isha/gaver/enosh.

Blessed are You, Present One, spirit of the world, who makes firm each person's path.

12. STRENGTH

בְּרוּכָה אַתְּ שְׁכִינָה אֱלֹהֵינוּ רוּחַ הָעוֹלָם אוֹזֶרֶת אוֹתִי בִּגְבוּרָה.

beruchah at shekhinah eloteinu ruach ha'olam ozeret oti bigevurah.

Blessed are You, Present One, spirit of the world, who girds me with strength.

13. BEAUTY

בְּרוּכָה אַתְּ שְׁכִינָה אֱלֹהֵינוּ רוּחַ הָעוֹלָם עוֹטֶרֶת אוֹתִי בְּתִפְאָרָה.

beruchah at shekhinah eloteinu ruach ha'olam oteret oti betifarah.

Blessed are You, Present One, spirit of the world, who crowns me with glory.

14. ENERGY

בְּרוּכָה אַתְּ שְׁכִינָה אֱלֹהֵינוּ רוּחַ הָעוֹלָם הַנוֹתֶנֶת לַיָעֵפָה/לַיָעֵף כֹּחַ.

beruchah at shekhinah eloteinu ruach ha'olam hanotenet le'yaefa/leya'ef koach.

Blessed are You, Present One, spirit of the world, who gives strength to the exhausted.

15. AWAKENING

בְּרוּכָה אַתְּ שְׁכִינָה אֱלֹהֵינוּ רוּחַ הָעוֹלָם הַמַּעֲבִירָה שֵׁנָה מֵעֵינַי וּתְנוּמָה מֵעַפְעַפָּי.

beruchah at shekhinah eloteinu ruach ha'olam hama'avirah sheinah me'einai utemunah me'afapai.

Blessed are You, Present One, spirit of the world, who lifts sleep from my eyes and slumber from my eyelids.

BIRCHOT HASHACHAR CHANT

בְּרוּכָה אַתְּ שְׁכִינָה

beruchah at shekhinah...	who grounds me
beruchah at shekhinah...	who reminds me that I know
beruchah at shekhinah...	who guides me
beruchah at shekhinah...	who gives me courage to let go

beruchah at shekhinah ruach ha'olam hameikhinah mitzadei isha

Ri J. Turner

KIVVUN HAYESODOT
WELCOMING THE ELEMENTS

In the Zohar, the four elements correspond to four levels of manifestation of divinity and world: assiyah (earth/body/action), yetzirah (water/heart/feeling), beriyah (air/mind/insight), and atzilut (fire/soul/essence).

1. FOUR WORLDS CHANT

Earth	my body	Earth	assiyah	nurture your body
Water	my blood	Water	yetzirah	heal your heart
Air	my breath	Air	briyah	experience your breath
Fire	my spirit	Fire	atzilut	open to Spirit

Taya Shere, adaptation of traditional circle song

2. BIRTH OF THE ELEMENTS

הַמַּיִם הָרוּ וְיָלְדוּ אֲפֵלָה   hamayim haru veyaldu afeilah
הָאֵשׁ הָרָה וְיָלְדָה אוֹר   ha'eish harah veyaldah or
הָרוּחַ הָרָה וְיָלְדָה חָכְמָה   haruach harah veyalda chochmah
הֶעָפָר הָרָה וְיָלְדָה חַיִּים   ha'afar harah veyalda chayim

In the beginning,
Water conceived and gave birth to darkness.
Fire conceived and gave birth to light.
Wind conceived and gave birth to wisdom.
Earth conceived and gave birth to life.

Adapted from Exodus Rabbah 13:3

3. LIFE IS BORN (DOR HOLECH)

dor holech vedor ba	דּוֹר הוֹלֵךְ וְדוֹר בָּא
veha'aretz le'olam omadet	וְהָאָרֶץ לְעוֹלָם עוֹמָדֶת
vezarach hashemesh uvahashamesh	וְזָרַח הַשֶּׁמֶשׁ וּבָא הַשָּׁמֶשׁ
ve'el mekomo shoef zoreiach	וְאֶל מְקוֹמוֹ שׁוֹאֵף זוֹרֵחַ
holech el darom	הוֹלֵךְ אֶל דָּרוֹם
vesovev el tzafon sovev sovev holech haruach	וְסוֹבֵב אֶל צָפוֹן סוֹבֵב סוֹבֵב הוֹלֵךְ הָרוּחַ
kol hanachalim holchim el hayam	כָּל הַנְּחָלִים הוֹלְכִים אֶל הַיָּם
vehayam einenu maleh	וְהַיָּם אֵינֶנּוּ מָלֵא
kach hatchalah zoremet	כָּךְ הַתְחָלָה זוֹרֶמֶת אֶל סוֹף
el sof keitz zorem el reishit	קֵץ זוֹרֵם אֶל רֵאשִׁית
ha'acharonah hi harishon	הָאַחֲרוֹנָה הִיא הָרִאשׁוֹן
hevel havalim havel hakol	הֲבֵל הֲבָלִים הֲבֵל הַכֹּל

Life is born and life moves on and the earth has held and will hold it all.
The sun rises and the sun sets and returns again to rise and fall.
The wind turns south and the wind turns north,
turning, turning, returning still.
The rivers run from the clouds to the sea
and become the rain, and the sea is never filled.
So the beginning moves to the end and the end flows on to begin again.
The one at the end is the one who begins and
the breath of breaths is within all things.

Jill Hammer, based on Ecclesiastes 1:1, 4-7, inspired by Nelly Sachs

4. BLESSING FOR THE ELEMENTS

O flame, mother of the light-spirits, shine on us!
O rain, father of the spirits of dark waters, soak us!
O wind, mother of the spirits of wisdom, make us wise!
O dirt, father of all that breathes, bless us with a good harvest.
Let us have eyes
to see the multiplicity
of your children.
And
let us have awareness
of the unseen world.
le'olam ulalmei almaya
in every world, in all the worlds,
we say amen.

Jill Hammer

WELCOMING THE ELEMENTS

SONG OF THE ARCHETYPES

The thirteen NETIVOT, or archetypes, are faces of the priestess (Goddess that the Kohenet community honors and seeks to reveal. Like the SEFIROT (ten divine aspects) of Jewish mystical tradition, the netivot are multiple aspects of sacred truth.

azkirah et ha'oreget, eim derachim tamcha pelech ki chol beitah levush shanim	אַזְכִּירָה אֶת הָאוֹרֶגֶת אֵם דְּרָכִים תָּמְכָה פֶלֶךְ כִּי כָל בֵּיתָהּ לָבֻשׁ שָׁנִים
azkirah et habetulah, eishet ne'urim od tadi tupayich veyatzat bimchol mesachakim	אַזְכִּירָה אֶת הַבְּתוּלָה אֵשֶׁת נְעוּרִים עוֹד תַּעְדִּי תֻפַּיִךְ וְיָצָאת בִּמְחוֹל מְשַׂחֲקִים
azkirah et haeim, birkot shadaim veracham meged geresh yerachim, meged givot olam	אַזְכִּירָה אֶת הָאֵם בִּרְכֹת שָׁדַיִם וָרָחַם מֶגֶד גֶּרֶשׁ יְרָחִים מֶגֶד גִּבְעוֹת עוֹלָם
azkirah et hagevirah, ziv hakavod tilbash malchut bechayil kaved me'od	אַזְכִּירָה אֶת הַגְּבִירָה זִיו הַכָּבוֹד תִּלְבַּשׁ מַלְכוּת בְּחַיִל כָּבֵד מְאֹד
azkirah et hameyaledet po'ah nishmat chayyim mitboseset bedamayich, bedamayich chayi	אַזְכִּירָה אֶת הַמְיַלֶּדֶת פּוֹעָה נִשְׁמַת חַיִּים מִתְבּוֹסֶסֶת בְּדָמַיִךְ בְּדָמַיִךְ חֲיִי
azkirah et hachachamah, inot tehom deracheha darchei noam, vekol netivoteha shalom	אַזְכִּירָה אֶת הַחֲכָמָה עֵינוֹת תְּהוֹם דְּרָכֶיהָ דַרְכֵי נֹעַם וְכָל נְתִיבוֹתֶיהָ שָׁלוֹם
azkirah et hamekonenet, re'utah kinah ki yeish sachar life'ulatah, tikvah le'acharitah	אַזְכִּירָה אֶת הַמְקוֹנֶנֶת וּרְעוּתָהּ קִינָה כִּי יֵשׁ שָׂכָר לִפְעֻלָּתָהּ תִּקְוָה לְאַחֲרִיתָהּ
azkirah et haneviah, et hatof beyada kol asher tomar elecha shma bekolah	אַזְכִּירָה אֶת הַנְּבִיאָה אֶת הַתֹּף בְּיָדָהּ כֹּל אֲשֶׁר תֹּאמַר אֵלֶיךָ שְׁמַע בְּקֹלָהּ
azkirah et hatzovah, l'shaarei hasipim ba'ah ha'isha hagoren hase'orim	אַזְכִּירָה אֶת הַצּוֹבְאָה לְשַׁעֲרֵי הַסִּפִּים בָּאָה הָאִשָּׁה הַגֹּרֶן הַשְּׂעֹרִים
azkirah et baalat ha'ov, eishet ein dor bemarot halailah habitu el makevet bor	אַזְכִּירָה אֶת בַּעֲלַת הָאוֹב אֵשֶׁת עֵין דּוֹר בְּמַרְאֹת הַלַּיְלָה הַבִּיטוּ אֶל מַקֶּבֶת בּוֹר
azkirah et hadoreshet holechet ledarkah mevaseret tzion shiti libech lamesilah	אַזְכִּירָה אֶת הַדּוֹרֶשֶׁת הוֹלֶכֶת לְדַרְכָּהּ מְבַשֶּׂרֶת צִיּוֹן שִׁתִי לִבֵּךְ לַמְסִלָּה
azkirah et ha'ohevet, kulach yafa bati legani pitchi li achoti kalah	אַזְכִּירָה אֶת הָאוֹהֶבֶת כֻּלָּךְ יָפָה בָּאתִי לְגַנִּי פִּתְחִי לִי אֲחֹתִי כַלָּה
azkirah et haleitzanit, lamah zeh tzahakah lev kesilim beveit hasimcha	אַזְכִּירָה אֶת הַלֵּיצָנִית לָמָּה זֶּה צָחֲקָה לֵב כְּסִילִים בְּבֵית הַשִּׂמְחָה
azkirah et haoreget matveh techelet ve'argaman oz vehadar levushah, vatischak leyom acharon	אַזְכִּירָה אֶת הָאוֹרֶגֶת מַטְוֶה תְּכֵלֶת וְאַרְגָּמָן עֹז וְהָדָר לְבוּשָׁהּ וַתִּשְׂחַק לְיוֹם אַחֲרוֹן

azkirah shekhinah, azkirah shekhinah

I call to mind Shekhinah
In all these ways I'm seeing Her....

I call to mind the Weaver, mother of the ways,
for with Her wheel She robes her house in change.

I call to mind the Maiden, woman of youth and grace,
who goes out with her timbrel in joyful song and praise!

I call to mind the Mother, blessings of breasts and womb,
the gifts of the hills, the stars and the moons.

I call to mind the Matriarch, garbed in shining splendor,
robed in Her power, in Her mighty valor.

I call to mind the Midwife, who breathes the breath of life.
She says: "You who are born in blood, through blood you are alive!"

I call to mind the Wise One, wellspring of the deep,
for Her ways are pleasant ways, and all Her paths are peace.

I call to mind the Mourning One. Grief is Her friend,
for there will be reward for Her sorrow in the end.

I call to mind the Prophetess. The drum is in her hand,
so listen to her vision and the justice she demands!

I call to mind the Shrinekeeper at the threshold's door.
She is the woman coming to the holy threshing floor.

I call to mind the Spirit Vessel, who keeps the well of names.
Through Her dreams, we journey to the place from which we came.

I call to mind the Seeker as She walks abroad,
Messenger to Zion, set your heart upon the road!

I call to mind the Lover, Her beauty vast and wide.
I have come into my garden, my sister, my bride!

I call upon the Fool. What makes Her laugh that way?
The heart of a fool lives in the house of play.

I call to mind the Weaver who holds it all together.
Strength and glory clothe Her; She has joy forever.

English and Hebrew: Jill Hammer, Music: Shoshana Jedwab

PRIESTESSES' KADDISH (KADDISH D'KOHANOT)

The KADDISH D'RABBANAN celebrates the chain of learning from one Torah sage to another. This KADDISH celebrates the connection among priestesses, and all who do holy work, from one generation to the next.

יִתְגַּדַל וְיִתְקַדַּשׁ שְׁמָהּ רַבָּא
בְּעָלְמָא דִּי בְרָאָה כִּרְעוּתָהּ
וְתַמְלִיךְ מַלְכוּתָהּ
בְּחַיֵּיכוֹן וּבְיוֹמֵיכוֹן
וּבְחַיֵּי דְכָל בֵּית יִשְׂרָאֵל
בַּעֲגָלָא וּבִזְמַן קָרִיב וְאִמְרוּ אָמֵן

yitgadal veyitkadash sh'mah rabbah
be'almah di vra chirutah
vetamlich malchutah.
bechayeichon uveyomeichon
uvechayei dechol veit yisrael
ba'agalah uvizman kariv ve'imru amein.

יְהֵא שְׁמָהּ רַבָּא
מְבָרַךְ לְעָלַם וּלְעָלְמֵי עָלְמַיָּא

yehei shmah rabbah
mevorach le'alam ulalmei almaya.

יִתְבָּרַךְ וְיִשְׁתַּבַּח וְיִתְפָּאַר וְיִתְרוֹמַם וְיִתְנַשֵּׂא
וְיִתְהַדָּר וְיִתְעַלֶּה וְיִתְהַלָּל שְׁמָהּ דְּקֻדְשָׁא
בְּרִיכָה הִיא
לְעֵלָּא מִן כָּל בִּרְכָתָא וְשִׁירָתָא
תֻּשְׁבְּחָתָא וְנֶחֱמָתָא דַּאֲמִירָן בְּעָלְמָא
וְאִמְרוּ אָמֵן

yitbarach veyishtabach veyitpaar veyitromam
veyitnasei veyithadar veyitalei
veyithalal sh'mah dekudsha brichah hi
le'eilah min kol birchata veshirata tushbechata
venechemata da'amiran be'alma
ve'imru amen.

עַל יִשְׂרָאֵל וְעַל כּוֹהֲנוֹתַן וְקְדוֹשֵׁיהוֹן
וְעַל דּוֹרוֹתֵיהוֹן וְעַל כָּל דּוֹרוֹת דּוֹרוֹתֵיהוֹן
וְעַל כָּל מָאן דְּעָסְקִין בְּאִילָנָא
דִּי בְאַתְרָא הָדֵין וְדִי לְכָל אֲתַר וַאֲתַר
יְהֵא לְהוֹן וּלְכוֹן שְׁלָמָא רַבָּא
חִנָּא וְחִסְדָּא וְרַחֲמִין וְחַיִּין
אֲרִיכִין וּמְזוֹנֵי רְוִיחֵי וּפֻרְקָנָא מִן קֳדָם
אִמָּהוֹן דִּי בִשְׁמַיָּא וְאַרְעָא וְאִמְרוּ אָמֵן

al yisrael ve'al kohanotan ukedosheihon
ve'al doroteihon ve'al kol dorot doroteihon
ve'al kol man de'oskin be'ilana
di ve'atra hadein ve di lechol atar ve'atar.
yehei lehon ulechon shlamah rabbah
chinah chisdah verachamin vechayyin arichin
umezonei revichei ufurkanah min kadam
imahon di vishamaya ve'arah ve'imru amein.

יְהֵא שְׁלָמָא רַבָּא מִן שְׁמַיָּא וְאַרְעָא
וְחַיִּים עָלֵינוּ וְעַל כָּל יִשְׂרָאֵל
וְעַל כָּל יוֹשְׁבֵי תֵבֵל וְאִמְרוּ אָמֵן

yehei shlamah rabbah min sh'maya ve'arah
vechayyim aleinu ve'al kol yisrael
ve'al kol yoshvei tevel ve'imru amen.

עֹשָׂה שָׁלוֹם בִּמְרוֹמֶיהָ
הִיא תַעֲשֶׂה שָׁלוֹם
עָלֵינוּ וְעַל כָּל יִשְׂרָאֵל
וְעַל כָּל יוֹשְׁבֵי תֵבֵל וְאִמְרוּ אָמֵן

osah shalom bimromeha
hi ta'aseh shalom
aleinu ve'al kol yisrael
ve'al kol yoshvei tevel ve'imru amen.

Holy and growing is God's great name in the world
which She has created
according to Her desire.
May She establish Her Presence
in our lifetime and our days
and in the lifetimes of all our people quickly, and say, Amen.

May Her great name be blessed
in this world and all the worlds.

Blessed and praised, beautified and exalted, raised up and glorified,
elevated and extolled be the Name of the Holiness,
blessed be She,
beyond all the blessings and hymns,
praises and consolations that are spoken in the world;
and say, Amen.

Upon the people and its priestesses
and all its holy people and their generations,
and the ones who continue their generations,
and upon all those who care for the Tree,
here and in all other places,
may they and we have much peace, grace,
kindness, compassion, long life, plentiful nourishment and salvation
before their Mother in Heaven and Earth, and say Amen.

May there be much peace from Heaven and Earth
and life for us and all Israel and all the world,
and say Amen.

May She who makes peace in Her shrines
make peace for us and all Israel
and all the world,
and let us say Amen.

WE LIVE IN THE SMALLEST HOUSE

we live in the smallest house this is where the work is
in the smallest house next to, in the shadow of, the larger house
this is where we come to pray,
say, I am here, before you, I stand at the turning point,
take me down, take me up, take me in and with you, the ice
is blossoming in the body, the
winter-flower leaning in the meadow, love-as-we-knew it is a glass jar
cracked open
the room is larger now, something breathes
something lumbers about in the meantime
wait,
wait,
wait,
meaning,
holding prism every face is a form of surrender
every form is a turning-it-over-to-Thee
your face my face the face of
as the cracking shoots out from the center
it would seem, ascending as if from the center
itself, it is a thread, it is a tendril, it is a stamen
of wanting, enter here, it says, as the earth
from the center splays out her many tiger-lily limbs

Nina Pick, from "A Luz"

PESUKEI DEZIMRAH
VERSES OF SONG

בָּרוּכָה שֶׁאָמְרָה וְהָיָה הָעוֹלָם b'rucha she'amra v'haya haolam.
בָּרוּכָה הִיא b'rucha hi.

בָּרוּכָה עֹשָׂה בְרֵאשִׁית b'rucha osah v'reshit.
בָּרוּכָה אוֹמֶרֶת וְעוֹשָׂה b'rucha omeret v'osah.
בָּרוּכָה גּוֹזֶרֶת וּמְקַיֶּמֶת b'rucha gozeret um'kayemet.
בָּרוּכָה מְרַחֶמֶת עַל הָאָרֶץ b'rucha m'rachemet al ha'aretz.
בָּרוּכָה מְרַחֶמֶת עַל הַבְּרִיּוֹת b'rucha m'rachemet al ha'briot.
בָּרוּכָה מְשַׁלֶּמֶת שָׂכָר טוֹב לִירֵאוֹתֶיהָ b'rucha m'shalemet sachar tov lirei'oteha.
בָּרוּכָה חַיָּה לָעַד וְקַיֶּמֶת לָנֶצַח b'rucha chaya la'ad v'kayemet lanetzach.
בָּרוּכָה פּוֹדָה וּמַצִּילָה b'rucha poda umatzilah.

ברוּך שְׁמָהּ baruch sh'mah.

Blessed is the one who
whispered at the world's birth.
Blessed is that voice.
Blessed is the one who births creation.
Blessed is the one who fulfills the promise.
Blessed is the one who watches over nature.
Blessed is the one who enfolds the earth.
Blessed is the one who rewards reverence.
Blessed is the weaver of time and space.
Blessed is the one
who spirals through creation
the thread of redemption.
Blessed is the name.

MEHULELET

בְּרוּכָה אַתְּ שְׁכִינָה מַלְכָּה מְהֻלֶּלֶת בַּתִּשְׁבָּחוֹת

b'rucha at shekhinah malka m'hulelet batishbachot

brucha at shechina (3x)

malka, malka

mehulelet batishbachot (3x)

malka, malka

Blessed are You Shekhinah,
Queen to whom we ululate in praise!

Ululate!!!! and repeat

Ketzirah Lesser

SHE/ZHE CREATES

She creates Her world as She speaks (2x)
Her world, She creates as She speaks

Zhe creates the world as Zhe… sings/drums/breathes/rests (2x)
This world, Zhe creates as Zhe… sings/drums/breathes/rests

We create our world as we… act/love/play/tend/dream (2x)
Our world, we create as we…. act/love/play/tend/dream

Taya Shere (This is a 'zipper' chant. Feel welcome to weave in or invite resonant ways of creating here…)

A PRAYER FOR WORDS

May fire glow within these words.
May breath bring them to life.
May earth root them in strength.
May water wash them away when the world changes.
In every world, in all the worlds, I say amen.

Jill Hammer, The Book of Earth

FROM "THE VOLCANO SEQUENCE"

it is said God spoke and the world came into being
now listen to this
holy one
a woman squats in a field
wheat stubble pricks her feet
smell of clods billows up
foggy middle of winter
air damp she shivers
she bleeds it helps the birth
of whatever means to be born

Alicia Ostriker

LEV TAHOR (PURE HEART)

לֵב טָהוֹר בְּרָא לִי אֱלֹהִים
וְרוּחַ נָכוֹן חַדֵּשׁ בְּקִרְבִּי

lev tahor bara li elohim
v'ruach nachon chadesh b'kirbi

For me, Weaver, please renew my core
I want a clear heart, please open the door

Hebrew: Psalm 51; English Ri J. Turner, adaptation by Taya Shere

CREATION

בְּרֵאשִׁית בָּרָא אֱלֹהִים אֵת הַשָּׁמַיִם וְאֵת הָאָרֶץ

bereisheet bara elohim et hashamayim v'et ha'aretz

She began to contract her womb
The whole world was born emerging from her tzimtzum
All of the sky, all of the sea,
all of the earth, inside of you and me

Taya Shere, from Genesis 1:1

PSALM 33

רַנְּנָה צַדִּיקוֹת בַּיהוֹה	ranenah tzadikot bahavaya
לַיְשָׁרִים נָאוָה תְהִלָּה	layesharim navah tehilah.
הוֹדוּ לַיהוֹה בְּכִנּוֹר	hodu lashekhinah bakinor
בְּנֵבֶל עָשׂוֹר זַמְּרָנָה לָהּ	benevel asor zamerna lah.
שָׁרְנָה לָהּ שִׁיר חָדָשׁ	sharna lah shir chadash
הֵיטִיבוּ נַגֵּן בִּתְרוּעָה	heitivu nagen b'teruah
כִּי יָשָׁר דְּבַר יהוֹה	ki yashar devar havayah
וְכָל מַעֲשֶׂיהָ בֶּאֱמוּנָה	vechol maaseha be'emunah
אֹהֶבֶת צְדָקָה וּמִשְׁפָּט	ohevet tzedakah umishpat chesed
חֶסֶד יהוֹה מָלְאָה הָאָרֶץ	shekhinah malah ha'aretz
בִּדְבַר יהוֹה שָׁמַיִם נַעֲשׂוּ	bidvar havayah shamayim naasu
וּבְרוּחַ פִּיהָ כָּל צְבָאָם	uveruach piha kol tzeva'am
כֹּנֶסֶת כַּנֵּד מֵי הַיָּם	koneset kaned mei hayam
נֹתֶנֶת בְּאוֹצָרוֹת תְּהוֹמוֹת	notenet be'otzarot tehomot
תִּרְאָנָה מֵיהוֹה כָּל הָאָרֶץ	tirena mehavayah kol ha'aretz
מִמֶּנָּה יָגוּרוּ כָּל יֹשְׁבֵי תֵבֵל	mimemah yaguru kol yoshvei tevel
כִּי הִיא אָמְרָה וַתֶּהִי הִיא צִוְּתָה וַתַּעֲמֹד	ki hi amrah vatehi hi tzivtah veta'amod
יהוֹה הֵפִירָה עֲצַת אוּמוֹת	havayah heiforah atzat umot
הֵנִיאָה מַחְשְׁבוֹת עַמִּים	heiniah machshevot amim
עֲצַת יהוֹה לְעוֹלָם תַּעֲמֹד	atzat shekhinah le'olam ta'amod
מַחְשְׁבוֹת לִבָּהּ לְכֹל דֹּר וָדֹר	machshevot libah lechol dor vador
אַשְׁרֵי הָאוּמָה אֲשֶׁר יהוֹה אֱלֹהֶיהָ	ashrei ha'umah asher havayah eloheha
הָעַמִּים בָּחֲרָה לְנַחֲלָה לָהּ	ha'amim bachrah lenachalah lah
מִשָּׁמַיִם הִבִּיטָה יהוֹה	mishamayim hibitah havayah
רָאֲתָה אֶת כָּל יְלוּדֵי אִשָּׁה	raatah et kol yeludei isha
מִמְּכוֹן שִׁבְתָּהּ הִשְׁגִּיחָה	mimechon shivtah hishgichah
אֶל כָּל יֹשְׁבוֹת הָאָרֶץ	et kol yoshvot ha'aretz
הַיֹּצֶרֶת יַחַד לִבָּן	hayotzeret yachad liban
הַמְּבִינָה אֶל כָּל מַעֲשֵׂיהֶם	hameivinah et kol maaseihem
אֵין הַמַּלְכָּה נוֹשַׁעַה	ein hamalkah nosha'ah berav chayil
בְּרָב חַיִל גְּבִירָה לֹא תִנָּצֵל בְּרָב כֹּחַ	gevirah lo tinatzel berav koach
שֶׁקֶר הַסּוּס לִתְשׁוּעָה וּבְרֹב חֵילוֹ לֹא יְמַלֵּט	sheker hasus liteshuah uverov cheilo lo yimaleit
הִנֵּה עֵין יהוֹה אֶל יְרֵאוֹתֶיהָ	hinei ein havayah al yereioteha
לַמְיַחֲלִים לְחַסְדָּהּ	lemeyachalim lechasdah
לְהַצִּיל מִמָּוֶת נַפְשָׁן וּלְחַיּוֹתָם בָּרָעָב	lehatzil mimavet nafshan ulechayotam bara'av
נַפְשֵׁנוּ חִכְּתָה לַיהוֹה	nafsheinu chiktah lehavayah
עֶזְרָתֵנוּ וּמָגִנָּתֵנוּ הִיא	ezrateinu umaginateinu hi
כִּי בָהּ יִשְׂמַח לִבֵּנוּ	ki vah yismach libeinu
כִּי בְשֵׁם קָדְשָׁהּ בָּטָחְנוּ	ki veshem kodshah vatachnu
יְהִי חַסְדֵּךְ יהוֹה עָלֵינוּ	yehi chasdeich havaya aleinu
כַּאֲשֶׁר יִחַלְנוּ לָךְ.	ka'asher yichalnu lach.

Rejoice, disciples, in the Source. How pleasant to praise that Being.
Give thanks in music, in instruments, in song.
Sing to Her an ever-renewed song:
play and shout for joy!
The substance of Spirit is good
and Her works can be trusted,
for She loves righteousness and justice—
Shekhinah's love fills the cosmos.
Her speech is the sky and the breath of Her mouth is the stars.
She piles the seawaters up like mountains,
and treasures the oceans in Her depths.
This is why the earth shakes
with the power of Her coming
and all earthdwellers live from Her essence.
For she created all the cosmos
and grounded all things that they might be real.
She overturns the thoughts of governments
and changes the minds of peoples.
Her plan alone shall stand,
and Her heart-wisdom, for all time.
Happy is the people who has the Source for Goddess:
those people she has taken to Herself.
She looks out from the cosmos
to see every living thing born.
She witnesses all creatures
from Her dwelling place, which is everywhere,
for She created their hearts
and understands their doings.
No powerful mortal can trust power,
no guardian is saved by her own strength.
No technology can save,
and no army can bring redemption,
yet that Eye is on all who tremble
and yearn for compassion,
to meet them in their death
and bring them alive again
out of their yearning.
Our spirits wait for the One
who is our Help and Shield,
and our hearts rejoice in Her
and trust Her names.
May the love of the Presence be upon us
as we have hoped.

ASHREI

Asherah (Lady who Walks on the Sea, or in Hebrew The Joyful One) is the ancient Canaanite goddess of fertility and creation. In ancient Israel, many people revered Asherah, who was worshipped by sacred trees or poles. The faces of the Divine feminine that appear in the Bible, like Lady Wisdom, are influenced by depictions of Asherah, and the menorah may be a stylized sacred tree. The word ashrei in Hebrew evokes the name Asherah, and we invite davveners to consider how this God-name sits with them as a name for Shekhinah (just as we still use the word El, an old Canaanite term for the supreme God, to refer to Adonai).

ASHREI (HAPPY PEOPLE)

אַשְׁרֵי יוֹשְׁבֵי בֵיתֶךָ עוֹד הַלְלוּךָ סֶּלָה
אַשְׁרֵי הָעָם שֶׁכָּכָה לוֹ אַשְׁרֵי הָעָם שֶׁיהוה אֱלֹהָיו

ashrei yoshvei veitecha od hallelucha selah
ashrei ha'am shekacha lo ashrei haam she'adonai elohav

Happy are people living in Your Temple,
May they always praise You Selah!
Joy to the ones who feel Your grace,
Oh happy people, happy people!
Hallelujah (x8)

קָרוֹב יהוה לְכָל קֹרְאָיו לְכֹל אֲשֶׁר יִקְרָאֻהוּ בֶאֱמֶת
וַאֲנַחְנוּ נְבָרֵךְ יָהּ מֵעַתָּה וְעַד עוֹלָם הַלְלוּיָהּ

karov adonai lechol korav, lechol asher yikrauhu bemet
vaanachnu nevareich yah, meata vead olam, hallelujah

You are near to everyone who's calling
To all who open up and feel Your truth
And we will go on blessing Yah
From now on and forever
Hallelujah (x8)

English by Shoshana Jedwab, based on Psalm 145

אַשְׁרֵי יוֹשְׁבֵי בֵיתֶיהָ עוֹד הַלְלוּהָ סֶלָה
אַשְׁרוֹת יוֹשְׁבוֹת בֵּיתֶיהָ עוֹד תְּהַלְלוּהָ סֶלָה
אֲשֵׁרָה יוֹשְׁבוֹת בֵּיתֵךְ עוֹד תְּהַלְלוּךְ סֶלָה

ashrei yoshvei veiteha od halleluha selah
ashrot yoshvot veiteha od tehalleluha selah
asherah yoshvot veiteich od tehallelookh selah

Happy are those dwelling in Her house and always singing to the Universe. Selah!
Asherah those who dwell in Your house will praise You always. Selah!

PSALM 148

הַלְלוּיָהּ	haleluyah
הַלְלוּ אֶת יהוה מִן הַשָּׁמַיִם	halelu et havayah min hashamayim
הַלְלוּהָ בַּמְּרוֹמִים	haleluha bameromim
הַלְלוּהָ כָל מַלְאָכָהּ	haleluha kol melacheha
הַלְלוּהָ כָּל צְבָאֶיהָ	haleluha kol tz'va'eha
הַלְלוּהָ שֶׁמֶשׁ וְיָרֵחַ	haleluha shemesh veyareiach
הַלְלוּהָ כָּל כּוֹכְבֵי אוֹר	haleluha kol kochvei or
הַלְלוּהָ שְׁמֵי הַשָּׁמָיִם	haleluha shmei hashamayim
וְהַמַּיִם אֲשֶׁר מֵעַל הַשָּׁמָיִם	vehamayim asher me'al hashamayim
יְהַלְלוּ אֶת שֵׁם יהוה	yehalelu et shem havayah*
כִּי הִיא צִוְּתָה וְנִבְרָאוּ	ki hi tzivtah venivra'u
וַיַּעֲמִידֵם לָעַד לְעוֹלָם	vetaamideim la'ad le'olam
חָק נָתְנָה וְלֹא יַעֲבוֹר	chok natnah velo yaavor
הַלְלוּ אֶת יְהוָה מִן הָאָרֶץ	hahelu et havayah min ha'aretz
תַּנִּינִים וְכָל תְּהֹמוֹת	taninim vechol tehomot
אֵשׁ וּבָרָד שֶׁלֶג וְקִיטוֹר	eish uvarad sheleg vekitur
רוּחַ סְעָרָה עֹשָׂה דְבָרָהּ	ruach saarah osah devarah
הֶהָרִים וְכָל גְּבָעוֹת עֵץ פְּרִי וְכָל אֲרָזִים	heharim vechol g'va'ot etz pri vechol arazim
הַחַיָּה וְכָל בְּהֵמָה	hachayah vechol beheimah
רֶמֶשׂ וְצִפּוֹר כָּנָף	remes vetzipor kanaf
מַלְכֵי אֶרֶץ וְכָל לְאֻמִּים	malchei aretz vechol le'umim
שָׂרִים וְכָל שֹׁפְטֵי אָרֶץ	sarim sarot vechol shoftei aretz
בַּחוּרִים וְגַם בְּתוּלוֹת זְקֵנִים עִם נְעָרִים	bachurim vegam betulot zekeinim im naarim
יְהַלְלוּ אֶת שֵׁם יהוה	yehalelu et shem havayah
כִּי נִשְׂגָּב שְׁמָהּ לְבַדָּהּ	ki nisgav sh'mah levadah
הוֹדָהּ עַל אֶרֶץ וְשָׁמָיִם	hodah al eretz veshamayim
וַיָּרֶם קֶרֶן לְעַמָּהּ	vayarem keren le'amah
תְּהִלָּה לְכָל חֲסִידֶיהָ	tehilah lechol hasideha
לִבְנֵי יִשְׂרָאֵל עַם קְרֹבָהּ	livnei uvnot yisrael am kerovah
הַלְלוּיָהּ	haleluyah

HAVAYAH: This Hebrew word for "Being" is a traditional Jewish name for God. It uses the four letters of the Divine Name (yud heh vav heh), but in a different order.

Halleluyah. Praise Havayah from the heavens!
Praise Her, o heights!
Praise Her, Her messengers!
Praise Her, her hosts!
Praise Her, moon and sun!
Praise her, stars of light!
Praise Her, heights of the heavens
and water that is above the heavens!
Praise the name of the Mother,
for She spoke and All became,
She weaves the All
from beginning to end.
Praise Havayah from the earth!
Praise Her, sea monsters and ocean depths!
Praise Her, fire and hail, snow and smoke
and storm that do Her will.
Mountains and hills, fruit trees and cedars,
wild and tame animals,
crawling things and birds,
rulers of the earth and peoples,
monarchs and judges of the earth,
all people, young and old.
Let all praise the name of Havayah,
for Her name is lifted up in all that is.
Her glory fills the heaven
and the earth.
Praise to all of Her faithful ones,
and to Her people close to Her.
Halleluyah.

SUN HALELUYAH (PSALM 148)

הַלְלוּהוּ שֶׁמֶשׁ וְיָרֵחַ הַלְלוּהוּ כָּל כּוֹכְבֵי אוֹר
הַלְלוּיָהּ מִן הַשָּׁמַיִם הַלְלוּהוּ בַּמְּרוֹמִים

haleluhu shemesh veyareiach, haleluhu kol kochvei or
haleluyah min hashamayim, haleluhu bameromim

Haleluyah, sun and moon and stars!
Haleluyah, sing the praise of God!

Shoshana Jedwab

VERSES OF SONG

PRAISE ELAH (PSALM 150)

הַלְלוּ אֱלָהּ אֱלָהּ
הַלְלוּ אֱלָהּ בְּקָדְשָׁהּ הַלְלוּיָהּ
הַלְלוּהָ בִּרְקִיעַ עֻזָּהּ הַלְלוּיָהּ
הַלְלוּהָ בִּגְבוּרֹתֶיהָ הַלְלוּיָהּ
הַלְלוּהָ כְּרֹב גֻּדְלָהּ הַלְלוּיָהּ
הַלְלוּהָ בְּתֵקַע שׁוֹפָר הַלְלוּיָהּ
הַלְלוּהָ בְּנֵבֶל וְכִנּוֹר הַלְלוּיָהּ
הַלְלוּהָ בְּתֹף וּמָחוֹל הַלְלוּיָהּ
הַלְלוּהָ בְּמִנִּים וְעֻגָב הַלְלוּיָהּ
הַלְלוּהָ בְּצִלְצְלֵי שָׁמַע הַלְלוּיָהּ
הַלְלוּהָ בְּצִלְצְלֵי תְרוּעָה הַלְלוּיָהּ
כֹּל הַנְּשָׁמָה תְּהַלֵּל יָהּ הַלְלוּיָהּ
כֹּל הַנְּשָׁמָה תְּהַלֵּל יָהּ הַלְלוּיָהּ
הַלְלוּ הַלְלוּ הַלְלוּ אֱלָהּ

hallelu elah elah, hallelu elah elah
hallelu elah b'kodsha, halleluyah
halleluha b'rkia uzah, halleluyah
halleluha b'gvuroteha, halleluyah
halleluha k'rov gudla, halleluyah
halleluha b'teikah shofar, halleluyah
halleluha b'neivel v'chinor, halleluyah
halleluha b'tof u'machol, halleluyah
halleluha b'minim v'ugav, halleluyah
halleluha b'tziltzelei shama, halleluyah
halleluha b'tziltzelei t'ruah, halleluyah
kol haneshama t'hallel yah   halleluyah
kol haneshama t'hallel yah   halleluyah
hallelu   hallelu   hallelu   elah

Praise Elah in Her shrine Halleluyah
Praise Her strength from sea to sky Halleluyah
Praise Her for Her mighty works Halleluyah
Praise the One so generous! Halleluyah
Praise Her with the horn and choir, Halleluyah
Praise Her with the harp and lyre, Halleluyah
Praise Her with the drum and flute, Halleluyah
Praise Her with guitar and lute, Halleluyah
Praise Her playing cymbals sounding, Halleluyah
Praise Her playing cymbals crashing, Halleluyah
May all who breathe keep praising Yah, Halleluyah (x2)

Feminized Hebrew and English by Shoshana Jedwab

NISHMAT
SABBATH SOUL-BREATH

OZI

עָזִי וְזִמְרָת יָהּ וַיְהִי לִי לִישׁוּעָה

ozi vezimrat yah vayehi li yeshuah

My strength, and the song of Yah, will be my deliverance.

Exodus 15:3

NISHMAT

נִשְׁמַת כָּל חַי תְּבָרֵךְ אֶת שְׁמֵךְ שְׁכִינָה אֱלֹתֵינוּ

nishmat kol chai tevarech et shmeich shekhinah eloteinu

The breath of all life praises you, Indwelling.

Traditional liturgy

RUMI NISHMAT

נִשְׁמַת כָּל חַי תְּבָרֵךְ אֶת שִׁמְךָ אֶת שְׁמֶךְ

nishmat kol chai tivarekh et shimcha et sh'mekh

The breathing of all life is blessing your name
The breathing of all life is blessing your name
But I have nothing to say
I have nothing to pray
I have nothing to say
I have nothing to pray
So spirit practice a song through me
Spirit practice a song through me
Spirit practice a song through me
Spirit practice a song through me

כָּל עַצְמוֹתַי תֹּאמַרְנָה יהוה מִי כָמוֹךָ

kol atzmotai tomarna adonai mi chamocha

All of my bones are speaking their truth
My Divine, who is like You?
All of my bones are speaking their truth
My Divine, who is like You?
But I have nothing to say
I have nothing to pray
So Spirit practice a song through me (4x)

בָּרְכִי נַפְשִׁי אֶת יהוה וְכָל קְרָבַי אֶת שֵׁם קָדְשׁוֹ

barchi nafshi et adonai v'chol k'ravai et shem kodsho

My body is blessing My Divine
The Holy Name-the song of my insides
My body is blessing My Divine
The Holy Name-the song of my insides
But I have nothing to say
I have nothing to pray
So spirit practice a song through me (4x)

Shoshana Jedwab, based on prayerbook and Rumi, Dedicated to Florette Blanc

ILU FINU

אִלּוּ פִינוּ מָלֵא שִׁירָה כַּיָּם

ilu finu malei shirah kayam…

If our mouths were as full with song as the sea…!

וּלְשׁוֹנֵנוּ רִנָּה כַּהֲמוֹן גַּלָּיו, וְשִׂפְתוֹתֵינוּ שֶׁבַח כְּמֶרְחֲבֵי רָקִיעַ
וְעֵינֵינוּ מְאִירוֹת כַּשֶּׁמֶשׁ וְכַיָּרֵחַ וְיָדֵינוּ פְרוּשׂוֹת כְּנִשְׁרֵי שָׁמַיִם וְרַגְלֵינוּ קַלּוֹת כָּאַיָּלוֹת
אֵין אֲנַחְנוּ מַסְפִּיקִים/מַסְפִּיקוֹת לְהוֹדוֹת לָךְ יָהּ אֱלֹתֵינוּ וֵאלֹהֵי הוֹרֵינוּ
וּלְבָרֵךְ אֶת שְׁמֵךְ עַל אַחַת מֵאָלֶף אֶלֶף אַלְפֵי אֲלָפִים
וְרִבֵּי רְבָבוֹת פְּעָמִים הַטּוֹבוֹת שֶׁעָשִׂית עִם הוֹרֵינוּ וְעִמָּנוּ

ulshoneinu rinah kahamon galai vesiftoteinu shevach k'merchavei rakia
ve'einenu me'irot kashemesh vechayareiach veyadeinu frushot kenishrei shamayim
veragleinu kalot ka'ayalot ein anachnu maspikim/maspikot lehodot lach
yah eloteinu ve'elohei horeinu ulevarech et shmeich al achat me'elef alfei alafim
veribei revavot pe'amim hatovot she'asit im horeinu ve'imanu.

…and our tongues with joy as the many waves,
and our lips as full with praise as the wide heavens,
and our eyes as bright as the sun and moon,
if our hands could spread out like the wings of eagles,
and our feet were as fleet as deer,
we could not finish praising you,
o life-power of all generations throughout time
or bless you for a thousand thousandth of the goodness
you have done for our ancestors and for us.

בָּרְכִי נַפְשִׁי אֶת נִשְׁמַת כָּל חַי
וְכָל קְרָבַי אֶת שֵׁם קָדְשָׁהּ

barchi nafshi et nishmat kol chai
vechol keravai et shem kodshah

Bless my soul the living Spirit, and all my inward being bless Her holy name.

BARCHU: CALL TO PRAYER

In ancient times the priest who watched over the Temple during the night would see the first glimmer of dawn and cry: BARKAI! This means: "First light, the moment of dawn."

The Barchu prayer is the call to worship. With the Barchu we move from personal to collective prayer, pooling our blessings.

LEADER

בָּרְכוּ אֶת הַבְּרֵכָה הַמְבֹרֶכֶת

barchu et habereichah hamevorechet

Give blessing to the Pool of Blessing!

PARTICIPANTS

בְּרוּכָה הַבְּרֵכָה הַמְבֹרֶכֶת לְעוֹלָם וָעֶד

beruchah habereichah hamevorechet le'olam va'ed

Give blessing to the Pool of Blessing from now until the end of time!

LEADER REPEATS

בְּרוּכָה הַבְּרֵכָה הַמְבֹרֶכֶת לְעוֹלָם וָעֶד

beruchah habereichah hamevorechet le'olam va'ed

Give blessing to the Pool of Blessing from now until the end of time!

GUARDIAN SONG/BARCHU

עוּרִי עוּרִי עוּרִי דְּבוֹרָה עוּרִי עוּרִי דַּבְּרִי שִׁיר

oori, oori, oori, devorah. oori, oori, oori, dabri shir

Awake, awake, awake, Deborah. Awake, awake, awake, utter a song.

Hear me, hear me, hear me Shekhinah.
Strengthen me, strengthen me, strengthen me in my tears.

מִימִינִי מִיכָאֵל וּמִשְׂמֹאלִי גַּבְרִיאֵל וּמִלְּפָנַי אוֹרִיאֵל וּמֵאֲחוֹרַי רְפָאֵל
עַל רֹאשִׁי שְׁכִינָה   עַל רֹאשִׁי שְׁכִינָה
מִיכָאֵל   גַּבְרִיאֵל   אוֹרִיאֵל   רְפָאֵל

miy'mini michaeil, umismoli gavriel
umil'fanai uri'eil, mei'achorai r'faeil
al roshi shekhinah (x2)
michaeil, gavriel, uriel, rafaeil

May Michael be at my right hand, Gabriel at my left,
before me Uriel, behind me Raphael, and above my head the Divine Presence.

בָּרְכוּ שְׁכִינָה   צִמְצְמַי   אֵל שַׁדַּי

barchu shekhinah, tzimtzemai, el shaddai (x2)

בָּרְכוּ אֶת הַבְּרֵכָה הַמְבֹרֶכֶת

barchu et habereichah hamevorechet (x2)

בְּרוּכָה הַבְּרֵכָה הַמְבֹרֶכֶת לְעוֹלָם וָעֶד

beruchah habereichah hamevorechet le'olam va'ed le'olam va'ed

Blessed is the Presence, the One who Makes Space, the Nurturing Divinity, blessed is
the Pool of Blessing that grants blessing, forever and ever.

Based on Judges 5:12, Judith 9:17 and 13:6, and traditional liturgy
English by Liviah Wessely; Barchu by Taya Shere and Jill Hammer.

BARCHU: CALL TO PRAYER **132**

MIMAINEI/BARCHU

מִמַּעַיְנֵי הַיְשׁוּעָה שְׁאַבְתֶּם מַיִם בְּשָׂשׂוֹן

mimainei hayeshuah shavtem mayim besasson

We will draw water in celebration
We will draw water in celebration
From the wellsprings of liberation
mayim chayim

Avra Shapiro and Yael Schonzeit

BLESS THE GODDESS/BARCHU

בָּרְכוּ אֶת שְׁכִינָה הַמְבֹרֶכֶת

barchu et shekhinah hamevorechet

ברוּכָה שְׁכִינָה הַמְבֹרֶכֶת לְעוֹלָם וָעֶד

beruchah shekhinah hamevorechet le'olam vaed

Bless the Goddess
Weaver of all the worlds
Bless the Goddess
From now til the end of time

beruchah shekhinah hamevorechet le'olam vaed

Elana Brody

COPPER MIRRORS

This chant is based on a biblical verse in which priestesses with mirrors serve at the gateway of the sacred shrine, the mishkan, where divine presence dwells:

וַיַּעַשׂ אֵת הַכִּיּוֹר נְחֹשֶׁת וְאֵת כַּנּוֹ נְחֹשֶׁת
בְּמַרְאֹת הַצֹּבְאֹת אֲשֶׁר צָבְאוּ פֶּתַח אֹהֶל מוֹעֵד

vayaas et hakiyor nechoshet ve'et kano nechoshet
b'marot hatzovot asher tzavu petach ohel mo'ed.

He made the washing-basin of copper and its stand of copper,
from the mirrors of the priestesses who served at the door to the tent of meeting.

Exodus 38:8

נְחֹשֶׁת בְּמַרְאֹת
בְּמַרְאֹת הַצֹּבְאֹת
אֲשֶׁר צָבְאוּ פֶּתַח אֹהֶל מוֹעֵד
אֹהֶל מוֹעֵד

nechoshet bemarot

bemarot hatzovot

asher tzavu petach

ohel moed, ohel moed

We are the ones tending shrine
with copper mirrors bending time
We embrace sacred space
there is blessing in this place

Taya Shere

SH'MA U'BIRKOTEHA
BLESSINGS OVER CREATION

בְּרוּכָה אַתְּ תְּהוֹמוֹת אֱלֹתֵינוּ רוּחַ הָעוֹלָם
יוֹצֶרֶת אוֹר וּבוֹרֵאת חֹשֶׁךְ עֹשָׂה שָׁלוֹם וּבוֹרֵאת אֶת הַכֹּל

beruchah at tehomot eloteinu, ruach ha'olam,
yotzeret or uvoreit hoshech, osah shalom uvoreit et hakol.

Blessed are You, Deep and Formless One, Wind of the Universe,
who forms light and births darkness,
who makes peace and brings all things into being.

Tiamat, the primordial sea goddess of the Babylonians, symbolizes the forces of chaos and formlessness. In myth, her body was torn apart to make the world. Tehomot, the Hebrew word for the deepest depths of the ocean, is a cognate for Tiamat, and is one Hebrew word for God/dess.

PRAYER FOR SIGHT

This invocation of faith I make:
I believe
in what I can see.
By leaf and berry,
word and stone,
I call:
shed on me the light
of humble things.

Jill Hammer

I CALL OUT TO YOU (ANI KRATICH)

אֲנִי קְרָאתִיךָ כִּי תַעֲנֵנִי אֵל

ani kratich ki ta'anini el

I call out to you for you will answer me, God

Annie Matan, Psalms 17:6

ON WEEKDAYS (INCLUDING FESTIVALS)

הַמְּאִירָה לָאָרֶץ וְלַדָּרִים עָלֶיהָ בְּרַחֲמִים וּבְטוּבָהּ מְחַדֶּשֶׁת בְּכָל יוֹם תָּמִיד מַעֲגַל בְּרֵאשִׁית מָה רַבּוּ מַעֲשֶׂיךָ עִלָּעָה כֻּלָּם בְּחָכְמָה עָשִׂית מָלְאָה הָאָרֶץ קִנְיָנַיִךְ

hame'irah la'aretz veladarim aleha berachamim. uvetuvah mechadeshet bechol yom tamid ma'agal vereishit. mah rabu maasayich ila'ah, kulam bechochmah asit malah ha'aretz kinyanayich.

She illuminates the earth and all who live on it in wombful compassion, and in her goodness she renews each day, constantly, the cycle of creation. How great are your works, Hidden One, you have made them all with Wisdom, and the earth is full of your creatures.

elah beruchah
gedolah deah heichinah
ufaalah zaharei chamah tov yatzrah
kevod lishmah meorot natnah sovevot uzah
pinot tzvaeha kedoshim romemei shadai tamid
mesaprim kevod elah ukedushatah

וּלְקַדְּשָׁתָהּ

Source of Blessing, Deep Wisdom sharpened the rays of the sun, made Goodness to dwell in, spread out lights to encircle Her dwelling. On four corners stand Her holy hosts, exalters of the Sustaining One, always telling of the Presence of the One and Her holiness flowing through everything.

SABBATH POEM OF THE SKIES

אֵלָה אֶדֶן לְכָל הַמַּעֲשִׂים	elah eden lekhol hama'asim
בְּרוּכָה וּמְבֹרֶכֶת בְּפִי כָּל נְשָׁמָה	beruchah umevorechet befi kol neshamah
גָּדְלָהּ וְטוּבָהּ מָלֵא עוֹלָם	gad'lah vetuvah malei olam
דַּעַת וּתְבוּנָה סֹבְבִים אוֹתָהּ:	da'at ut'vunah sovevim otah:
הַמִּתְגָּאֶה עַל חַיּוֹת הַקֹּדֶשׁ	hamitga'eh al chayot hakodesh
וְנֶהְדָּר בְּכָבוֹד עַל הַמֶּרְכָּבָה	venehedar bechavod al hamerkavah
זְכוּת וּמִישׁוֹר לִפְנֵי כִסְאוֹ	zechut umishor lifnei kiso
חֶסֶד וְרַחֲמִים לִפְנֵי כְבוֹדָהּ	chesed verachamim lifnei kevodah
טוֹבִים מְאוֹרוֹת שֶׁבָּרָא אֱלֹהֵינוּ	tovim me'orot shebara eloheinu
יְצָרָם בְּדַעַת בְּבִינָה וּבְהַשְׂכֵּל	yetzaram b'da'at b'vinah uvhas'kel
כֹּחַ וּגְבוּרָה נָתַן בָּהֶם	ko'ach ug'vurah natan bahem
לִהְיוֹת מוֹשְׁלִים בְּקֶרֶב תֵּבֵל	lihyot moshlim bekerev tevel
מְלֵאִים זִיו וּמְפִיקִים נֹגַהּ	mele'im ziv um'fikim nogah
נָאֶה זִיוָם בְּכָל הָעוֹלָם	na'eh zivam bechol ha'olam
שְׂמֵחִים בְּצֵאתָם וְשָׂשִׂים בְּבוֹאָם	s'mechim betzetam vesassim bevo'am
עוֹשִׂים בְּאֵימָה רְצוֹן קוֹנָתָם	osim b'eimah retzon konatam
פְּאֵר וְכָבוֹד נוֹתְנִים לִשְׁמָהּ	pe'er vechavod not'nim lish'mah.
צָהֳלָה וְרִנָּה לְזֵכֶר מַלְכוּתָהּ	tzahalah verinah lezecher malchutah.
קְרָאָה לַשֶּׁמֶשׁ וַיִּזְרַח אוֹר	karah lashemesh vayiz'rach or
רָאֲתָה וְהִתְקִינָה צוּרַת הַלְּבָנָה	ra'atah vehit'kinah tzurat halevanah
שֶׁבַח נוֹתְנִים לוֹ כָּל צְבָא מָרוֹם	shevach not'nim lo kol tz'va marom.
תִּפְאֶרֶת וּגְדֻלָּה	tif 'eret ugedulah
שְׂרָפִים וְאוֹפַנִּים וְחַיּוֹת הַקֹּדֶשׁ	serafim ve'ofanim vechayot hakodesh.

Elah is the foundation of all creation, blessed and re-blessed is She by every soul.
Her greatness and goodness fill the world knowledge and wisdom surround Her.
He is exalted above the celestial constellation-animals,
and beautified in glory upon the Divine chariot
merit and justice stand before His seat, kindness and compassion swirl around Her
Good are the lights that our God created,
they were made with knowledge, wisdom and insight
He placed in them energy and power to watch over the world
They fill with splendor and sparkle brightness;
Beautiful is their radiance throughout all the worlds.
They take joy in their rising and are glad in their setting
performing with reverence the desire of their Creator
They give glory and honor to the Divine essence and joyous song to Her immanence.
She called forth the sun, and it shone with light;
She gazed, and fixed the changing form of the moon.
All the hosts of heaven give Him praise;
All the celestial beings, glory and lavishness.

קְדוֹשָׁה קְדוֹשָׁה קְדוֹשָׁה שַׁדַּי צְבָאוֹת
מְלֹא כָל הָאָרֶץ כְּבוֹדָהּ

☐ kedoshah kedoshah kedoshah shaddai tzevaot
melo chol ha'aretz kevodah

קָדוֹשׁ קָדוֹשׁ קָדוֹשׁ יהוה צְבָאוֹת
מְלֹא כָל הָאָרֶץ כְּבוֹדוֹ

△ kadosh kadosh kadosh adonai tzevaot
melo chol ha'aretz kevodo

קְדוֹשֶׁה קְדוֹשֶׁה קְדוֹשֶׁה הויה צְבָאוֹת
מְלֹא כָל הָאָרֶץ כְּבוֹדֶה

⊖ kedosheh kedosheh kedosheh havayah tzevaot
melo chol ha'aretz kevodeh

Holy, holy, holy is the One of Multitudes: the whole earth is full of Their presence.

HOLY

Holy (x10)

Holy is the silence and holy is the sound
Holy is each one of us and holy is the ground
Holy is the darkness and holy is the light
Holy is the morning and holy is the night

קָדוֹשׁ קָדוֹשׁ קָדוֹשׁ יהוה צְבָאוֹת מְלֹא כָל הָאָרֶץ כְּבוֹדוֹ

kadosh kadosh kadosh adonai tzevaot melo chol ha'aretz kevodo

lyrics and music by Taya Shere, additional verse Jill Hammer

אוֹר חָדָשׁ עַל צִיּוֹן תָּאִירִי וְנִזְכֶּה כֻלָּנוּ מְהֵרָה לְאוֹרוֹ. בְּרוּכָה אַתְּ עֲנַן הַכָּבוֹד יוֹצֶרֶת הַמְּאוֹרוֹת.

or chadash al tzion ta'iri venizkeh chulanu meheirah le'oro. beruchah at anan hakavod, yotzeret hame'orot.

Blessed are You, Cloud of Glory, who illuminates us with light.

BLESSINGS OVER CREATION

PRAYER OF LOVE (AHAVAH RABAH)

אַהֲבָה רַבָּה אֲהַבְתָּנוּ יהוה אֱלֹהֵינוּ

ahavah rabbah ahavtanu adonai eloheynu…

with an abounding love

אַהֲבָה רַבָּה אֲהַבְתִּינוּ שְׁכִינָה אֱלָתֵנוּ

ahavah rabbah ahavtinu shekhinah elateinu…

with an astounding love

we shall lift each other up
as you have lifted us G!ddess
we shall lift each other up

Taya Shere, adaptation of Ixchele Greentree circle song

אַהֲבָה רַבָּה אֲהַבְתִּינוּ שְׁכִינָה אֱלָתֵנוּ חֶמְלָה גְדוֹלָה וִיתֵרָה חָמַלְתְּ עָלֵינוּ.
אִמֵּנוּ מוֹרָתֵנוּ בַּעֲבוּר אִמּוֹתֵינוּ שֶׁבָּטְחוּ בָךְ וַתְּלַמְּדָן חֻקֵּי חַיִּים כֵּן תְּחָנֵּנוּ וּתְלַמְּדֵנוּ.
אִמֵּנוּ הָאֵם הָרַחֲמָנָה הָרַחֵם רַחֲמֵי עָלֵינוּ וּתְנִי בְּלִבֵּנוּ
לְהָבִין וּלְהַשְׂכִּיל
לִשְׁמֹעַ לִלְמֹד וּלְלַמֵּד
לִשְׁמֹר וְלַעֲשׂוֹת וּלְקַיֵּם
אֶת כָּל דִּבְרֵי תַלְמוּד תּוֹרָתֵךְ
בְּאַהֲבָה.

ahavah rabbah ahavtinu shekhinah elateinu chemlah gedolah vitera chamalt aleinu. imeinu morateinu, ba'avur imoteinu shebatchu vach vatelamdim chukei chayyim. ken techaninu ut'lamdinu imeinu ha'em harachamanah harechem rachmi aleinu vetni bilibeinu lehavin ulchaskel lishmoa lilmod ulelamed lishmor vela'asot ulkayyem et kol divrei talmud torateich be'ahavah.

With a great love have you loved us, Shekhinah. A great tenderness have you spread over us. Our mother, our teacher, our mothers trusted in you, and you taught them the paths of life. Be gracious to us, compassionate mother, and make our hearts understand and hear and learn Your teachings.

וְהָאֵר עֵינֵינוּ בְּתוֹרָתֶךְ וְדַבֵּק לִבֵּנוּ בְּמִצְוֹתֶיךָ וְיַחֵד לְבָבֵנוּ לְאַהֲבָה וּלְיִרְאָה אֶת שְׁמֶךָ וְלֹא נֵבוֹשׁ לְעוֹלָם וָעֶד: כִּי בְשֵׁם קָדְשְׁךָ הַגָּדוֹל וְהַנּוֹרָא בָּטָחְנוּ, נָגִילָה וְנִשְׂמְחָה בִּישׁוּעָתֶךָ

veha'er einenu betoratecha vedabek libeynu bemitzvotecha veyached levaveinu le'ahavah ulirah et shmecha. velo neivosh le'olam va'ed ki veshem kodshecha hagadol vehanorah batachnu, nagila venishmecha biyeshuatecha.

Let our eyes be bright in your Wisdom, let our hearts cling to your doings, and let our hearts be united to love and revere your Name. Then we will never be shamed, for we have put our trust in Your great and awesome name. We will be glad and rejoice in your wholeness!

וַהֲבִיאֵנוּ לְשָׁלוֹם מֵאַרְבַּע כַּנְפוֹת הָאָרֶץ וְתוֹלִכֵנוּ קוֹמְמִיּוּת לְאַרְצֵנוּ כִּי אֵלָה פּוֹעֶלֶת יְשׁוּעוֹת אָתְּ וּבָנוּ בָחַרְתְּ עִם כָּל עַם וְלָשׁוֹן. וְקֵרַבְתָּנוּ לְשִׁמְךָ הַגָּדוֹל סֶלָה בֶּאֱמֶת לְהוֹדוֹת לָךְ וּלְיַחֶדְךָ בְּאַהֲבָה. בְּרוּכָה אַתְּ שְׁכִינָה הַבּוֹחֶרֶת בְּעַמָּהּ יִשְׂרָאֵל בְּאַהֲבָה.

vehavi'inu leshalom mearba kanfot ha'aretz vetolichinu komemiut le'artzeinu ki elah poelet yeshuot at uvanu vachart im kol am velashon. vekeravtinu lishmeich hagadol sela be'emet lehodot lach uleyachdeich be'ahavah. beruchah at shekhinah habocheret be'amah yisrael be'ahavah.

THE TZITZIT ARE GATHERED TOGETHER

Bring us in peace from the four wings of the earth and bring us to stand on our land. For you are a wonder-working Goddess and have harvested us among all the other peoples of the earth. You have drawn us close to your essence so that we may be grateful to you and seek your unity of spirit.

Blessed are You, Shekhinah, who gathers your communities with love.

MEDITATION FOR TZITZIT

As you gather the tzitzit to the center,
open to your own fringes, the edges, margins and knots.
Open to immerse in wholeness, in shalom.

As you hold the tzitzit, open your heart wide.
Open yourself to welcome, to offer shalom for all beings
at the edges, the margins, and those in exile, refugees.
Open to all beings at the fringes of our worlds.

Open to the wisdom
of compassion and courage.
Breathe deep, and honor the powers of sacred presence.

Sharon Shosh Lulyanit

BLESSINGS OVER CREATION

SH'MA (THE PRAYER FOR ONENESS)

The mystics understood the Shema as a means for bringing what is separate into wholeness. They would recite intentions before the Shema, inviting the Shekhinah to unite with the Holy One of Blessing. We invite you to contemplate one of the following unification prayers, using a variety of languages about the divine, before reciting the Shema.

לְשֵׁם יִחוּד קוּדְשָׁא בְּרִיךְ הוּא וּשְׁכִינְתֵּא

l'shem yichud kudsha brich hu ushekhintei.

For the sake of the unification of the Holy One and the Shekhinah, God and Goddess.

or

לְשֵׁם יִחוּד אִמָּא עִלָּאָה וְאִמָּא תַחְתּוֹנָה

l'shem yichud immah ilaah veimmah tachtonah.

For the sake of the unification of Binah and Shekhinah,
the Mother and Daugher, the Cosmos and Earth.

or

לְשֵׁם יִחוּד אָרִיךְ אַנְפִּין וְזָאִיר אַנְפִּין

l'shem yichud arikh anpin uze'ir anpin.

For the sake of the unification of Chochmah and Tiferet,
the Lover and the Beloved.

or

לְשֵׁם יִחוּד כָּל פְּנֵי אֱלוֹהוּת

l'shem yichud kol p'nei elohut.

For the sake of the unification of all aspects of deity, all faces of God/dess.

It is customary to cover the eyes when reciting the Shema. As you recite each word, you can use the kabbalistic custom of placing the six words in the six directions as a reminder of the oneness all around. Use whatever name for God calls you. Use whatever name for your people calls you. Multiple options for the Shema are presented here.

שְׁמַע יִשְׂרָאֵל יהוה אֱלֹהֵינוּ יהוה אֶחָד

△ sh'ma yisrael adonai eloheinu adonai echad

שְׁמַע יִשְׂרָאֵל שְׁכִינָה אֱלָתֵינוּ שְׁכִינָה אַחַת

□ sh'ma yisrael shekhinah eloheinu shekhinah achat

שִׁמְעָה יִשְׂרָאֵל הויה אֱלֹהֵינוּ הויה אֶחֵד

⊖ shim'eh yisrael havayah eloheinu havayah ached

שִׁמְעִי יִשְׂרָאֵלָךְ שְׁכִינָה אֱלָתֵינוּ שְׁכִינָה אַחַת

□ shimi yisraelah shekhinah eloteinu shekhinah achat

שִׁימְעִי תִּשְׂרָאֵלָה תהוה אֱלוֹהֹתֵינוּ תהוה אַחַת

□ shimi tisraelah tehovah elohoteinu tehovah achat

Hear, Godwrestler: The Present One is the Creator, the Present One is One.

RECITE SILENTLY

בָּרוּךְ שֵׁם כְּבוֹד מַלְכוּתָהּ לְעֹלָם וָעֶד

baruch shem kevod malchutah le'olam va'ed

Blessed is the name of the glory of the Shekinah forever.

The final version of SHMA here is from *Toratah: The Regendered Bible* by Yael Kanarek and Tamar Biala.

BLESSINGS OVER CREATION

TZIMTZEMAI SH'MA

> The trees of Jerusalem were of cinnamon, and when they were harvested their smell would carry through all the land of Israel. When Jerusalem was destroyed they were hidden away, and only a few remained. They may be found in the treasure house of Queen Tzimtzemai.
>
> *Babylonian Talmud, Shabbat 63a*

This mysterious text suggests that Tzimtzemai is one of the names of Shekhinah. Tzimtzemai means "she who makes herself smaller." This name connects to the kabbalistic process of *tzimtzum*, in which God becomes smaller in order for there to be space for the universe to grow.

שְׁמַע יִשְׂרָאֵל צִמְצֲמַי אֱלֹתֵינוּ צִמְצֲמַי אַחַת

shema yisrael tzimtzemai eloheinu tzimtzemai achat

Hear, O Israel, the One who Makes Space is Our God, the One who Makes Space is One.

SILENTLY

בָּרוּךְ שֵׁם כְּבוֹד מַלְכוּתָהּ לְעוֹלָם וָעֶד

baruch shem kevod malchutah le'olam va'ed

Blessed is the name of the glory of the Shekinah forever.

ALTERNATE SH'MA FROM THE SONG OF SONGS (5:2, 6:9)

אֲחֹתִי רַעְיָתִי יוֹנָתִי תַמָּתִי אַחַת הִיא

achoti rayati yonati tamati achat hi

My sister, my love, my dove, my pure one, she is one.

YOU SHALL LOVE

v'ahavt et Shekhinah elohayich
b'chol levavech u'vchol nafshech u'vchol m'odech

You shall love the holy one with all your heart, with all your body,
with all your breath, with all your being

Taya Shere, from the liturgy

AND YOU SHALL LOVE (VE'AHAVTA)
PART I: ADAPTED FROM DEUTERONOMY 6:4-9

☐ FEMININE

וְאָהַבְתְּ אֵת שְׁכִינָה אֱלֹהַיִךְ בְּכָל לְבָבֵךְ וּבְכָל נַפְשֵׁךְ וּבְכָל מְאֹדֵךְ וְהָיוּ הַדְּבָרִים הָאֵלֶּה אֲשֶׁר אָנֹכִי מְצַוָּתֵךְ הַיּוֹם עַל לְבָבֵךְ. וְשִׁנַּנְתִּים לְבָנַיִךְ וּלִבְנוֹתַיִךְ וְדִבַּרְתְּ בָּם בְּשִׁבְתֵּךְ בְּבֵיתֵךְ וּבְלֶכְתֵּךְ בַּדֶּרֶךְ וּבְשָׁכְבֵּךְ וּבְקוּמֵךְ. וּקְשַׁרְתִּים לְאוֹת עַל יָדֵךְ וְהָיוּ לְטֹטָפֹת בֵּין עֵינָיִךְ וּכְתַבְתִּים עַל מְזֻזוֹת בֵּיתֵךְ וּבִשְׁעָרָיִךְ

ve'ahavt et shekhinah elohayich, bechol levavech, uvechol nafshech, uvechol me'odech. vehayu hadevarim ha'eleh, asher anochi metzavatech hayom al levavech. veshinantim l'vanayich uvnotayich, vedibart bam beshivtech beveitech u'velechtech vaderech, uveshachbech uvekumech. ukshartim le'ot al yadech, vehayu letotafot bein einayich. uchetavtim al mezuzot beitech uvisharayich.

△ MASCULINE

וְאָהַבְתָּ אֵת יהוה אֱלֹהֶיךָ בְּכָל לְבָבְךָ וּבְכָל נַפְשְׁךָ וּבְכָל מְאֹדֶךָ. וְהָיוּ הַדְּבָרִים הָאֵלֶּה אֲשֶׁר אָנֹכִי מְצַוְּךָ הַיּוֹם עַל לְבָבֶךָ. וְשִׁנַּנְתָּם לְבָנֶיךָ וְדִבַּרְתָּ בָּם בְּשִׁבְתְּךָ בְּבֵיתֶךָ וּבְלֶכְתְּךָ בַדֶּרֶךְ וּבְשָׁכְבְּךָ וּבְקוּמֶךָ וּקְשַׁרְתָּם לְאוֹת עַל יָדֶךָ וְהָיוּ לְטֹטָפֹת בֵּין עֵינֶיךָ וּכְתַבְתָּם עַל מְזֻזוֹת בֵּיתֶךָ וּבִשְׁעָרֶיךָ.

ve'ahavta et adonai elohecha, bechol levavcha, uvechol nafshecha, uvechol me'odecha. vehayu hadevarim ha'eleh, asher anochi metzavcha hayom al levavecha. veshinantam l'vanecha vedibarta bam beshivtecha be'veitecha, uvelechtecha va'derech, u've'shochbecha u'vekumecha. uk'shartam le'ot al yadecha, vehayu letotafot bein einecha. uch'tavtam al mezzuzot beitecha u'visharecha.

⊖ NONBINARY

וְאָהַבְתֶּ אֵת רוֹיה אֱלֹהֶיךֶ בְּכָל לְבָבֶךְ וּבְכָל נַפְשֶׁךְ וּבְכָל מְאֹדֶךְ. וְהָיוּ הַדְּבָרִים הָאֵלֶּה אֲשֶׁר אָנֹכִי מְצַוְּתֶךְ הַיּוֹם עַל לְבָבֶךְ. וְשִׁנַּנְתֶּם לַבָּנוֹל בָּךְ וְדִבַּרְתֶּ בָּם בְּשִׁבְתֶּךְ בְּבֵיתֶךְ וּבְלֶכְתֶּךְ בַּדֶּרֶךְ וּבְשָׁכְבֶּךְ וּבְקוּמֶךְ. וּקְשַׁרְתֶּם לְאוֹת עַל גּוּפֶךְ וְהָיוּ לְטֹטָפֹת עַל רֹאשֶׁךְ. וּכְתַבְתֶּם עַל מְזֻזוֹת בֵּיתֶךְ וּבִשְׁעָרֶךְ.

ve'ahavteh et havayah elohecheh, bechol levavcheh, uvechol nafshecheh, uvechol me'odecheh. vehayu hadevarim ha'eleh, asher anochi metzavetcheh hayom al levavcheh. veshinantem labanol bach vedibarteh bam beshivtecheh be'veitecheh, uvelechtecheh va'derech, u've'shochbecheh u'vekumecheh. uk'shartem le'ot al gufecheh, vehayu letotafot al roshecheh. uch'tavtem al mezzuzot beitecheh u'visharecheh.

You shall love Becoming your God with all your heart, with all your life-force, with all your gifts. These words which I tell you this day you shall take into your heart. You shall teach them to your children, and speak of them when you sit in your house and when you walk on the path, when you lie down and when you rise up. Tie them as a sign upon your hand and let them be ornaments between your eyes. Write them on the doorposts of your house and on your gates.

BLESSINGS OVER CREATION

SPRING AND AUTUMN RAIN (VE'HAYAH)
PART II: ADAPTED FROM DEUTERONOMY 11:13-21

□ FEMININE

וְהָיָה אִם-שָׁמֹעַ תִּשְׁמַעְנָה אֶל-מִצְוֹתַי אֲשֶׁר אָנֹכִי מְצַוָּה אֶתְכֶן הַיּוֹם לְאַהֲבָה אֶת יְהוָֹה אֱלֹהֵיכֶן וּלְעָבְדָהּ בְּכָל-לְבַבְכֶן וּבְכָל נַפְשְׁכֶן: וְנָתַתִּי מְטַר-אַרְצְכֶן בְּעִתּוֹ יוֹרֶה וּמַלְקוֹשׁ וְאָסַפְתְּ דְּגָנֵךְ וְתִירֹשֵׁךְ וְיִצְהָרֵךְ: וְנָתַתִּי עֵשֶׂב בְּשָׂדֵךְ לִבְהֶמְתֵּךְ וְאָכַלְתְּ וְשָׂבָעְתְּ: הִשָּׁמְרָנָה לָכֶן פֶּן-יִפְתֶּה לְבַבְכֶן וְסַרְתֶּן וַעֲבַדְתֶּן אֱלֹהִים אֲחֵרִים וְהִשְׁתַּחֲוִיתֶן לָהֶם: וְחָרָה אַף-שְׁכִינָה בָּכֶן וְעָצְרָה אֶת-הַשָּׁמַיִם וְלֹא-יִהְיֶה מָטָר וְהָאֲדָמָה לֹא תִתֵּן אֶת-יְבוּלָהּ וַאֲבַדְתֶּן מְהֵרָה מֵעַל הָאָרֶץ הַטֹּבָה אֲשֶׁר יְהוָֹה נֹתֶנֶת לָכֶם: וְשַׂמְתֶּן אֶת דְּבָרַי אֵלֶּה עַל-לְבַבְכֶן וְעַל-נַפְשְׁכֶן וּקְשַׁרְתֶּן אֹתָם לְאוֹת עַל-יֶדְכֶן וְהָיוּ לְטוֹטָפֹת בֵּין עֵינֵיכֶן: וְלִמַּדְתֶּן אֹתָם אֶת-בְּנוֹתֵיכֶן וּבְנֵיכֶם לְדַבֵּר בָּם בְּשִׁבְתֵּךְ בְּבֵיתֵךְ וּבְלֶכְתֵּךְ בַדֶּרֶךְ וּבְשָׁכְבֵּךְ וּבְקוּמֵךְ: וּכְתַבְתָּם עַל-מְזוּזוֹת בֵּיתֵךְ וּבִשְׁעָרֶיךְ: לְמַעַן יִרְבּוּ יְמֵיכֶן וִימֵי בְנוֹתֵיכֶן וּבְנֵיכֶן עַל הָאֲדָמָה אֲשֶׁר נִשְׁבְּעָה שְׁכִינָה לְאִמּוֹתֵיכֶן וְלַאֲבוֹתֵיכֶן לָתֵת לָהֶן כִּימֵי הַשָּׁמַיִם עַל-הָאָרֶץ:

vehaya im shamoa tishmanah el mitzvotai asher anochi mitzavah etchen hayom, l'ahava et havaya eloheychen ule'avdah bechol levavchen uv'chol nafshechen: v'natati metar artzechen b'ito yoreh umalkosh v'asaft deganech v'tirshech v'yitzharech v'natati eisev b'sadech livhemteich v'achalt v'savat: hishamarna lachen pen yifteh l'vavchen vesarten v'avadeten elohim acheirim v'hishtachaviten lahem: v'charah af shekhinah bachem v'atzar et hashamayim velo yihyeh matar veha'adamah lo titein et yevulah va'avadten meheira me'al ha'aretz hatova asher havayah notenet lachem: v'shamten et dvarai eileh al levavchen v'al nafshechen uksharten otam l'ot al yed'chen, v'hayu l'totafot bein eineichen: v'limadten otem et b'neichem uv'noteichen l'dabeir bam, b'shivteich b'veiteich, uv'lechteich vaderech, uveshachbeich uvekumeich uchtavtim al mezuzot beiteich uvish'arayich: lma'an yirbu y'meichen vimei v'noteichen uv'neichen al ha'adamah asher nishba'ah shekhinah l'imoteichen v'la'avoteichen lateit lahen kimei hashamayim al ha'aretz:

△ MASCULINE

וְהָיָה אִם-שָׁמֹעַ תִּשְׁמְעוּ אֶל-מִצְוֹתַי אֲשֶׁר אָנֹכִי מְצַוֶּה אֶתְכֶם הַיּוֹם לְאַהֲבָה אֶת יְהוָֹה אֱלֹהֵיכֶם וּלְעָבְדוֹ בְּכָל-לְבַבְכֶם וּבְכָל נַפְשְׁכֶם: וְנָתַתִּי מְטַר-אַרְצְכֶם בְּעִתּוֹ יוֹרֶה וּמַלְקוֹשׁ וְאָסַפְתָּ דְגָנֶךָ וְתִירֹשְׁךָ וְיִצְהָרֶךָ: וְנָתַתִּי עֵשֶׂב בְּשָׂדְךָ לִבְהֶמְתֶּךָ וְאָכַלְתָּ וְשָׂבָעְתָּ: הִשָּׁמְרוּ לָכֶם פֶּן-יִפְתֶּה לְבַבְכֶם וְסַרְתֶּם וַעֲבַדְתֶּם אֱלֹהִים אֲחֵרִים וְהִשְׁתַּחֲוִיתֶם לָהֶם: וְחָרָה אַף-יְהוָֹה בָּכֶם וְעָצַר אֶת-הַשָּׁמַיִם וְלֹא-יִהְיֶה מָטָר וְהָאֲדָמָה לֹא תִתֵּן אֶת-יְבוּלָהּ וַאֲבַדְתֶּם מְהֵרָה מֵעַל הָאָרֶץ הַטֹּבָה אֲשֶׁר יְהוָֹה נֹתֵן לָכֶם: וְשַׂמְתֶּם אֶת דְּבָרַי אֵלֶּה עַל-לְבַבְכֶם וְעַל-נַפְשְׁכֶם וּקְשַׁרְתֶּם אֹתָם לְאוֹת עַל-יֶדְכֶם וְהָיוּ לְטוֹטָפֹת בֵּין עֵינֵיכֶם: וְלִמַּדְתֶּם אֹתָם אֶת-בְּנֵיכֶם וּבְנוֹתֵיכֶם לְדַבֵּר בָּם בְּשִׁבְתְּךָ בְּבֵיתֶךָ וּבְלֶכְתְּךָ בַדֶּרֶךְ וּבְשָׁכְבְּךָ וּבְקוּמֶךָ: וּכְתַבְתָּם עַל-מְזוּזוֹת בֵּיתֶךָ וּבִשְׁעָרֶיךָ: לְמַעַן יִרְבּוּ יְמֵיכֶם וִימֵי בְנֵיכֶם וּבְנוֹתֵיכֶם עַל הָאֲדָמָה אֲשֶׁר נִשְׁבַּע יְהוָֹה לַאֲבֹתֵיכֶם וְלַאֲבוֹתֵיכֶם לָתֵת לָהֶם כִּימֵי הַשָּׁמַיִם עַל-הָאָרֶץ:

△ MASCULINE CONTINUED

vehaya im shamoa tishme'u el mitzvotai asher anochi metzaveh etchem hayom le'ahavah et havayah eloheichem ul'avdo bechol l'vavchem uvechol nafesheichem. venatati m'tar artzechem be'ito yoreh umalkosh ve'asafta d'ganecha vetiroshecha veyitzharecha. venatati eisev besadecha uvhemtecha ve'achalta vesavata. hishamru lachem pen yifteh levavchem vesartem ve'avadtem elohim acherim vehishtachavitem lachem. vehara af havaya bachem ve'atzar et hashamayim velo yihiyeh matar veha'adamah lo titen et yevulah ve'avadtem meheirah me'al ha'aretz hatovah asher havayah noten lachem. vesamtem et devarai eileh al levachem ve'al nafsheichem ukshartem otam le'ot al yadchem vehayu letotafot bein eineichem. velimadtem otam el beneichem uvnoteichem ledaber bam beshivtecha beveitecha uvlecttecha vaderech uveshachbecha uvekumecha uktavtem al mezuzot beitecha uvishe'arecha. lma'an yirbu yemeichem viymei vnoteichem uvneichem al ha'adamah asher nishba havayah l'imoteichem vela'avoteichem latet lahem kiymei shamayim al ha'aretz.

Spring and autumn rain
corn and wine and oil you shall have
if only you will love
Becoming itself
and sit with it at home
and walk with it on your journeys
and lie down with it in your dreams
and rise up with it in your hopes
you will eat and be satisfied
and if you will close your heart
and turn away
from your nefesh-wisdom
and your communion with the world
and serve gods that are Other than Becoming
the earth will not yield her fruit
and the skies will shut their doors
and you will be lost from the good land
that Becoming gives you
yet if you will love Becoming
with heart, body, and soul
and weave it into the thoughts of your mind
and the works of your hands
and teach it to your children
and tell it in your stories
then your days will be long and whole
as the days of the sky above the earth.

I place my hands
on the roots of the tree of life:
this stone and clay,
these fertile grains of dust.
This is the covenant:
think of the earth
and she will ground you,
as it is written
ask the earth
and she will teach you.
This is the covenant:
sink your roots in her,
and when rain comes,
spring and autumn,
you will be watered
with her.

Jill Hammer

FRINGES (VA'YOMER)
PART III: ADAPTED FROM NUMBERS 13:37-41

□ FEMININE

וַיֹּאמֶר יְהוָֹה אֶל־מִרְיָם וּמֹשֶׁה לֵּאמֹר: דַּבְּרִי אֶל־בְּנוֹת וּבְנֵי יִשְׂרָאֵל וְאָמַרְתְּ אֲלֵהֶן: וְעָשׂוּ לָהֶן צִיצִת עַל־כַּנְפֵי בִגְדֵיהֶן לְדֹרֹתָן וְנָתְנוּ עַל־צִיצִת הַכָּנָף פְּתִיל תְּכֵלֶת: וְהָיָה לָכֶן לְצִיצִת וּרְאִיתֶן אֹתוֹ וּזְכַרְתֶּן אֶת־כָּל־מִצְוֹת יְהוָֹה וַעֲשִׂיתֶן אֹתָן וְלֹא תָתֻרְנָה מֵאַחֲרֵי לְבַבְכֶן וְאַחֲרֵי עֵינֵיכֶן אֲשֶׁר־אַתֶּן זָנוֹת מֵהֵן: לְמַעַן תִּזְכּוֹרְנָה וַעֲשִׂיתֶן אֶת־כָּל־מִצְוֹתָי וִהְיִיתֶן קְדֹשׁוֹת לֶאֱלַתְכֶן אֲנִי יְהוָֹה אֱלַתְכֶן אֲשֶׁר הוֹצֵאתִי אֶתְכֶן מֵאֶרֶץ מִצְרַיִם לִהְיוֹת לָכֶם לְאֵלָה אֲנִי יְהוָֹה אֱלַתְכֶן:

vayomer havayah el miryam lemor: dabri el b'not uvnei yisrael ve'amart aleihen ve'asu lahen tzitzit al kanfei bigdeihen ledorotan venatnu al tzitzit hakanaf ptil tcheilet. vehaya lahen letzitzit ure'iten oto uzecharten et kol mitzvot havayah velo tatorna acharei levavchen ve'acharei eineihen asher aten zanot meihen. lema'an tizkornah va'asiten et kol mitzvotai, vehiyten kedoshot l'elatchen. ani havayah elatchen, asher hotzeiti etchen me'eretz mitzrayim lihiyot lachem l'elah. ani havayah elatchen.

△ MASCULINE

וַיֹּאמֶר יְהוָֹה אֶל־מֹשֶׁה וּמִרְיָם לֵּאמֹר: דַּבֵּר אֶל־בְּנוֹת וּבְנֵי יִשְׂרָאֵל וְאָמַרְתָּ אֲלֵהֶם: וְעָשׂוּ לָהֶם צִיצִת עַל־כַּנְפֵי בִגְדֵיהֶם לְדֹרֹתָם וְנָתְנוּ עַל־צִיצִת הַכָּנָף פְּתִיל תְּכֵלֶת: וְהָיָה לָכֶם לְצִיצִת וּרְאִיתֶם אֹתוֹ וּזְכַרְתֶּם אֶת־כָּל־מִצְוֹת יְהוָֹה וַעֲשִׂיתֶם אֹתָן וְלֹא תָתוּרוּ מֵאַחֲרֵי לְבַבְכֶם וְאַחֲרֵי עֵינֵיכֶם אֲשֶׁר־אַתֶּם זָנִים מֵהֶם: לְמַעַן תִּזְכְּרוּ וַעֲשִׂיתֶם אֶת־כָּל־מִצְוֹתָי וִהְיִיתֶם קְדֹשִׁים לֵאלֹהֵיכֶם אֲנִי יְהוָֹה אֱלֹהֵיכֶם אֲשֶׁר הוֹצֵאתִי אֶתְכֶם מֵאֶרֶץ מִצְרַיִם לִהְיוֹת לָכֶם לֵאלֹהִים אֲנִי יהוה אֱלֹהֵיכֶם:

vayomer havayah el moshe lemor: daber el bnot uvnei yisrael va'amarta aleihem ve'asu lahem tzitzit al kanfei bigdeihem ledorotam venatnu al tzitzit hakanaf ptil tcheilet. vehaya lahem letzitzit ure'item oto uzechartem et kol mitzvot havayah velo taturu acharei levavchem ve'acharei eineichem asher atem zanim meihem. lema'an tizkeru va'asitem et kol mitzvotai, vehiyten kedoshim lelohechem. ani havayah eloheichem, asher hotzeiti etchem me'eretz mitzrayim lihiyot lachem l'elohim. ani havayah eloheichem.

God said to Miriam and Moshe: Speak to the children of Israel and say to them that they should make fringes on the corners (wings) of their garments throughout their generations, and they should put upon the fringe of the corner a thread of blue. They will be fringes for you, and you will look at them and remember the desires of the Eternal your God, and you will not turn aside from the knowing of your hearts or the understanding your eyes by which you nourish yourselves. Thus shall you remember my desires and be holy to the Infinite. I, Havayah, am the Infinite who led you out of Egypt to be infinite to you. I, the Infinite, am your God.

INCULCATION

An inculcation is a teaching or prayer repeated regularly in order to impress it upon the mind. This poem, inspired by the V'AHAVTA, was written for the divine feminine within.

> Mother, sister, daughter,
> crone, widow, orphan,
> neighbor, oppressor, stranger—
> Lay down your burden.
> There is a reservoir
> waiting to be filled
> with your tears.
>
> Take these inculcations
> into your womb.
> Speak of them when you rise up
> and when you lie down,
> in the place where you
> momentarily make your home
> and in the heart where your soul resides.
>
> Remove the bindings from your eyes.
> Let your deeds of justice be your davening.
> Revision halakhah, releasing stuck regimen.
> Listen to earth's law, defining new ritual.
> Let these words become a signpost
> that you may cultivate
> a forest of living waters
> sprouting from your every pore.
> May you sweat your prayers,
> nourish your fingertips and your hip bones,
> and pour the gratitude for
> these gritty moments
> daily over your body.
>
> Shower your spirit with this one phrase of
> truths and histories:
> I am alive. Goddess is within me.
> I am free. I am liberated by surrender.
> I am alive. Goddess is within me.
>
> *Rae Abileah*

NOTES ON SH'MA

In the above section, the God-name usually pronounced as Adonai has been rendered as YHWH (the Tetragrammaton) with the pronunciation Havayah (Havayah means Being, and a permutation of the name YHWH). This name has been translated Becoming (another possible translation of YHWH), or simply as Havayah. This is with the understanding that individuals will use the God-name that is right for them.

There has been a change from the original Torah text in the third section, in the biblical passage regarding fringes. The original passage says: "do not wander after your hearts or your eyes, after which you stray/act like a whore." In the interests of promoting the intuition of the heart, and removing the prostitute imagery, the passage has been rendered: 'do not wander away from your heart and your eyes, which nourish you." (The Hebrew for "to lust" and "to feed or nourish" are similar.)

While according to the Torah, the texts of these passages were given to Moshe (Moses) and not to Miriam, we include the priestess and prophetess Miriam's name as a reminder that inspiration was also received by prophetesses and priestesses. In this siddur, we include that wisdom in what we hold sacred.

MI CHAMOCHA
BLESSING FOR REDEMPTION

1.

umalchuto beratzon kiblu aleihem
moshe umiriam uvnei yisrael
lecha anu shirah besimcha rabah
veamru kulam

mi chamocha ba'elim adonai
mi kamocha nedar bakodesh
norah tehilot oseh feleh

malchutcha ra'u vanecha
bokea yam lifnei moshe umiryam
zeh eli anu ve'amru:
adonai yimloch le'olam va'ed

☐ vene'emar ki fadah havayah et yaakov
uge'alo miyad chazak mimenu.

△ vene'emar ki fad'ah havayah et hagar
uge'alah miyad hazakah mimenah.

beruchah at shekhinah, ga'alah yisrael.

וּמַלְכוּתוֹ בְּרָצוֹן קִבְּלוּ עֲלֵיהֶם
מֹשֶׁה וּמִרְיָם וּבְנֵי יִשְׂרָאֵל
לְךָ עָנוּ שִׁירָה בְּשִׂמְחָה רַבָּה
וְאָמְרוּ כֻלָּם

מִי כָמֹכָה בָּאֵלִים יהוה
מִי כָּמֹכָה נֶאְדָּר בַּקֹּדֶשׁ
נוֹרָא תְהִילֹת עֹשֵׂה פֶלֶא

מַלְכוּתְךָ רָאוּ בָנֶיךָ
בּוֹקֵעַ יָם לִפְנֵי מֹשֶׁה וּמִרְיָם
זֶה אֵלִי עָנוּ וְאָמְרוּ
יהוה יִמְלֹךְ לְעוֹלָם וָעֶד

☐ וְנֶאֱמַר: כִּי פָדָה יהוה אֶת יַעֲקֹב
וּגְאָלוֹ מִיַּד חָזָק מִמֶּנּוּ.

△ וְנֶאֱמַר: כִּי פְדָתָה הויה אֶת הָגָר
וּגְאָלָהּ מִיַּד חֲזָקָה מִמֶּנָּה.

בְּרוּכָה אַתְּ שְׁכִינָה גָּאֲלָה יִשְׂרָאֵל.

Your children acclaimed your sovereignty,
Moses and Miriam and the Israelites sang:

Who is like you, Adonai, among all powers of the world?
Who is like you, glorious in holiness,
Awesome in praises, doing wonders?

The Source of Life preserves the journeyer amid vast obstacles,
and guides wanderers like Hagar and Jacob to the places they seek.

Blessed is Shekhinah, the Redeemer of Israel.

2. SPIRIT IS FLOWING

mi chamocha ba'elim adonai
mi kamocha nedar bakodesh
norah tehilot oseh feleh

מִי כָמֹכָה בָּאֵלִים ירהוה
מִי כָּמֹכָה נֶאְדָּר בַּקֹּדֶשׁ
נוֹרָא תְהִילֹת עֹשֵׂה פֶלֶא

The Spirit is flowing, flowing and growing
The Spirit is flowing, through you and me

HaShem guide me, be faithfully beside me
HaShem guide me, and bless how I be

The Spirit is flowing, flowing and growing
The Spirit is flowing, through you and me

Shekhinah, reside in me, your wisdom lives inside of me
Shekhinah, reside in me, oh Holy of Holies!

Taya Shere, adaptation of traditional circle song

3. GROVE SONG

mi kamoha baeylim shaddai
mi kamoha hadar bakodesh
nor'ah tehilot osah feleh

מִי כָמוֹהָ בָּאֵילִים שָׁדַּי
מִי כָּמוֹהָ הָדָר בַּקֹּדֶשׁ
נוֹרָאָה תְהִילֹת עֹשָׂה פֶלֶא

Who is like Her, the Nourishing One, in all the groves?
Who is like Her, the glory in the sanctuary,
mysterious in praise, doing wondrously?

Jill Hammer

4. VATIKACH MIRIAM

vatikach miriam haneviah
achot aharon et hatof beyada
vatetzena khol hanashim achareha

וַתִּקַּח מִרְיָם הַנְּבִיאָה
אֲחוֹת אַהֲרֹן אֶת הַתֹּף בְּיָדָהּ
וַתֵּצֶאןָ כָל הַנָּשִׁים אַחֲרֶיהָ

And Miriam the prophetess
sister of Aharon, took a drum in her hand
and all the women went out after her.

Exodus 15:20, melody by Tziona Achishena

JOURNEY

between
a pillar of cloud
and a pillar of fire
the sea yawns
birth canal
labyrinth
blood-painted door
we enter joyful
that the future is just ahead
we enter afraid
of what pursues us
we enter
not knowing
we have escaped slavery
someone bought our freedom
we're not sure who
ancestors
children
prophets
all-weaver
angel of death
to either side
the water is mirrors
is windows
is a glimpse of the deep
just ahead
is darkness
is a light shining
is the sound of singing
and the pounding of feet

Jill Hammer

LABYRINTH

Go forward, always down, and never left or right.
Instructions given to Ariadne, keeper of the labyrinth.

Here is the real
in the throat and the sternum
and the feet and the churning of the gut.

Not the past,
not the law,
not the wish,
not the fear,
not the story.
Trust what the body tells you.
Everyone else is lying.

The girl with the lantern is here,
disorganized, stubborn,
to take you through the dark tunnels.
You don't want to trust her,

but she knows the way.
You know this;
do not let yourself forget
as you so often have
to your regret.

Follow her down
into the arms of the earth:
the other disorganized, stubborn body
that never lies.

Do not turn left or right.
Below the skin,
the pulse is singing.
Follow that sound.

Jill Hammer

AMIDAH

DOORWAYS INTO THE AMIDAH

You will find, here and elsewhere in the siddur, a variety of traditional and creative options for entering the Amidah prayer, to be used by themselves or in combination.

Amidah I   Traditional Shabbat Amidah with Feminine God-Language, page 154
Amidah II   Shrine Meditation (Shabbat, Festivals, or Weekdays), page 164
Amidah III   Seven Blessings: A Guided Meditation Amidah (all occasions), page 166
Amidah IV   Elemental Amidah (Shabbat, Festivals, or Weekdays), page 167
Amidah V   Circle of Life Amidah (for Weekdays), page 168
Amidah VI   Earth-based Meditations for the Amidah (for Weekdays), page 171

For Traditional Weekday Amidah with feminine God-language, see page 64
For Traditional Festival Amidah with gender-balanced God-language, see page 76

PRAYER BEFORE THE AMIDAH

△ אֲדֹנָי שְׂפָתַי תִּפְתָּח וּפִי יַגִּיד תְּהִלָּתֶךּ
☐ שְׁכִינָה שְׂפָתַי תִּפְתְּחִי וּפִי יַגִּיד תְּהִלָּתֵךְ

△ adonai s'fatai tiftach ufi yagid t'hilatecha
☐ shekhinah s'fatai tiftechi ufi yagid t'hilateich

Open up my lips Oh G!d and I will sing your praise

ANCESTOR CHANT

We are the old people, we are the new people
We are the same people, stronger than before

> You bless us Elohei Sarah
> You bless us Elohei Rivka
> You bless us Elohei Rachel
> You bless us Elohei Leah
> You bless us Elohei Avraham
> You bless us Elohei Yitzhak
> You bless us Elohei Yaakov
> You bless us Elohei Yisrael

"We are an Old People" chorus by morning feather / Will Shepardson, adaptation Taya Shere

SEVEN BREATH MEDITATION

Breathing in, I take breath into myself.
Breathing out, I join the web of being.
Breathing in, I rest in the present.
Breathing out, I am part of past and future.
Breathing in, I honor the shrine of my body.
Breathing out, I honor the shrine of the cosmos.
Breathing in, Presence fills me.
Breathing out, Presence enfolds me.
Breathing in, I witness what is broken.
Breathing out, I bow to what is perfect.
Breathing in, I offer gratitude for what is.
Breathing out, I accept that all changes.
Breathing in, I pray for peace for myself.
Breathing out, I pray for peace for all beings.

AMIDAH

I. SHABBAT AMIDAH WITH FEMININE GOD-LANGUAGE

1. BLESSING FOR ANCESTORS (IMAHOT, AVOT, DOROT

beruchah at shekhinah eloteinu	בְּרוּכָה אַתְּ שְׁכִינָה אֱלֹתֵינוּ וֵאלֹהֵי
ve'elohei imoteinu va'avoteinu vedoroteinu	אִמּוֹתֵינוּ וַאֲבוֹתֵינוּ וְדוֹרוֹתֵינוּ
elohei sarah, elohei rivka,	אֱלֹהֵי שָׂרָה אֱלֹהֵי רִבְקָה
elohei rachel, ve'elohei leah	אֱלֹהֵי רָחֵל וֵאלֹהֵי לֵאָה
(ve'elohei bilhah ve'elohei zilpah)	וֵאלֹהֵי בִּלְהָה וֵאלֹהֵי זִלְפָּה
elohei avraham elohei yitzchak ve'elohei yaakov	אֱלֹהֵי אַבְרָהָם אֱלֹהֵי יִצְחָק וֵאלֹהֵי יַעֲקֹב
ha'elah hagedolah hagiborah vehanora'ah	הָאֵלָה הַגְּדוֹלָה הַגִּבּוֹרָה וְהַנּוֹרָאָה
elah ilaah	אֱלָהּ עִלָּאָה
gomelet chasadim tovim	גּוֹמֶלֶת חֲסָדִים טוֹבִים
vekonah hakol vezocheret chasdei avot ve'imahot	וְקוֹנָה הַכֹּל וְזוֹכֶרֶת חַסְדֵּי אָבוֹת וְאִמָּהוֹת
umeviah goelet livnot venoteihen	וּמְבִיאָה גּוֹאֶלֶת לִבְנוֹת בְּנוֹתֵיהֶן
(velivnei v'neihem)	וְלִבְנֵי בְנֵיהֶם
lma'an shmah be'ahavah.	לְמַעַן שְׁמָהּ בְּאַהֲבָה

BETWEEN ROSH HASHANAH AND YOM KIPPUR   בעשרת ימי תשובה

zochrinu lechayim ruach chafetzet bachayim	זָכְרִינוּ לְחַיִּים רוּחַ חֲפֵצֶת בַּחַיִּים
vekitvinu lesefer hachayyim	וְכִתְבִינוּ בְּסֵפֶר הַחַיִּים
lema'anech ma'yan chayim.	לְמַעֲנֵךְ מַעְיַן חַיִּים

malka ozeret u'moshiah u'mayan.	מַלְכָּה עוֹזֶרֶת וּמוֹשִׁיעָה וּמָעְיָן.
beruchah at shekhinah,	בְּרוּכָה אַתְּ שְׁכִינָה
ma'yan avraham ve'ezrat sarah.	מָעְיָן אַבְרָהָם וְעֶזְרַת שָׂרָה.

Blessed are You, Shekhinah, our Source and Source of our parents:
Life-force of Sarah, Rebekah, Rachel, Leah, Bilhah, and Zilpah,
of Abraham, Isaac and Jacob.
Great Goddess, strong, revered, exalted,
pouring out Your abundant kindness on all beings,
forming the All and all things in it,
weaving a web of connection for our ancestors,
bringing wholeness to all generations
for the sake of your Name that dwells with us in love.

BETWEEN ROSH HASHANAH AND YOM KIPPUR
Remember us for life, Spirit who desires life
and write us in the book of life, for your sake, Source of Life.

Ruler of the cosmos and its servant,
aiding us in our brokenness and bringing us to wholeness:
Blessed are You, shield of Abraham, helper of Sarah.

2. BLESSING FOR THE CIRCLE OF LIFE (GEVUROT)

at gevirah le'olam shadai   אַתְּ גְּבִירָה לְעוֹלָם שָׁדָי
mechayah meitim at rav lehoshia   מְחַיָּה מֵתִים אַתְּ רַב לְהוֹשִׁיעַ

BETWEEN SHEMINI ATZERET AND PASSOVER   בין ש״ע ופסח
   meishivah haruach umoridah hagashem   מַשִּׁיבָה הָרוּחַ וּמוֹרִידָה הַגֶּשֶׁם

mechalkelet chayim bechesed   מְכַלְכֶּלֶת חַיִּים בְּחֶסֶד
mechayah meitim berachamim rabim   מְחַיָּה מֵתִים בְּרַחֲמִים רַבִּים
somechet noflot verofeit cholim   סוֹמֶכֶת נוֹפְלוֹת וְרוֹפֵאת חוֹלִים
umatirah asurot   וּמַתִּירָה אֲסוּרוֹת
umekayemet emunatah lishnot afar   וּמְקַיֶּמֶת אֱמוּנָתָהּ לִישֵׁנוֹת עָפָר
mi chamoch gevirat gevurot   מִי כָמוֹךְ גְּבִירַת גְּבוּרוֹת
umi domah lach   וּמִי דּוֹמָה לָךְ
malkah meimitah umechayah   מַלְכָּה מְמִיתָה וּמְחַיָּה
umatzmichat yeshuah   וּמַצְמִיחַת יְשׁוּעָה

BETWEEN ROSH HASHANAH AND YOM KIPPUR   בעשרת ימי תשובה
  mi chamoch eim harachamim   מִי כָמוֹךְ אֵם הָרַחֲמִים
  zocheret yetzureha lechayyim berachamim   זוֹכֶרֶת יְצוּרֶיהָ לְחַיִּים בְּרַחֲמִים

vene'emanah at lehachayot meitim   וְנֶאֱמָנָה אַתְּ לְהַחֲיוֹת מֵתִים.
beruchah at shekhinah,   בְּרוּכָה אַתְּ שְׁכִינָה
mechayah hameitim   מְחַיָּה הַמֵּתִים.

> You are eternally gatekeeper and nurturer
> turning life to death and death to life,
> rescuing us from the void, sustaining life in love,
> enlivening what dies in your great womb,
> making what falls rise again
> healing the hurt, freeing the enslaved, weaving all that sleeps in earth
> into the bond of life.
> Who could be like you, most potent
> Queen who turns the wheel of death and life and makes redemption flower.

BETWEEN ROSH HASHANAH AND YOM KIPPUR

> Who is like you, mother of mercy,
> transforming your creatures in Your womb of compassion?

> Faithful are you in turning the wheel from death to life.
> Blessed are You, Presence who turns the wheel
> from death to life.

3. KEDUSHAH

נְקַדֵּשׁ אֶת שְׁמָהּ בָּעוֹלָם כְּשֵׁם שֶׁמַּקְדִּישׁוֹת אוֹתָהּ בִּשְׁמֵי מָרוֹם
כַּכָּתוּב עַל יַד נְבִיאוֹתֶיךָ וְקָרְאָה זֹאת אֶל זֹאת וְאָמְרָה

קְדוֹשָׁה קְדוֹשָׁה קְדוֹשָׁה שְׁכִינָה צוֹבָאוֹת מְלֹא כָל הָאָרֶץ כְּבוֹדָהּ

אָז בְּקוֹל רַעַשׁ גָּדוֹל אַדִּיר וְחָזָק מַשְׁמִיעוֹת קוֹל מִתְנַשְּׂאוֹת לְעֻמַּת שְׂרָפוֹת לְעֻמָּתָם בָּרוּךְ יֹאמֵרוּ

בָּרוּךְ כְּבוֹד שְׁכִינָה מִמְּקוֹמָהּ

מִמְּקוֹמֵךְ רוּחֵנוּ תּוֹפִיעָה וְתִמְלוֹךְ עָלֵינוּ כִּי מְחַכּוֹת אֲנַחְנוּ לָךְ מָתַי תִּמְלוֹךְ בְּצִיּוֹן בְּקָרוֹב בְּיָמֵינוּ לְעוֹלָם וָעֶד תִּשְׁכּוֹן תִּתְגַּדַּל וְתִתְקַדַּשׁ בְּתוֹךְ יְרוּשָׁלַיִם עִירֵךְ לְדוֹר וָדוֹר וּלְנֵצַח נְצָחִים וְעֵינֵינוּ תִרְאֶינָה מַלְכוּתֵךְ כַּדָּבָר הָאָמוּר בְּשִׁירֵי עֻזֵּךְ עַל יְדֵי דָּוִד מְשִׁיחַ צִדְקֵךְ

תִּמְלוֹךְ שְׁכִינָה לְעוֹלָם אֱלֹהַיִךְ צִיּוֹן לְדוֹר וָדוֹר הַלְלוּיָהּ

לְדוֹר וָדוֹר נַגִּיד גָּדְלֵךְ וּלְנֵצַח נְצָחִים קְדֻשָּׁתֵךְ נַקְדִּישׁ וְשִׁבְחֵךְ אֱלוֹתֵנוּ מִפִּינוּ לֹא יָמוּשׁ לְעוֹלָם וָעֶד כִּי אֵלָה מַלְכָּה גְּדוֹלָה וּקְדוֹשָׁה אָתְּ. בְּרוּכָה אַתְּ שְׁכִינָה הָאֵלָה הַקְּדוֹשָׁה.

nekadeish et sh'mah ba'olam k'shem shemakdishot otah bishmei marom
kakatuv al yad nevioteha vekarah zot el zot ve'amrah

kedosha kedoshah kedoshah shekhinah tzovot
melo chol ha'aretz kevodah

az bekol raash gadol adir vehazak mashmiot kol
mitnasot le'umat serafot le'umatam baruch yomeiru

baruch kevod shekhinah mimekomah

mimekomeich rucheinu tofiah vetimloch aleinu ki mechakot anachnu lach matai timloch betzion bekarov beyameinu l'olam va'ed tishkon titgadal vetitkadash betoch yerushalayim irech ledor vador ulnetzach netzachim ve'eyneynu tirena malchutech kadavar ha'amur beshirei uzech al yedei david meshiach tzidkeich

timloch shekhinah le'olam elohayich tzion ledor vador haleluyah

l'dor vador nagid gadlecha ulenetzach netzachim kedushatcha nakdish veshivchech eloteinu mipinu lo yamush le'olam vaed ki elah malkah gedolah ukedoshah at beruchah at shekhinah ha'elah hakedoshah

Let us mark Her presence in the world just as the beings of light mark Her presence in the sky, as the seers said, they call to one another and say:

holy, holy, holy is the Presence among the shrinekeepers of heaven, the fullness of the cosmos is Her being.

Then with the voice of thunder the world resounds and the angelic breath-song rises, meeting beings of fire and crying: "Blessed!"

Blessed is the presence of the Presence throughout space and time.

From the Place of all places, our Soul, appear and guide us. We all wait for you. When will She dwell among us? Now? Forever? Be abundant, be sanctified in Your holy places through all the generations, through all ages. May our eyes see your Indwelling just as Your beloved, Your anointed, sang to you with the harp.

May Shekhinah reign everywhere.

May You be everywhen.

Halleluyah.

From one age to another we tell the story of Your vastness.
From forever to forever we are part of Your vitality
and our selves do not cease to utter song to You even in our brokenness
for You are the Real and You are the Holy.
Blessed are You, Living Presence, Holy Source.

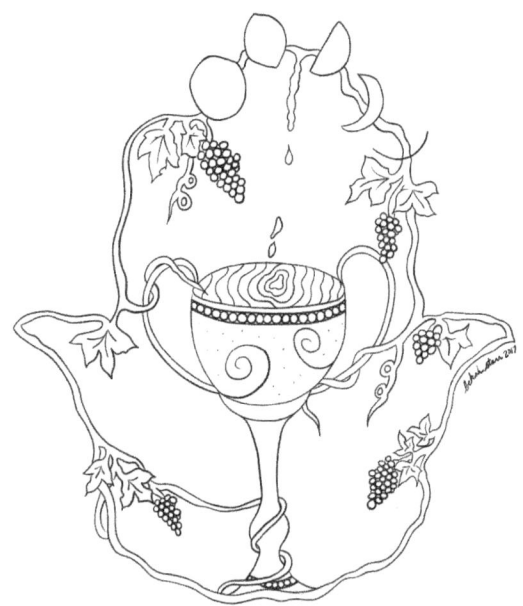

4. HOLINESS OF THE DAY
(KEDUSHAT HAYOM)

תִּשְׂמַח מִרְיָם בְּמַתְנַת חֶלְקָהּ כִּי עוֹבֶדֶת וְאוֹמֶנֶת נִקְרָאָה. כְּלִילַת תִּפְאֶרֶת בְּרֹאשָׁהּ בְּעָמְדָהּ תַּחְתִּית הָהָר. וְלוּחַ אֲבָנִים הֶעֱלָה מֵאֲדָמָה וְכָתוּב בּוֹ שְׁמִירַת שַׁבָּת. וְכֵן כָּתוּב בְּתוֹרָתָהּ:

tismach miriam bematnat chelkah ki ovedet ve'omenet nikra'ah. kelilat tiferet berosha be'amadah tachtit hahar, uluach avanim he'alah me'adamah vekatuv bo shemirat shabbat, vekein katuv betoratah:

Miriam rejoiced in the gift of her destiny, for she was called to be a priestess for the people. A garland of grace was on her head as she stood under the Sinai mountain, bringing up the teachings of time from the depths. And there was inscribed the keeping of Shabbat, and so it is written:

וְשָׁמְרוּ דוֹרוֹת יִשְׂרָאֵל אֶת הַשַּׁבָּת לַעֲשׂוֹת אֶת הַשַּׁבָּת לְדֹרֹתָם בְּרִית עוֹלָם. בֵּינִי וּבֵין דוֹרוֹת יִשְׂרָאֵל אוֹת הִיא לְעוֹלָם, כִּי שֵׁשֶׁת יָמִים עָשְׂתָה שְׁכִינָה אֶת הַשָּׁמַיִם וְאֶת הָאָרֶץ. וּבַיּוֹם הַשְּׁבִיעִי שָׁבְתָה וַתִּנָּפַשׁ.

v'shamru dorot yisrael et hashabbat, la'asot et hashabbat ledorotam berit olam. beini uvein dorot yisrael ot hi le'olam, ki sheishet yamim asta shekhinah et hashamayim ve'et ha'aretz, u'vayom hashvi'i shavta va'tinafash.

The people of Israel shall watch over Shabbat, making Shabbat throughout their generations as an eternal covenant. Between me and the generations of Israel it is a sign forever, that in six days the Shekhinah formed the sky and the earth, and on the seventh she found peace, and rested.

אֱלֹהֵינוּ וֵאלֹהֵי הוֹרֵינוּ רְצֵה נָא
בִּמְנוּחָתֵנוּ קַדְּשֵׁנוּ בְּמִצְוֺתֶיךָ וְתֵן חֶלְקֵנוּ
בְּתוֹרָתֶךָ שַׂבְּעֵנוּ מִטּוּבֶךָ וְשַׂמְּחֵנוּ
בִּישׁוּעָתֶךָ, וְטַהֵר לִבֵּנוּ לְעָבְדְּךָ בֶּאֱמֶת
וְהַנְחִילֵנוּ הוֹיה אֱלֹהֵינוּ בְּאַהֲבָה
וּבְרָצוֹן שַׁבַּת קָדְשֶׁךָ וְיָנוּחוּ בָהּ יִשְׂרָאֵל
מְקַדְּשֵׁי שְׁמֶךָ.

בְּרוּכָה אַתְּ שְׁכִינָה
מְקַדֶּשֶׁת הַשַּׁבָּת.

eloheinu ve'elohei horeinu, retzei na vimenuchateinu kadsheinu bemitzvotecha vetein chelkeinu betoratecha sabeinu mituvecha vesamcheinu biyeshuatecha vetahei libeinu leavdecha be'emet vehanchileinu havaya eloheinu be'ahavah bveratzon shabbat kodshecha veyanuchu vah yisrael mekadshei shemecha.

beruchah at shekhinah,
mekadeshet hashabbat

O Holiness, revered of our ancestors, delight in our rest. Keep us vibrant through engaging us with mitzvot, and may your teachings be as nourishing as the earth we cultivate. Satisfy us with your abundance and awaken us to the ever-unfolding spiral of life's journey. Clarify our hearts that we may serve the world through truth, and allow us to inherit the love that is Shabbat. May all who wrestle with the Divine and with the holy come to find rest on this day.

Blessed is the Tree of Life
that sanctifies Shabbat.

↵

THE RETURN OF MIRIAM

When Miriam came back
from the wilderness
where her brother and his God
had cast her,

when she returned
from her seven days of exile,

the wind came back with her.

So did the soil,
and the wings of the eagles,
and the enduring thornbush,
the pillar-shaped clouds
and the sun and moon—

the whole world-sanctuary,
wide as space and time,
came with her,
crowding into the camp.
She shone with the light
of the desert stars

and her eyes were full of the well
that rises up everywhere,

and she no longer fit
into the tiny tabernacle
from which they had excluded her.

Jill Hammer

AMIDAH

5. BLESSING FOR PRAYER (R'TZI)

retzi shekhinah eloteinu	רְצִי שְׁכִינָה אֱלֹתֵינוּ
bedorot yisrael uvitefilatan	בְּדוֹרוֹת יִשְׂרָאֵל וּבִתְפִלָּתָן
vehashvi et ha'avodah lidvir beiteich	וְהָשְׁבִי אֶת הָעֲבוֹדָה לִדְבִיר בֵּיתֵךְ
ve'ishei yisrael utefilatan be'ahavah	וְאִשֵׁי יִשְׂרָאֵל וּתְפִלָּתָן בְּאַהֲבָה
tekabli beratzon utehi leratzon tamid	תְּקַבְּלִי בְּרָצוֹן וּתְהִי לְרָצוֹן תָּמִיד
avodat yisrael ameich	עֲבוֹדַת יִשְׂרָאֵל עַמֵּךְ
vetechezena eineinu beshuvech	וְתֶחֱזֶינָה עֵינֵינוּ בְּשׁוּבֵךְ
letzion berachamim.	לְצִיּוֹן בְּרַחֲמִים.
beruchah at shekhinah	בְּרוּכָה אַתְּ שְׁכִינָה
hamachazirah shekhinatah letzion.	הַמַּחֲזִירָה שְׁכִינָתָהּ לְצִיּוֹן.

Be glad, Shekhinah, in the generations of our tribe and their prayers, and return the rituals to your holy shrine, the earth. Accept the offerings of the people and their prayers in love, and may our ceremonies always rise to join with your desire. May our eyes see Your return to the land in compassion. Blessed are You, Shekhinah returning to Zion and to all sacred earth.

6. BLESSING FOR GRATITUDE (MODIM)

modim anachnu lach she'at hi	מוֹדִים אֲנַחְנוּ לָךְ שָׁאַתְּ הִיא
havayah eloheinu ve'elohei avoteinu ve'imoteinu	הֲוָיָה אֱלֹהֵינוּ וֵאלֹהֵי אֲבוֹתֵינוּ וְאִמּוֹתֵינוּ
leolam va'ed tzur chayeinu	לְעוֹלָם וָעֶד צוּר חַיֵּינוּ
magein yisheinu at hi ledor vador	מָגֵן יִשְׁעֵנוּ אַתְּ הִיא לְדוֹר וָדוֹר
nodeh lach unesaper tehilatech	נוֹדֶה לָךְ וּנְסַפֵּר תְּהִלָּתֵךְ
al chayeinu hamseurim beyadech	עַל חַיֵּינוּ הַמְּסוּרִים בְּיָדֵךְ
ve'al nishmoteinu hapekudot lach	וְעַל נִשְׁמוֹתֵינוּ הַפְּקוּדוֹת לָךְ
ve'al niseich shebechol yom imanu	וְעַל נִסֵּיךְ שֶׁבְּכָל יוֹם עִמָּנוּ
ve'al niflotayich vetovotayich shebechol eit	וְעַל נִפְלְאוֹתַיִךְ וְטוֹבוֹתַיִךְ שֶׁבְּכָל עֵת
erev vavoker vetzaharayim	עֶרֶב וָבֹקֶר וְצָהֳרָיִם
hatov ki lo chalu rachamayich	הַטּוֹב כִּי לֹא כָלוּ רַחֲמָיִךְ
vehamerachemet shelo tamu chasadayich	וְהַמְרַחֶמֶת כִּי לֹא תַמּוּ חֲסָדָיִךְ
me'olam kivinu lach	מֵעוֹלָם קִוִּינוּ לָךְ

We give thanks to You, Being and Becoming, Strength of our ancestors, Rock on which our lives evolve, our protecting Shell within which we transform. You are That, for all generations, and we are grateful. You hold our bodies in your hands and keep the archive of our spirits. We thank You, for You are daily miracles, those of morning, noon, and night. You are the abundance of creation, in which compassion and creativity are endless. We have hoped in You since the beginning of the world.

ON CHANUKAH AND PURIM   בחנוכה ופורים

al hanisim ve'al hapurkan
ve'al hag'vurot ve'al hatshuot
ve'al hatekufot sheasit ledoroteinu
bayamim haheim bazman hazeh.

עַל הַנִּסִּים וְעַל הַפֻּרְקָן
וְעַל הַגְּבוּרוֹת וְעַל הַתְּשׁוּעוֹת
וְעַל הַתְּקֻפוֹת שֶׁעָשִׂיתָ לְדוֹרוֹתֵינוּ
בַּיָּמִים הָהֵם בַּזְּמַן הַזֶּה.

For the miracles and changes and triumphs worked in the world
for our ancestors and us, we are grateful.

ve'al kulam yitbarach sh'meich
rucheinu tamid le'olam va'ed.

וְעַל כֻּלָּם יִתְבָּרַךְ וְיִתְרוֹמַם שְׁמֵךְ
רוּחֵנוּ תָּמִיד לְעוֹלָם וָעֶד

And for all these things, many-named one, we are grateful.

ON THE TEN DAYS OF REPENTANCE   בעשרת ימי תשובה

uchitvi lechayyim tovim kol b'nei vriteich

וּכְתְבִי לְחַיִּים טוֹבִים כָּל בְּנֵי בְרִיתֵךְ

Scribe of Life, inscribe for abundant life all who are children of your web of life.

vekol hachayim yoduch selah
vihallelu et shmeich be'emet
ha'el yeshuateinu ve'ezrateinu selah.
beruchah at shekhinah
hatov shimech velach naeh lehodot.

וְכֹל הַחַיִּים יוֹדוּךְ סֶּלָה
וִיהַלְלוּ אֶת שְׁמֵךְ בֶּאֱמֶת
הָאֵל יְשׁוּעָתֵנוּ וְעֶזְרָתֵנוּ סֶלָה.
בְּרוּכָה אַתְּ שְׁכִינָה
הַטּוֹב שִׁמֵךְ וְלָךְ נָאֶה לְהוֹדוֹת.

All life sings to the essence of life, the Changer who changes us. Blessed are You who hold the many names and the abundant voices calling out in praise.

AMIDAH

PRIESTEXXLY BLESSING

תְּבָרְכֵךְ שַׁדַּי וְתִשְׁמְרֵךְ	□ tevarcheich shadai vetishmereich
תָּאֵר שַׁדַּי פָּנֶיהָ אֵלַיִךְ וִתְחֻנֵּךְ	ta'er shadai paneha elayich vit'chuneich
תִּשָּׂא שַׁדַּי פָּנֶיהָ אֵלַיִךְ	tisa shadai paneha elayich
וְתָשֵׂם לָךְ שָׁלוֹם	vetasem lach shalom
יְבָרֶכְךָ יהוה וְיִשְׁמְרֶךָ	△ yevarechecha adonai veyishmerecha
יָאֵר יהוה פָּנָיו אֵלֶיךָ וִיחֻנֶּךָּ	ya'er adonai panav elecha viychuneka
יִשָּׂא יהוה פָּנָיו אֵלֶיךָ	yisa adonai panav eilecha
וְיָשֵׂם לְךָ שָׁלוֹם	veyasem lecha shalom
יְבָרְכֹךְ הויה וְיִשְׁמְרֹךְ	⊖ yevarchocheh havayah vishmerocheh
יָאֱרֶה הויה פָּנֶיהֶ אֵילֶיחֶ וִיחֳנֹכֶה	yaeyreh havayah paneheh eilecheh viychonocheh
יִשְׂאֶה הויה פָּנֶיהֶ אֵילֶיחֶ	yiseh havayah paneheh eilecheh
וְיָשֵׂמֶה לֶחֶ שָׁלוֹם	veyaseymeh leche shalom

May the One of Being bless you and keep you.
May the One Who Is shine the Divine faces on you and show you grace.
May the Who Is Becoming lift up the Divine faces to you,
and grant you wholeness and peace.

PRIESTESS BLESSING

May She bless you and May She keep you

As She shines Her face

May you embody grace

May Zhe bless you and may Zhe keep you

As Zhe brings release

May you embody peace (alt: May you give birth to peace)

Taya Shere

simi shalom tovah uvrachah	שִׂימִי שָׁלוֹם טוֹבָה וּבְרָכָה
chein vachesed verachamim aleinu ve al ameich.	חֵן וָחֶסֶד וְרַחֲמִים עָלֵינוּ וְעַל כָּל עַמֵּךְ
barcheinu imeinu kulanu ke'echad be'or panayich	בָּרְכֵנוּ אִמֵּנוּ כֻּלָּנוּ כְּאֶחָד בְּאוֹר פָּנָיִךְ
ki ve'or panayich natat lanu shaddai eloteinu	כִּי בְאוֹר פָּנָיִךְ נָתַתְּ לָנוּ שַׁדַּי אֱלֹתֵינוּ
torat chayim ve'ahavat chesed	תּוֹרַת חַיִּים וְאַהֲבַת חֶסֶד
utzdakah uvrachah verachamim vechayim veshalom.	וּצְדָקָה וּבְרָכָה וְרַחֲמִים וְחַיִּים וְשָׁלוֹם
vetov be'eineich levarech et amech yisrael	וְטוֹב בְּעֵינַיִךְ לְבָרֵךְ אֶת עוּמוֹתַיִךְ
vekol umotayich bechol eit uvechol sha'ah bishlomeich.	בְּכָל עֵת וּבְכָל שָׁעָה בִּשְׁלוֹמֵךְ

Plant peace, abundance, blessing, grace, love, compassion in us and all Your people. Bless us, our Mother, one and all, with the light of Your Faces, for by that light you have given us life-wisdom and a love of love itself, and justice and blessing and compassion and life and peace. For it is good in your eyes to bless this Godwrestling people, and all peoples, at all times, with Your peace.

☐ brucha at shechina
   hamevorechet amah yisrael
   ve'et kol yoshvei tevel bashalom

בְּרוּכָה אַתְּ שְׁכִינָה
הַמְבָרֶכֶת אֶת עַמָּה יִשְׂרָאֵל
וְאֶת כָּל יוֹשְׁבֵי תֵבֵל בַּשָּׁלוֹם.

⊖ berucheh ateh yah
   hamevarecheh et ameh yisrael
   ve'et kol yoshvei tevel bashalom

בְּרוּכֶה אַתֶּה יָהּ
הַמְבָרְכֶה אֶת עַמֶּה יִשְׂרָאֵל
וְאֶת כָּל יוֹשְׁבֵי תֵבֵל בַּשָּׁלוֹם.

      Blessed are You, Yah-Shekhinah, who blesses your people Israel
            and all those who dwell on earth with peace.

II. SHRINE MEDITATION

Stand with weight balanced on both feet. If this is too uncomfortable feel free to sit. Begin by taking a couple of deep, full, breaths and on the out breath release that top layer of stress and tension.

As you begin breathing slowly, comfortably and easily, invite your body to relax and to let go of any unnecessary tension. Notice the tension in your body, where do you feel it the most?

Take the time to bring your attention to each part of your body, and invite it to release and relax, letting go, easily, comfortably.

Open your mind to the possibilities of the Universe. Let your mind float from your body. Slowly you find yourself in the doorway of a room with eight sides. Seven of the sides house small, ancient shrines — the eighth, just the door. Turn and walk towards the shrine closest to you.

1. You find yourself looking at a shrine to your ancestors. Take a moment and absorb the imagery of the shrine. What artifacts are there? Who is represented? What relics of your parents, grandparents and great-grandparents do you see? Look for something to leave as an offering — incense, candles, flowers, food, or wine and make an offering to your ancestors. Through your offering renew your connection to all of the past that made you what you are. Turn and move to the next shrine.

2. You see a fountain that seems to replenish itself. All around there are images of birth and death. This fountain is the water of life. It flows and flows giving life and taking life to continue the circle. Run your hands under the water, let refresh and revive you. When you are ready move to the next shrine.

3. This shrine is a wall of words. Look closely and you'll see every name of everything and everyone. You'll see your name, the one your parents gave you and the secret one you call yourself. You'll see the name the Divine has for you and the name you have for the Divine. These names are creation. Through these names we connect to everything that is and was. Find the names that have the most meaning for you and take them into yourself. Let these sacred names connect you to creation and let these names connect creation to you. When you are ready move to the next shrine.

4. In this shrine there is a mirror with the words "Today is forever, forever is now" written above it. Look into the mirror and what is reflected back is the promises you have made to the universe about how you will live your life. Which promises have you kept? Which have you broken? Take a moment to renew those promises that need to be kept and release those which do not. Take a deep breath and release it. Move on to the next shrine.

5. It is a shrine of the home and hearth, the place where you feel safe and warm and welcome. Take the time to look at the shrine and let the feeling of safety wash over you. Let the warmth and safety of home envelope you. Find something to leave as an offering to the hearth so it may replenished for all who may need it. Slowly move to the next shrine.

6. In the shrine is an image of deity as you see it. All around are offerings of gratitude. Find something to give as a give of gratitude. Reflect on all of the blessings in your life and all of the things for which you are grateful. Let the joy of the shrine fill you as you move to the next.

7. As you stand at the next shrine you see a cup with a prayer etched into it. "Eternal wellspring of peace, may we be drenched with the longing for peace that we may give ourselves over as the earth to the rain to the dew, until peace overflows our lives as living water overflow the seas." Drink from the cup and feel peace. Walk back to the door and look into the room. Reflect on what you have learned, seen and felt. Take a deep breath in... and exhale. Turn and walk out of the room.

Ketzirah Lesser, inspired by Marcia Falk's Shabbat Amidah in The Book of Blessings

III. SEVEN BLESSINGS

Each of these meditations is based on one of the seven blessings in the Shabbat Amidah. You can engage all seven, or just one.

1. ANCESTORS

You are at the shore of an ocean. As you look out to sea, you observe waves coming toward you, carrying the voices of your ancestors. Each wave contains a generation of your people. Listen carefully for the voices: maybe your name, maybe song. Say the prayer that arises as the waves comes to shore.

2. THE CIRCLE OF LIFE

You are witnessing an immense tree. Some of the tree's leaves are just opening. Some of the leaves are full and green, and some are scarlet and gold. Some of the tree's leaves are withered. Say the prayer that arises as you observe the great tree's cycle of life and death.

3. HOLINESS

You are on a mountaintop. A wind rushes toward you. As the wind whirls around you, all thoughts and ways of being that are smallminded, confused, or unnecessary are carried away. Only clarity remains. Say the prayer that arises out of this clarity.

4. SHABBAT

Before you is an unlit lamp with seven branches. The lamp begins to light itself. As the lights appear, think of memories of the week. When the seventh light appears, be in this moment. Say the prayer that arises out of this moment.

5. PRAYER

You are in a sacred space that holds an altar. Make three offerings on the altar: one on your own behalf, one on behalf of your tribe or community (whatever that means to you), and one on behalf of the world. Say the prayer that accompanies this offering.

6. GRATITUDE

Before you is a book. When you open the book, you discover in it a record of your blessings. Find at least one of the blessings. Say the prayer that arises as you contemplate the presence of this blessing in your life.

7. PEACE

You are in a grove of trees. The roots of this grove go down into the depths of the earth. Feel how all the roots connect underneath the soil. Say the prayer that arises you feel the power of this connection.

Jill Hammer

IV. ELEMENTAL AMIDAH

Spirits of the house, spirits of the fields,
spirits of the ancestors,
come near to us,
or, if you are walking past,
walk around us.

We summon the spirit of earth
where it flows like water,
where it curves and rises like a mansion,
where it curls like an embryo of stone.

We summon the ground of life
to life.

When I speak, hide words under my tongue.
Hint to me your signs.
Help me say truth, or help me be silent.
I stand at the crossroads of time.
Point a direction for my heart.

I listen
for the footsteps of the real.
I listen
for the omens of the possible.
I listen
for the breath behind the breath.

From the earth, a rising-up blessing.
From the water, a seeping-in blessing.
From the wind, a diving-down blessing.
From the fire, a breaking-through blessing.

Circle, open:
release this soul
into the larger circle.

le'olam ul'almei almaya

In every world, in all the worlds, we say amen.

Jill Hammer

V. ALTERNATIVE AMIDAH: BETWEEN THE PARTS

Bless the parts that become a whole
The whole that is made up of parts
The cracks, the edges of transformative stories
The place of meeting that constantly moves
The fiddling of fate, the meddling of desperation
A million desert prayers
That is why the sand glistens
Tears have become the sun's reflection
Go for yourself, for yourself you go
Where you go I'll go, but at times you must go at it alone
Vibrating narratives of long ago
Shifting the occipital lobe
The desert strips your layers
And you can lie no more
Bless the truth, the truth that unfolds
That becomes as it is told
That shapes the worlds yet to be born
You thought it, you thunk it, you think it and it is so

You've been enmeshed too long
You speak and your voice is not your own
You mimic, you chameleon, you mirror on
Thinking this is the way of survival, the way you'll belong
Oh holy one who etched names on souls
Counted hairs, and promised heirs
Who foretold, told and post told
Only possibility, only if you dare
The ions and eons, the nucleus and its shell
The protons and neutrons
Shema, you've designed it all
Nothing is analog
Like an ancient galactic memory,
I saw you knit together the fabric of our reality
Like a yesterday, a today and a tomorrow
Changing names to teach people to change lanes
Let those who must go, go
Stop thinking the hagars are a substitute
Stop banishing the work of your hands
As if a multitude can not be born

You are not the only one with a plan
For what knoweth you of the grains of sand
The stars in the skies
Interpret what you must
Make sense of what you can
But do not put the infinite in a box
Or try to overstand
Your lot is the inbetween
The place of covenant
three heifers, three goats, three rams, a turtle dove and a young bird
Liberation, Determination, Steadfastness, Fidelity
and the ability to perceive new dimensions

Will you oh holy one, pass between
Will you oh holy one, pass between
Will you oh holy one, pass between

The who we are becoming and the parts we no longer need
If life is the sacrifice, then take that which has ceased to be
Take thing 1, thing 2 and thing 3
We are sowing new seeds,
Let us aggregate, assemble, collect, crowd, turn out
And witness the great number
Of the ways things come about,
birthed forward and prolifically self populating
Abraham, Sarai, Hagar, Lot and dem folx
Were given a promise for their context
We have been given a different dream, a new hope
One in which trauma doesn't have the lead
One in which belonging is not weaponized
And houses not built by genocide

And so with this said, I give thanks
For all things I don't understand
For the power of innerstanding
The gift of a new seed
The process to let it go on as a blossom
And the trust that allows us to move through the inbetween

Angelique Rivera

BAT ADAMAH

עֲלִי לְמַעְלָה, עֲלִי	ali lema'alah ali
עֲלִי לְמַעְלָה	ali lema'alah
עֲלִי בַּת עָפָר	ali bat afar
עֲלִי לְמַעְלָה, עֲלִי	ali le ma'alah ali
כִּי כֹחַ עַז לָךְ,	ki ko-ach az lach
יֵשׁ לָךְ כַּנְפֵי רוּחַ,	yesh lach kanfei ruach(2x)
כַּנְפֵי נְשָׁרִים אַבִּירִים.	kanfei n'sharim abirim
אַל תְּכַחֵשׁ בָּם,	al tekachashi bam, pen
פֶּן יְכַחֲשׁוּ לָךְ	ye'cha'cha'shu lach
דִּרְשִׁי אוֹתָם –	dirshi otam, dirshi bat afar
וְיִמָּצְאוּ לָךְ מִיָּד.	v'yim-atzu lach miyad

Children of the earth
rise children rise
take your wings where the eagles fly
and rise children rise

Traci Marx, based on a poem of Abraham Isaac Kook

VI. EARTH-BASED MEDITATIONS for the AMIDAH

This earth-based prayer meditation is based on a teaching of Rabbi Shneur Zalman of Liadi, who said that the divine shefa (energetic flow) exists in very great measure in the earth. This truth is also expressed in indigenous spiritual traditions around the world. This meditation contains nineteen sections based on the nineteen benedictions of the weekday Amidah.

1. ANCESTORS

Connect to the earth with your feet or your hands. Imagine that the earth is filled with the energy of divine presence. You can imagine it as light or a humming sound or a feeling in your palms. Feel this energy come into contact with you. Experience it as light or sound or touch or in any other way that you feel it. Feel that this energy has been in contact with your ancestors. Receive the blessing of your ancestors, all of your ancestors as you understand them, through the contact you now have with the earth.

2. THE CIRCLE OF LIFE

Feel that this energy is what gives life to trees, creatures, and human beings. Feel that it is revitalizing what is faded and wilted, what is decayed and broken. Feel the potential of this everyday resurrection of all things.

3. HOLINESS

Feel that the strength you receive from the earth at this moment is the same strength that flowed to priests in the temple and to sages in the synagogue. Feel that the energy of which you are now aware is holy and has been served by many throughout time.

4. WISDOM

Feel the wisdom of the earth's cycles and seasons. Feel that you receive from the earth the wisdom you need to make right choices at this moment on your journey.

5. TURNING

Feel the change within the earth. The elements of the earth are always combining and decaying. Feel the power of change, of teshuvah in your own life.

6. FORGIVENESS

Feel how the earth holds everyone and everything no matter how small, frail, or broken. From this place of acceptance, explore the possibility of forgiveness toward yourself and others.

7. REDEMPTION

Feel that the radiance of the earth draws you into integrity, integrating you with all life that exists now and all life that has ever existed. Feel that everything separating you from this oneness ceases to separate you, and you are able to enter into it fully.

8. HEALING

Perceive that many plants that grow from the earth have healing properties. In fact, the earth itself has healing properties through its microbes and minerals. Take in healing from the earth and ask for healing for others.

9. ABUNDANCE

Pray for the earth to have a bountiful year, producing a harvest that sustains all life. Intend that this prayer should benefit many peoples and many species.

10. INGATHERING

Remember that there is a place (or places) on the earth to which you feel particularly connected, a place that have given you deep gifts. Summon in your mind such a place, and ask for the possibility to return there and re-experience those gifts.

11. JUSTICE

Know as you take in the earth's energy that what happens to the earth affects the poor and vulnerable. Know that care for the earth makes possible justice for the poor and the afflicted. Commit yourself to the pursuit of justice on this earth that is our home.

12. PROTECTION

Feel that there are forces out of balance within nature. Feel that there are forces out of balance within you. Ask for these forces to come back into balance so that harm is minimized for all. Ask for good health and good action for yourself and for all beings.

13. THE RIGHTEOUS

Feel that the earth has many guardians and caretakers who are or have been engaged in lovingkindness and in the protection of life. Pray for the needs of these guardians and caretakers. Feel that perhaps you are one yourself and pray for your own benefit.

14. THE LAND

Feel in this moment a connection to the landscape that shaped your ancestors. Pray for abundance, wholeness, justice, and peace to inhabit that landscape, and all who dwell there, and all who love that land. Pray for all peoples to inhabit their full and authentic connection to the earth, free of oppression and fear.

15. THE FUTURE

Feel that there is potential for peace and healing within all the life-forms present in the cosmos, even if we cannot yet perceive it. Invite this peace and healing to manifest itself around you, within you, and through you. Commit yourself to letting this peace and healing come through you to the world.

16. PRAYER

Look inward to discover: what is the prayer of your heart? See this prayer as a flower blossoming inside you. Present this flower to the Source. Envision the Source receiving the flower. Take a moment to listen for the response.

17. PRESENCE

Feel that the earth and all of its creatures are praying with you. Feel that the power of their life-force is added to your prayer. Feel how great your prayer becomes as all the creatures around you add their blessings to your prayer. Feel that the Divine Presence also prays your prayer.

18. GRATITUDE

Express your gratitude for the gifts of this body, formed of the elements of the earth, and for the gifts of this earth, formed of the elements of the cosmos. Offer thanks for all you have received and experienced as a living being, and for what you receive and experience in this moment.

19. PEACE

Breathing in and breathing out, feel the peace of being part of all this. Pray for peace for yourself and your loved ones. Pray for peace for all beings. Pray for peace for the earth, one immense being that grounds and sustains all of us. Feel, see, and hear the divine presence within and around you, emanating in the power and beauty of the earth you are touching in this moment.

Jill Hammer

TORAH SERVICE

1. WHERE WERE YOU?

Where were you when I laid the earth's foundations?
Where were you, where were you?
Where were you when I laid the earth's foundations?
Where were you, where were you?

I was there when You laid out the heavens
I was there when You circled round the deep
I was there when You set the edge of heaven
When you drew forth the fountains from the deep

I was there when You assigned the sea its limits
So the waters never disobey your word
I was there when You laid the earth's foundation
I am the instructions that You heard.

Annie Matan, from Job 38:4 and Proverbs 8:27-30

2. THE BEGINNING OF WISDOM

רֵאשִׁית חָכְמָה יִרְאַת הויה שֵׂכֶל טוֹב לְכָל מַעֲשֶׂיהָ

reishit chochmah yirat havayah seichel tov lechol maaseha

The beginning of wisdom is reverence for Being.
May all Her creatures have good judgment.

Sarah Bracha Gershuny, from Proverbs 9:10

3. ELAH MALKAH

אֱלָה מַלְכָּה נֶאֱמָנָה

elah malkah ne'emanah
She, Mother Earth, we love and honor
elah malkah ne'emanah
She is the Queen there is none beyond Her
She is the Tree there is none beyond Her

Taya Shere

TORAH ORAH

torah orah torah
Fire from the mountain
torah orah torah
She's a desert-dwelling fountain

torah orah torah
Wheels of wisdom rolling
torah orah torah
She's the tree of life we're holding

And we bring her round
And we're singing loud
torah orah torah
Practice liberation
Feed the stranger and the orphan

torah orah torah
Gather round and listen
torah orah torah
To what's written and what's missing

torah orah torah
For ancestors and children
torah orah torah
Heal the planet, keep her rhythm

Shoshana Jedwab

SONG FOR MY SISTERS

This is a song for my sisters.
This is a song for my mothers.
This is a song for my daughters.
This is a song from our ancestors

May you be counted in every circle.
May you speak in every house.
May you know that your prayers are the prayers of God/dess/dexx.

This is a song for my brothers.
This is a song for my fathers.
This is a song for my sons.
This is a song from our ancestors.

May you bear witness in every circle.
May you hear singing in every house.
May the wisdom of Shechinah be a blessing in your heart.

This is a song for all bodies.
This is a song for all hearts.
This is a song for all minds.
This is a song for all souls.

May you see the world in circles.
May you sing in every house.
May you know your wholeness in the holiness of All.

Annie Matan

TORAH SERVICE

WHEN THE ARK WOULD TRAVEL (VAYEHI BINSOA)

וַיְהִי בִּנְסֹעַ הָאָרֹן וַיֹּאמֶר מֹשֶׁה: קוּמָה יְהוָה וְיָפֻצוּ אֹיְבֶיךָ וְיָנֻסוּ מְשַׂנְאֶיךָ מִפָּנֶיךָ
אָז יָשִׁיר יִשְׂרָאֵל אֶת הַשִּׁירָה הַזֹּאת עֲלִי בְאֵר עֱנוּ לָהּ

vayehi binsoa ha'aron vayomer moshe, kumah adonai veyafutzu oyvecha veyanusu misanecha mipanecha. az yashir yisrael et hashirah hazot:
ali be'er enu lah!

When the Ark would travel forward, Moses would say; Arise, Adonai, and may all ill in the world flee from your face. And Israel would sing to Miriam's well:
Arise, o well, sing to Her!

כִּי מִצִּיּוֹן תֵּצֵא תוֹרָה וּדְבַר הויה מִירוּשָׁלָיִם
בְּרוּכָה שֶׁנָּטְעָה תוֹרָה בְּעַמָּהּ יִשְׂרָאֵל בִּקְדֻשָּׁתָהּ

ki mitzion tetzeh torah ud'var havaya miyrushalayim
beruchah shenatnah torah le'amah yisrael bikedushatah

Torah shall go out of Zion, and the word of Being from Jerusalem.
Blessed is the Tree of Life who plants Torah in Her people Israel in holiness.

ON SHABBAT

שְׁמַע יִשְׂרָאֵל יהוה אֱלֹהֵינוּ יהוה אֶחָד
אַחַת אֱלָתֵינוּ רַבּוֹת פָּנֶיהָ רַבּוֹת פָּנֵינוּ

shema yisrael adonai eloheinu adonai echad
achat elateinu rabot paneha rabot paneinu

Hear O Israel, Adonai is our God, Adonai is one.
One is our Goddess, many are Her faces, many are our faces.

ON ALL DAYS WE CONTINUE

גַּדְּלוּ לַיהוה אִתִּי וּנְרוֹמְמָה שְׁמוֹ יַחְדָּו

gadlu l'adonai iti uneromemah shemo yachdav.

Glorify the Connected One with me and let us praise that Being together.

לְךָ יהוה הַגְּדֻלָּה וְהַגְּבוּרָה וְהַתִּפְאֶרֶת וְהַנֵּצַח וְהַהוֹד כִּי כֹל בַּשָּׁמַיִם וּבָאָרֶץ: לְךָ יהוה הַמַּמְלָכָה
וְהַמִּתְנַשֵּׂא לְכֹל לְרֹאשׁ: רוֹמְמוּ יהוה אֱלֹהֵינוּ וְהִשְׁתַּחֲווּ לַהֲדֹם רַגְלָיו קָדוֹשׁ הוּא רוֹמְמוּ יהוה אֱלֹהֵינוּ
וְהִשְׁתַּחֲווּ לְהַר קָדְשׁוֹ
כִּי קָדוֹשׁ יהוה אֱלֹהֵינוּ

lecha havayah hagedulah vehagevurah vehatiferet vehanetzah vehahod ki chol bashamayim uva'aretz. lecha havaya hamamlachah vehamitnaseh lechol lerosh.

To Being belongs love and strength, beauty, eternity, humility, and all that is in heaven and earth. To Being belongs the rule of creation, for it is the start of everything.

CROSSROADS

"If one sees two women sitting at a crossroads,
facing one another, they are engaged in witchcraft." *Babylonian Talmud, Pesachim 111a*

We have been sitting
at a crossroads:
the place where text
meets hurt.
The breezes bring us
characters, stories, silence.
We catch and discuss, dissect,
sew phrases together
with hairs from our own heads,
release the words,
let them float off down the road.
In the evenings, we work parchment through our hands,
making it soft and pliable.

If travelers come by, they pass quickly.
It is not true, mostly, that we eat souls,
but sometimes
we steal someone's complacency
and now and again we do turn someone
into something else.
We are a conspiracy of gardeners.
We seed ourselves
in the Torah like a fungus,
spreading up and down the tree of life
in fat shelves. Slowly, painfully,
using the microbes of our own bodies,
we are turning her into mulch.
At the place where the two roads meet,
a heap of anger, like dung.
Tourists step over it,
but we will be here when the dung is soil,
and the song runs clear and light,
and a living tree grows between us
at the crossroads.

Jill Hammer

WISE WOMAN CHANT

the wise woman sits at the crossroads
the wise woman chants at the crossroads
the wise woman rants at the crossroads
the wise woman plants at the crossroads

the wise woman sits at the crossroads
the wise woman flows at the crossroads
the wise woman grows at the crossroads
the wise woman knows at the crossroads

the wise woman sits at the crossroads
the wise woman lives at the crossroads
the wise woman gives at the crossroads
the wise woman forgives at the crossroads

the wise woman sits at the crossroads
the wise woman cries at the crossroads
the wise woman flies at the crossroads
the wise woman dies at the crossroads

the wise woman sits at the crossroads
the wise woman bleeds at the crossroads
the wise woman needs at the crossroads
the wise woman feeds at the crossroads

the wise woman sits at the crossroads
the wise woman hip-hops at the crossroads
the wise woman flip-flops at the crossroads
the wise woman don't stop at the crossroads

the wise woman sits at the crossroads
the wise woman leads at the crossroads
the wise woman plants seeds at the crossroads
the wise woman proceeds at the crossroads

the wise woman sits at the crossroads
the wise woman shakes hips at the crossroads
the wise woman does flips at the crossroads
the wise woman smacks lips at the crossroads

the wise woman sits at the crossroads
the wise woman drums at the crossroads
the wise woman hums at the crossroads
the wise woman comes at the crossroad

the wise woman sits at the crossroads
the wise woman feels at the crossroads
the wise woman yields at the crossroads
the wise woman heals at the crossroads

Taya Shere

TORAH SERVICE

BLESSINGS *BEFORE* TORAH

THOSE TAKING THE ALIYAH SAY

□ בָּרְכוּ אֶת חָכְמָה הַמְבֹרֶכֶת
△ בָּרְכוּ אֶת יהוה הַמְבֹרָךְ
⊖ בָּרְכוֹל אֶת הויה הַמְבֹרְכֶה

□ barchu et chochmah hamevorechet
△ barchu et adonai hamevorach
⊖ barchol et havayah ham'vorecheh

Blessed is Wisdom, the fountain of blessing.

THE CONGREGATION RESPONDS

□ בְּרוּכָה חָכְמָה הַמְבֹרֶכֶת לְעוֹלָם וָעֶד
△ בָּרוּךְ יהוה הַמְבֹרָךְ לְעוֹלָם וָעֶד
⊖ בְּרוּכֶה הויה הַמְבֹרְכֶה לְעוֹלָם וָעֶד

□ beruchah chochmah hamevorechet le'olam va'ed
△ baruch adonai hamevorach le'olam vaed
⊖ berucheh havayah ham'vorecheh le'olam va'ed

Blessed is Wisdom, the fountain of blessing forever.

THOSE TAKING THE ALIYAH CONTINUE ON THE FOLLOWING PAGE

□ beruchah chochmah hamevorechet le'olam va'ed. בְּרוּכָה חָכְמָה הַמְבֹרֶכֶת לְעוֹלָם וָעֶד.
beruchah at shekhinah eloteinu ruach ha'olam, בְּרוּכָה אַתְּ שְׁכִינָה אֱלֹתֵינוּ רוּחַ הָעוֹלָם
asher bachrah banu im kol ha'amim venatnah אֲשֶׁר בָּחֲרָה בָּנוּ עִם כָּל הָעַמִּים
lanu et toratah וְנָתְנָה לָנוּ אֶת תּוֹרָתָהּ.
beruchah at shekhinah, notenet hatorah בְּרוּכָה אַתְּ שְׁכִינָה נוֹתֶנֶת הַתּוֹרָה

△ baruch adonai hamevorach le'olam va'ed. בָּרוּךְ יהוה הַמְבֹרָךְ לְעוֹלָם וָעֶד.
baruch ata adonai eloheinu melekh ha'olam בָּרוּךְ אַתָּה יהוה אֱלֹהֵינוּ מֶלֶךְ הָעוֹלָם
asher bachar banu mikol ha'amim אֲשֶׁר בָּחַר בָּנוּ מִכָּל הָעַמִּים
venatan lanu et torato וְנָתַן לָנוּ אֶת תּוֹרָתוֹ.
baruch ata adonai, noten hatorah בָּרוּךְ אַתָּה יהוה נוֹתֵן הַתּוֹרָה

⊖ berucheh havayah ham'vorecheh le'olam va'ed. בְּרוּכֶה הֲוָיָה הַמְבֹרְכֶה לְעוֹלָם וָעֶד.
berucheh ateh havayah eloheinu chei haolamim בְּרוּכֶה אַתֶּה הֲוָיָה אֱלֹהֵינוּ חֵי הָעוֹלָמִים
asher kibletnu mikol ha'amim אֲשֶׁר קִבְּלֶתְנוּ מִכָּל הָעַמִּים
venatneh lanu et torateh וְנָתְנֶה לָנוּ אֶת תּוֹרָתֶה.
berucheh ateh havayah, notenei hatorah בְּרוּכֶה אַתֶּה הֲוָיָה נוֹתְנֶה הַתּוֹרָה

Blessed is Wisdom, the fountain of blessing forever.
Blessed is the Indwelling, spirit of the world, who has ripened us along with the peoples of the earth, and has given us the unique wisdom of the Torah.
Blessed are You, Shekhinah, who is always giving the Torah.

BLESSINGS AFTER TORAH

□ beruchah at shekhinah בְּרוּכָה אַתְּ שְׁכִינָה
eloteinu ruach ha'olam אֱלֹתֵינוּ רוּחַ הָעוֹלָם
asher natnah lanu torat emet אֲשֶׁר נָתְנָה לָנוּ תּוֹרַת אֱמֶת
vechayei olam natah betocheinu וְחַיֵּי עוֹלָם נָטְעָה בְּתוֹכֵנוּ
beruchah at shekhinah, notenet hatorah בְּרוּכָה אַתְּ שְׁכִינָה נוֹתֶנֶת הַתּוֹרָה

△ baruch ata adonai בָּרוּךְ אַתָּה יהוה
eloheinu melekh ha'olam אֱלֹהֵינוּ מֶלֶךְ הָעוֹלָם
asher natan lanu torat emet אֲשֶׁר נָתַן לָנוּ תּוֹרַת אֱמֶת
vechayei olam natah betocheinu וְחַיֵּי עוֹלָם נָטַע בְּתוֹכֵנוּ
baruch ata adonai, noten hatorah בָּרוּךְ אַתָּה יהוה נוֹתֵן הַתּוֹרָה

□ berucheh ateh havayah בְּרוּכָה אַתֶּה הֲוָיָה
eloheinu chei haolamim אֱלֹהֵינוּ חֵי הָעוֹלָמִים
asher natneh lanu torat emet אֲשֶׁר נָתְנֶה לָנוּ תּוֹרַת אֱמֶת
vechayei olam nateh betocheinu וְחַיֵּי עוֹלָם נָטְעָה בְּתוֹכֵנוּ
beruchah ateh havayah, notenei hatorah בְּרוּכָה אַתֶּה הֲוָיָה נוֹתְנֶה הַתּוֹרָה

Blessed is the Indwelling, spirit of the world, who has given us a teaching of truth, and planted the life of the universe within us. Blessed are You, Shekhinah, who gives Torah.

HEALING PRAYERS

1. ANA ELAH NA

אָנָא אֱלָה נָא רְפָאִי נָא לָה

▢ ana elah nah reefee na lah

Please God heal them, body and spirit.
Body and spirit, may they be whole.

Goddess heal us, body and spirit.
Body and spirit, may we be whole.

Numbers 12:13, English by Taya Shere

2. ANA EL NA

אָנָא אֵל נָא רְפָא נָא לָה

△ ana el nah refah na lah

Please Great Spirit, please Great Spirit heal them.
(Please Goddess, please Goddess, heal us.)

Renee Finkelstein/Radharani

3. HEALING PRAYER OF THE PRECANTADORAS

Viene para sanarte milesinarte como Miriam a Levy
Qui sinava y milseinava yo todo mal
Se lo quitava y a la mar lo echava

This comes to heal you and bring you medicine like Miriam the Levite who would bring medicine and heal and take all the illness away and throw it to the bottom of the sea.

From Derya F. Agis, "Beliefs of the American Sephardic Woman Related to the Evil Eye" (2010)

4. GENEROUS SUN (SHEMESH TZEDAKAH)

I can't believe all you have done for me
Healing me with kindness and a love I can feel
Keep far away all trouble and pain
Protect me protect me
Please keep me safe
And may these words that I dare to say
And may these words that I dare to say
Be your will my Rock who saves
And always shine on me a generous sun
With wings of light healing me with love
Always shine on me a generous sun
With wings of light healing me with love
Healing me with love

קָטֹנְתִּי מִכָּל הַחֲסָדִים אֲשֶׁר עָשִׂיתָ עִמָּדִי
הַרְחֵק מֵעָלַי כָּל צָרָה וְתוּגָה
שָׁמְרֵנִי מִכָּל רָע
יִהְיוּ לְרָצוֹן אִמְרֵי פִי צוּרִי וְגוֹאֲלִי
וְזָרְחָה לִי תָּמִיד שֶׁמֶשׁ צְדָקָה וּמַרְפֵּא בִּכְנָפֶיהָ

katonti katonti m'kol hahasadim asher aseetah imadee
harcheik mealai kol tzarah v'tugah
shomreinee shomreinee shomreinee mikol rah
yihiyu l'ratzon imrei fi tzuri v'goali
v'zarcha li tamid shemesh tzedakah (3x)
umarfeh biknafehah

Our lives are the gift of Your mercy and delight
Oh generous Lover of life
But even heartbreak can heal cause in the darkness I find
You near shining love like a light
So always shine on me a generous sun
With wings of light healing me with love
Always shine on me a generous sun
With wings of light healing me with love
Healing me with love

Prayer Upon Recovery From Illness. Based on the Sim Shalom prayer book
Music and English lyrics by Shoshana Jedwab. Based on Malachi 3:18

HEALING PRAYERS

5. HEALER OF THE BROKENHEARTED

□ FEMININE

הָרֹפֵאת לִשְׁבוּרֵי לֵב וּמְחַבֶּשֶׁת לְעַצְבוֹתָן
מוֹנָה מִסְפָּר לַכּוֹכָבִים לְכֻלָּם שֵׁמוֹת תִּקְרָא

harofeyt lishvrei lev um'chabeshet leatzvotan
monah mispar lachochavim lechulam sheimot tikrah

△ MASCULINE

הָרֹפֵא לִשְׁבוּרֵי לֵב וּמְחַבֵּשׁ לְעַצְבוֹתָם
מוֹנֶה מִסְפָּר לַכּוֹכָבִים לְכֻלָּם שֵׁמוֹת יִקְרָא

harofeh lishvurei lev um'chabesh leatzvotam
moneh mispar lachochavim lechulam sheimot yikrah

⊖ NONBINARY

הָרֹפֵאה לִשְׁבוּרוֹל לֵב וּמְחַבֶּשֶׁה לְעַצְבוֹתָל
מוֹנֶת מִסְפָּר לַכּוֹכָבִים לְכֻלָּם שֵׁמוֹת יִקְרָאֶה

harofei'ah lishvurol lev um'chabesheh leatzvotol
monet mispar lachochavim lechulam sheimot yikre'eh

Healer of the brokenhearted, binder of our/their wounds
Counter of uncountable stars You know who we/they are

הַלְלוּ יָהּ

halleluyah (x4)

אָנָא אֵל/אֱלָה נָא רְפָא/רְפָאִי/רְפָאֶה נָא לָהּ

△ ana el nah refah na lah (x2)
□ ana elah nah rifee na lah (x2)
⊖ ana el nah rifeh na lah (x2)

Based on Psalm 147:3-4, English and melody by Shir Meira Feit

6. THE SKY'S REPLY

מִן הַמֵּצַר קָרָאתִי יָהּ
עָנָנִי בַמֶּרְחָב יָהּ

min hametzar karati yah

ah'nani vamerchav yah

To You I call, feeling scared and small.
And You reply with the vastness of the sky!

אָנָּא אֵל נָא רְפָא נָא לָהּ

ana el nah refah na lah

Heal them, hold them
Underneath your wing

Joshua Blaine, Psalm 118:5 with inspiration from Siddur haKohenet translation, Healing verses added by Keshira haLev Fife

7. HEALING CHANT

אָנָּא אֱלָהּ נָא רְפָאִי נָא לָהּ

□ ana elah nah reefee na lah

Please God heal them/us body and soul
Body and spirit, may they/we be whole

Numbers 12:13, English by Liviah Wessely

EITZ CHAYIM HEE: SHE IS THE TREE (ABRIDGED VERSION)

She is the Tree
She is the Tree
The Tree of Life for you and me
Limbs reaching out in all directions
Connecting us with Infinity
Rooting us to our own power
To mend the world for peace and equality

eitz chayim hee (x2) lamachazikot bah
v'tom'cheha m'ushar (x2)
deracheha darchei noam
v'chol n'tivoteha shalom.
hashivinu havayah elayich v'nashuva
chadshi yameinu k'kedem (x2)

Eitz Chayim Hee
She is the Tree
Embrace Her into your body
Feel the bliss She brings
Wrapped up within Her rings
So much pleasure to find in Her journeys
Connecting us to each other
And to our communities
Connecting us to the Old Ones
Without whom we would not be

Eitz Chayim Hee
She is the Tree
Dance Her into your body
We called Her Asherah
We call Her Torah
Reminding us everyday that we are free
Connecting us with our own glory
Rooting us to our collective stories
Giving us the sense to question what they say
Connecting with the text in our own ways

Eitz Chayim Hee
She is the Tree
She is already in your body
In every cell and strand
In our hearts and our hands
In every single nook and cranny
She's in the oxygen
She breathes out, we breathe in
In our souls infusing them with Her peace

Eitz Chayim Heh*
Zhe** is the Web
Zhe is the Weaver
Zhe is the thread
Connecting everything to each other
To all that's Living and to the Dead
Connecting us to past and future
But holding us in the present moment
Reminding us to tap into
And to really feel how we all connect

Eitz Chayim Hee
We are the Tree
In sacred commUnities
Writing our own Torah
Our Love as the ink
An endless connection of link upon link
Black on white fire but mostly hues of grey
Allowing our hearts to lead the way

Eitz Chayim Hee
She is the Tree
The Tree of Life
For you and me

*ALY/Ahavah Lilith evershYne,
Hebrew from Proverbs 3:18, 3:17*

הֶא ("Heh"): Nonbinary 3rd person singular pronoun created by the Nonbinary Hebrew Project by Lior Gross and Eyal Rivlin.
*** Zhe: Nonbinary 3rd person singular pronoun taught to me by my teacher Taya Shere who learned it from her beloved collaborator Ibrahim Baba haKohenet.*

תְּהַלֵּלְנָה אֶת שֵׁם הויה
כִּי נִשְׂגָּב שְׁמָהּ לְבַדָּהּ
הוֹדוֹ עַל אֶרֶץ וְשָׁמָיִם
וַיָּרֶם קֶרֶן לְעַמּוֹ
תְּהִלָּה לְכָל חֲסִידֶיהָ
לְבָנֶיהָ עַם קְרוֹבָהּ הַלְלוּיָהּ

tehallelna et shem havayah
ki nisgav shemah levadah
hodo al eretz veshamayim
vayarem keren le'amo
tehilah lechol hasideha
levaneha am kerovah halleluyah

Let us praise the name of Being, for that name alone is exalted.
The glory of Being rests on heaven and earth, and exalts the horns of the people.
Praise to all Being's lovers, to Being's children, to the people close to her. Halleluyah.

עֵץ
חַיִּים הִיא
לַמַּחֲזִיקוֹת בָּהּ וְתֹמְכֶיהָ מְאֻשָּׁר
דְּרָכֶיהָ דַרְכֵי נֹעַם וְכָל נְתִיבוֹתֶיהָ שָׁלוֹם

הֲשִׁיבִינוּ הויה אֵלַיִךְ וְנָשׁוּבָה חַדְּשִׁי יָמֵינוּ כְּקֶדֶם

etz chayim hee

lemachazikot bah vetomcheha me'ushar

deracheha darchei noam vechol netivoteha shalom

hashivinu havayah elayich venashuvah chadshi yameinu kekedem

She is a tree of life to those who hold her fast, and her supporters are happy.
Her ways are ways of pleasantness, and all her paths are peace.
Return us to you, Circle of Life, and we shall return
renew our days as you have since the world's beginning.

HEALING PRAYERS **188**

GROUNDING PRAYERS

AND WE WILL SEE SHEKHINAH (ALEINU)

יִהְיֶה יְהֹוָה אֶחָד וּשְׁמוֹ אֶחָד
תִּהְיֶה הֲוָיָה אַחַת וְרוּחָהּ אַחַת

yihiyeh adonai echad, ushemo echad (x3)
tihiyeh havaya achat, verucha achat (x3)

And we will see Shekhinah

in the wind across the land

we are a circle within her circle

And we will be Shekhinah

in the work of our hearts and our hands

She is a circle, within our circle

Taya Shere adaptation of "We Are A Circle" by Rick Hamouris ("v'rucha achat" lyric by Jill Hammer)

VEHASHEIVOTA

△ וַהֲשֵׁבֹתָ אֶל לְבָבֶךָ כִּי יְהֹוָה הוּא הָאֱלֹהִים
▢ וַהֲשֵׁבֹת אֶל לְבָבֵיךְ כִּי שְׁכִינָה הִיא הָאֱלֹהִים
⊖ וַהֲשֵׁבֹתֶה אֶל לְבָבֶךֶה כִּי הֲוָיָה הֵא הָאֱלֹהִים

△ vehasheivota el levavecha ki adonai hu ha'elohim
▢ vehasheivot el levaveich ki shekhinah hi ha'elohim
⊖ vehasheivoteh el levavecheh ki havayah heh ha'elohim

וְנֶאֱמַר וְהָיָה הֲוָיָה לְרוּחַ עַל כָּל הָאָרֶץ
בַּיּוֹם הַהוּא יִהְיֶה הֲוָיָה אַחַת וּשְׁמָהּ אֶחָד

vene'emar vehaya havayah leruach al kol ha'aretz
bayom hahu tihiyeh havayah achat ush'ma echad

And it is written; one day we will see that the "one who rules is the wind blowing across the earth. On that day we will know that Being is one, and Being's name is one."

Shir Meira Feit based on Deuteronomy 4:39 and the Aleinu prayer

A PRAYER TO THE SHEKHINAH

"For I will turn their mourning into joy, and I will comfort them, and make them rejoice from their sorrow."

Jeremiah 31:13

Come be our mother	we are your young ones
Come be our bride	we are your lover
Come be our dwelling	we are your inhabitants
Come be our game	we are your players
Come be our punishment	we are your sinners
Come be our ocean	we are your swimmers
Come be our victory	we are your army
Come be our laughter	we are your story
Come be our Shekhinah	we are your glory
We believe that you live	
though you delay	we believe you will certainly come....

Shekhinah bless us and keep us

Shekhinah shine your face on us

Shekhinah turn your countenance

To us and give us peace

Alicia Ostriker

SHIELDING PRAYERS

When reciting the first line, draw energy up from the earth
and raise your arms over your head touching your fingers together.

When reciting the second line, move the energy
around above your head by circling your arms over your head.

When reciting the third line, release the energy
down over your body by releasing your hands and arms.

WEEKDAY

May I be guarded, shielded, guided, and protected from accidentally, unknowingly, unintentionally, or unjustly harming myself.

May I be guarded, shielded, guided, and protected from accidentally, unknowingly, unintentionally, or unjustly harming others.

May I be guarded, shielded, guided, and protected from accidentally, unknowingly, unintentionally, or unjustly being harmed by others.

SHABBAT

May I be enveloped, wrapped and enrobed in the peace of the Sabbath, so I may not accidentally, unknowingly, unintentionally, or unjustly harm myself.

May I be enveloped, wrapped and enrobed in the peace of the Sabbath, so I may not accidentally, unknowingly, unintentionally, or unjustly harm others.

May I be enveloped, wrapped and enrobed in the peace of the Sabbath, so I may not accidentally, unknowingly, unintentionally, or unjustly be harmed by others.

Ketzirah Lesser

WE ARE A SPIRAL (KI AFAR AT)

כִּי עָפָר אַתְּ וְאֶל עָפָר תָּשׁוּבִי

ki afar at ve'el afar tashuvi

Earth we are and earth we will be
We are a spiral coming home

Taya Shere

ALL OF IT, ALWAYS, EARTH

All of it, always, earth.
This multitude of worms,
this radiance of butterflies,
the name of your fourth grade teacher,
death.
All of it, always, earth.

All of it, always, earth:
Your body, your heart, your mind, your temple.
The beautiful delusions of your grandeur,
The secret mushroom of your shame.
This slow and instant awakening. This constant birth.
All of it, always, earth.

All of it, always, earth:
Your first goodbye, your last hello.
The hand of your beloved, your mother, your child.
All families.
All tribes.
All of it. Always. Earth.

Tamuz Shiran

EYL MALEI

אֵל מָלֵא רַחֲמִים שׁוֹכֵן בַּמְּרוֹמִים
הַמְצֵא מְנוּחָה נְכוֹנָה עַל כַּנְפֵי הַשְּׁכִינָה

eyl malei rachamim shocheyn bam'romim
hamtzei menucha n'chona al kanfei hashekhina

Compassionate One who dwells on high,
Give rest to these souls and help them fly.
Wrap them in Shekhinah's wings.
Protection, comfort and peace please bring.

Taya Shere

LEAN BACK

Lean back, they say (x3)
We're right here (x2)

We are at your back
Feel the waters of ancestral blessing
We are at your back
We're right here (x2)

In the curls of your hair
In the fire of your stare
In the drops of your blood
And when you speak (x2)

In the air that you breathe
In the knowledge that you seek
In the wisdom of your hands
And in your bones

Sarah Salem

GROUNDING PRAYERS

KADDISH

The true mysteries of the Sacred Feminine are not about cryptic codes, secret messages, and hidden hoards of treasure. They are the most ordinary, everyday things of life, which we all experience: birth, growth, death, and regeneration.

Starhawk

MOURNER'S KADDISH (KADDISH YATOM)

yitgadal veyitkadash shemeh rabbah	יִתְגַּדַּל וְיִתְקַדַּשׁ שְׁמֵהּ רַבָּא.
be'almah di vra chirutei veyamlich malchutei	בְּעָלְמָא דִּי בְרָא כִרְעוּתֵיהּ וְיַמְלִיךְ מַלְכוּתֵיהּ
bechayeichon uveyomeichon	בְּחַיֵּיכוֹן וּבְיוֹמֵיכוֹן
uvechayei dechol veit yisrael	וּבְחַיֵּי דְכָל בֵּית יִשְׂרָאֵל.
ba'agalah uvizman kariv ve'imru amein.	בַּעֲגָלָא וּבִזְמַן קָרִיב וְאִמְרוּ אָמֵן

yehei shmei rabbah mevorach	יְהֵא שְׁמֵהּ רַבָּא מְבָרַךְ
le'alam ulalmei almaya.	לְעָלַם וּלְעָלְמֵי עָלְמַיָּא

yitbarach veyishtabach	יִתְבָּרַךְ וְיִשְׁתַּבַּח
veyitpaar veyitromam veyitnasei	וְיִתְפָּאַר וְיִתְרוֹמַם וְיִתְנַשֵּׂא
veyithadar veyitaleh veyithalal,	וְיִתְהַדָּר וְיִתְעַלֶּה וְיִתְהַלָּל
shemei dekudsha brich hu	שְׁמֵהּ דְּקֻדְשָׁא בְּרִיךְ הוּא
le'eilah min kol birchata veshirata	לְעֵלָּא (בעשי״ת וּלְעֵלָּא מִכָּל) מִן כָּל בִּרְכָתָא וְשִׁירָתָא
tushbechata venechemata	תֻּשְׁבְּחָתָא וְנֶחֱמָתָא
da'amiran be'alma ve'imru amen.	דַּאֲמִירָן בְּעָלְמָא, וְאִמְרוּ אָמֵן

yehei shlamah rabbah min sh'maya	יְהֵא שְׁלָמָא רַבָּא מִן שְׁמַיָּא
vechayyim aleinu ve'al kol yisrael	וְחַיִּים (טוֹבִים) עָלֵינוּ וְעַל כָּל יִשְׂרָאֵל
ve'imru amen.	וְאִמְרוּ אָמֵן

osah shalom bimromeha	עֹשָׂה שָׁלוֹם בִּמְרוֹמֶיהָ
hi taaseh shalom aleinu ve'al kol yisrael	הִיא תַּעֲשֶׂה שָׁלוֹם עָלֵינוּ וְעַל כָּל יִשְׂרָאֵל
ve'al kol yoshvei tevel ve'imru amen.	וְעַל כָּל יוֹשְׁבֵי תֵבֵל וְאִמְרוּ אָמֵן

May the great name, which includes all names that have been and will be, be blessed in this world and all the worlds. Amen.

May the One who makes peace in the high places make peace for us and all Israel and all the world. Amen.

STONE BY STONE

stone by stone, tear by tear
we release and create right here

what is gone we build upon

thread by thread, bone by bone
we remember
as we journey home

holy ground is all around

Taya Shere

SHALOM CHAVEROT

Shalom, shalom chaverot, shalom (x2)

Tzeitchen l'shalom (x3)
Shalom chaverot, shalom

L'hitraot, shalom chaverot, shalom (x2)

Od od od od… od od od od… od od od od… od! (x2)

Kehilla kedoshah, shalom chaverot, shalom (x2)

Od od od od… od od od od… od od od od… od! (x2)

Shalom, shalom chaverot, shalom (x2)

L'hitraot, shalom chaverot, shalom (x2)
L'hitraot, until we meet again.

Peace, friends. Peace to the sacred community. Until we meet again, farewell and peace.

Traci Marx, inspired by the folk song Shalom Chaverim

COME TO THE WELL

Come come to the well
Come come and be held
Draw up the waters of peace
Your voices flow through me

Come come to the well
Come come for your help
Drink from the waters you need
Your voices flow through me

ezri ezri me'im osah shamayim (x2)

Come come to the well
Come come where I dwell
Bathe in the waters of dreams
Your voices flow through me

ezri ezri me'im osah shamayim (x2)

ezri ezri Your voices flow through me...

Traci Marx, inspired by Psalm 121

WHERE YOU GO

Where you go, I will go, Beloved*

Where you go, I will go

(x2)

And where you lie, I will lie, Beloved

Where you lie, I will lie

(x2)

And your people are my people

Your people are mine

Your people are my people

Your Divine my Divine

* repeat verses replacing Beloved with
Refugee/Mother Earth/Children/Ancestors/Goddess/Priestess

Shoshana Jedwab

CIRCLE OF LOVE

We are a circle, circle, circle of love

galgalay ahavah, galgalay ahava
ahava raba, ahavat olam

Through time and space, eternity,
we are a circle of love.

Geela Rayzel Raphael

CLOSING THE CIRCLE

*Everything in the sky has its counterpart on earth,
and everything on earth has its counterpart in the sea,
and yet all form a unity.*

Zohar II, 20a

לִשְׁמָה

לִשְׁמוֹ

לְשֵׁם עָלְמַיָּא

אַרְעָה יָמָא וּשְׁמַיָּא

אֲנוּ עָשִׂין עִיגוּל נָפְשַׁיָּא

lishmah lishmo leshem almaya
ar'ah, yama, veshamaya
anu osin igul nafshaya
we are the earth, wind, water and fire

lishmah lishmo leshem almaya
ar'ah, yama, veshamaya
anu osin igul nafshaya
may our souls circle deeper and higher

In Her name, in His name, in the Name of the worlds,
earth, sea, and sky
we make a circle of our souls.

Jill Hammer & Taya Shere

MINCHAH
AFTERNOON PRAYERS

The *Mincha* prayer, or afternoon prayer, is recited sometime between noon and sundown. It corresponds to the afternoon offering in Temple times. *Mincha* means "gift," and specifically refers to a grain-offering—a cooked meal offering with oil, offered for Shabbat and festivals and many other kinds of occasions. The mincha offering was also known as the offering of the poor because it was inexpensive. This suggests the *kavvanah* or intention of humility and gratitude when praying this prayer. *Mincha* is like a Sabbath within the day, asking us to take time out to tend our relationship with spirit even in the middle of a busy afternoon.

The traditional mincha prayer consists of *Ashrei*, the *Hatzi Kaddish*, the *Amidah*, the *Aleinu*, and the Mourner's Kaddish. Our Mincha prayer offers meditations and rituals for invoking sacred connection as part of one's daily practice.

ASHREI (HAPPY PEOPLE)

אַשְׁרֵי יוֹשְׁבֵי בֵיתֶךָ עוֹד הַלְלוּךָ סֶּלָה
אַשְׁרֵי הָעָם שֶׁכָּכָה לוֹ אַשְׁרֵי הָעָם שֶׁיְהֹוָה אֱלֹהָיו

ashrei yoshvei veitecha od hallelucha selah
ashrei ha'am shekacha lo ashrei haam she'adonai elohav

Happy are people living in Your Temple,
May they always praise You Selah!
Joy to the ones who feel Your grace,
Oh happy people, happy people!
Hallelujah (x8)

קָרוֹב יְהֹוָה לְכָל קֹרְאָיו לְכֹל אֲשֶׁר יִקְרָאֻהוּ בֶאֱמֶת
וַאֲנַחְנוּ נְבָרֵךְ יָהּ מֵעַתָּה וְעַד עוֹלָם הַלְלוּיָהּ

karov adonai lechol korav, lechol asher yikrauhu bemet
vaanachnu nevareich yah, meata vead olam, hallelujah

You are near to everyone who's calling
To all who open up and feel Your truth
And we will go on blessing Yah
From now on and forever
Hallelujah (x8)

English by Shoshana Jedwab, based on Psalm 145

אַשְׁרֵי יוֹשְׁבֵי בֵיתֶיהָ עוֹד הַלְלוּהָ סֶּלָה
אַשְׁרוֹת יוֹשְׁבוֹת בֵּיתֶהָ עוֹד תְּהַלְלוּהָ סֶּלָה
אֲשֵׁרָה יוֹשְׁבוֹת בֵּיתֵךְ עוֹד תְּהַלְלוּךְ סֶּלָה

ashrei yoshvei veiteha od halleluha selah
ashrot yoshvot veiteha od tehalleluha selah
asherah yoshvot veiteich od tehallelookh selah

Happy are those dwelling in Her house and always singing to the Universe. Selah!
Asherah those who dwell in Your house will praise You always. Selah!

AFTERNOON PRAYERS 202

MINCHA MEDITATION I. SEALS OF THE SEVEN DIRECTIONS

According to the Sefer Yetzirah, the Divine "seals" the six directions of the world in order to allow the world to exist. Each of these directions has a combination of letters (yud, heh, and vav) that is its seal, and each of these combinations corresponds to an element and a gender. At Kohenet, we use these elemental seals to create a protected sacred space within which we will pray, play and work.

This meditation can be used at afternoon prayer or at any time to create a bounded sacred space around yourself. You may want to associate each of the seals of the directions with a color, image, or sound. Reciting or envisioning the seals of the six directions is a way of creating a temple around yourself.

You can tone the letters using the sounds provided while focusing on the six directions. You can envision the entities of air, fire, and water as you face in the six directions. Or, you can use the letters as a visual meditation, focusing on each trio of letters as you turn toward or concentrate on each direction.

Here are two variations on this ancient ritual technology. In sealing the six directions, we ask for our own space to be clear, peaceful and protected, and we participate in guarding creation.

A.

In this visualization, each direction is sealed and protected by a combination of the letters of the divine name, as explained in Sefer Yetzirah Chapter One.

Face east.

Look up	and visualize the letters Yud Hei Vav:	י ה ו
Look down	and visualize the letters Heh Yud Vav:	ה י ו
Look forward	and visualize the letters Vav Yud Heh:	ו י ה
Look backward	and visualize the letters Vav Hei Yud:	ו ה י
Look right	and visualize the letters Yud Vav Heh:	י ו ה
Look left	and visualize the letters Hei Vav Yud:	ה ו י
	Visualize the letters of God's name within yourself:	י ה ו ה

Invoke any intention or prayer that you have at this time.

The seal is complete.

B.

In this visualization, each direction is sealed by a sacred presence guarding that direction, and by a combination of letters of the divine name. This visualization is based on the seals of the six directions in Chapter One of the ancient book Sefer Yetzirah, as well as the seals of the elements in Chapter Three of that book. The names of the sounded letters are provided, should you wish to intone them using different vowels.

Face east.

יהו   Visualize a watery feminine presence above you.
Intone: Yahava (Yud Hei Vav).

היו   Visualize a fiery feminine presence below you.
Intone: Hayava (Heh Yud Vav).

ויה   Visualize an airy masculine presence in front of you.
Intone: Vayaha (Vav Yud Heh).

והי   Visualize an airy feminine presence behind you.
Intone: Vahaya (Vav Hei Yud).

יוה   Visualize a watery masculine presence to your right.
Intone: Yavaha (Yud Vav Heh).

הוי   Visualize a fiery feminine presence to your left.
Intone: Havaya (Hei Vav Yud).

הויה   Feel the Source-presence within, however it appears to you.
Intone: Havayah (Hei Vav Yud Hei).

Invoke any intention or prayer that you have at this time.

The seal is complete.

MINCHA MEDITATION II. HEART PRAYER

may this heart be held
by the heart of the world
and feed the roots of the world

may this heart's joy
become the roots of the Tree of Life

may this heart move with the moon
be blessed by the tides
be at the center of all peacemaking

may this heart provide the rhythm for my dancing

may this heart be
healed by all the crying of the world
nourished by all the belly laughter of the world
blessed by all of the beauty of the world
received in every moment

may this heart be awakened tenderly and gently
all the days of my life

may this heart
and may all Creation be blessed
and may this heart
be the best and most beautiful heart
in my whole ribcage

may i be wholehearted

Ilana Streit

MINCHA MEDITATION III. SILENCE

Lie down on the floor or stand so that you feel the solid ground and the gravity of the earth beneath. Allow yourself to commune with the sea of being, with divinity as you understand it. If you wish, you may meditate on one or more of the following themes:

 remembering the ancestors
 renewal of life
 holiness
 the gifts of the mind
 repentance (change
 forgiveness
 help from the universe
 healing
 abundance of the earth
 return from exile
 justice
 protection from harm
 kindness toward the righteous and the community
 shelter for Jerusalem
 hope for a better future
 the hearing of prayer
 the return of the Shekhinah
 a heart full of gratitude
 peace for all the living

When you have finished meditating, feel your body in connection with the earth. Allow an answer to your prayer to arise in you. See what is in your heart. When you are ready, conclude.

Doorways into the Amidah prayers for Shabbat, festivals, and weekdays can be found on page 152.

AND WE WILL SEE SHEKHINAH

יִהְיֶה יְרוֹרָה אֶחָד וּשְׁמוֹ אֶחָד
יִהְיֶה הֲוָיָה אַחַת וְרוּחָהּ אַחַת

yihiyeh adonai echad
ushemo echad x3
tihiyeh havaya achat
verucha achat x3

And we will see Shekhinah in the wind across the land
we are a circle within her circle
And we will be Shekhinah
in the work of our hearts and our hands
She is a circle within our circle

Taya Shere, adaptation of "We Are A Circle" by Rick Hamouris ("v'rucha achat" lyric by Jill Hammer)

MOURNER'S KADDISH

CONCLUDE ON PAGE 194

HALLEL

The Hallel prayer is a series of psalms proclaiming joy and celebrating deliverance from hardship. It is recited on all festivals and new moons, and is particularly associated with Sukkot, festival of the harvest. It is the ultimate form of thanksgiving prayer.

On Sukkot, Jews wave the lulav in the six directions during Hallel, inviting the presence of the sacred cosmos, the All represented by the directions. While there is no tradition to wave a barley sheaf during Passover or a loaf of bread during Shavuot, this would be an appropriate custom, since priests waved sheaves of barley on the second day of Passover, and also waved the bread-offering during Shavuot.

בְּרוּכָה אַתְּ שְׁכִינָה אֱלֹתֵינוּ רוּחַ הָעוֹלָם אֲשֶׁר קִדְּשַׁתְנוּ בְּמִצְוֹתֶיהָ וְצִוַּתְנוּ לִקְרוֹא אֶת הַהַלֵּל

beruchah at shekhinah eloteinu ruach ha'olam
asher kidshatnu bemitzvoteha vetzivatnu likro et hahalel.

Blessed are You, Weaver of the Year, who has made us wise with your wisdom
and has invited us to sing songs of praise.

IF TAKING THE LULAV (ON SUKKOT)

בְּרוּכָה אַתְּ שְׁכִינָה אֱלֹתֵינוּ רוּחַ הָעוֹלָם אֲשֶׁר קִדְּשַׁתְנוּ בְּמִצְוֹתֶיהָ וְצִוַּתְנוּ עַל נְטִילַת לוּלָב

beruchah at shekhinah eloteinu ruach ha'olam
asher kidshatnu bemitzvoteha vetzivatnu al netilat lulav.

Blessed is the Indwelling Spirit in space
that invites us to shake the lulav in all directions.

בְּרוּכָה אַתְּ שְׁכִינָה אֱלֹהֵינוּ רוּחַ הָעוֹלָם שֶׁהֶחֱיָתְנוּ וְקִיְּמָתְנוּ וְהִגִּיעָתְנוּ לַזְּמַן הַזֶּה

beruchah at shekhinah eloheinu ruach ha'olam
shehecheyatnu vekiymatnu vehigiatnu lazman hazeh.

Blessed is the Indwelling Spirit in time
that enlivens us and sustains us and allows us to reach this joyful moment.

PSALM 113

m'kimi me'afar dal
moshivi akeret habayit
eim hanbanim s'meichah
halleluyah!

מְקִימִי מֵעָפָר דָּל
מוֹשִׁיבִי עֲקֶרֶת הַבַּיִת
אֵם הַבָּנִים שְׂמֵחָה
הַלְלוּיָהּ

Raising the poor up from the earth—
Returning the Root of the House, the happy Mother of children!
Halleluyah!

PSALM 114

betzeit yisrael mimitzrayim	בְּצֵאת יִשְׂרָאֵל מִמִּצְרָיִם
beit yaakov me'am loez	בֵּית יַעֲקֹב מֵעַם לֹעֵז
haytah yehudah lekodshah	הָיְתָה יְהוּדָה לְקָדְשׁוֹ
yisrael mamsheloteha	יִשְׂרָאֵל מַמְשְׁלוֹתָיו
hayam ra'ah vayanos	הַיָּם רָאָה וַיָּנֹס
hayarden yisov le'achor	הַיַּרְדֵּן יִסֹּב לְאָחוֹר
heharim rakdu ke'eilim	הֶהָרִים רָקְדוּ כְאֵילִים
geva'ot kivnei tzon	גְּבָעוֹת כִּבְנֵי צֹאן
mah lecha hayam ki tanus	מַה לְּךָ הַיָּם כִּי תָנוּס
hayarden tisov le'achor	הַיַּרְדֵּן תִּסֹּב לְאָחוֹר
heharim rakdu ke'eilim	הֶהָרִים תִּרְקְדוּ כְאֵילִים
geva'ot livnei tzon	גְּבָעוֹת כִּבְנֵי צֹאן
milifnei adan chuli aretz	מִלִּפְנֵי אָדוֹן חוּלִי אָרֶץ
milifnei eloha yaakov	מִלִּפְנֵי אֱלוֹהַּ יַעֲקֹב
hahofchi hatzur agam mayim	הַהֹפְכִי הַצּוּר אֲגַם מָיִם
chalamish lemaino mayim	חַלָּמִישׁ לְמַעְיְנוֹ מָיִם

When Israel went forth from the narrow place, they became holy to the Divine. The sea saw and leaped, the Jordan ran backwards! The mountains danced like rams, and the hills like lambs. Why did they do this? Because of the Connector of the earth, who can turn stones to water, and flint into flowing streams!

FROM PSALM 116

כּוֹס יְשׁוּעוֹת אֶשָּׂא וּבְשֵׁם שַׁדַּי אֶקְרָא

kos yeshuot esa uveshem shaddai ekra

I lift up this cup of transformation
this womb of renewal
and call upon Shaddai

עָזִּי וְזִמְרָת יָהּ וַיְהִי לִי לִישׁוּעָה

ozi ve'zimrat yah vay'hi li li'shuah

My strength, and the Divine song, will be my deliverance.

Exodus 15:3

מִן הַמֵּצַר קָרָאתִי יָהּ עֲנָתַנִי בַמֶּרְחָב יָהּ

min hametzar karati yah anatani vamerchav yah

I called to Yah from the narrow place, and was answered with the sky's wideness

אָנָּא יהוה הוֹשִׁיעָה נָּא
אָנָּא שְׁכִינָה הוֹשִׁיעִי נָּא

ana adonai hoshia na
ana shekhinah hoshi'i na

Please o holy open us

אָנָּא יהוה הַצְלִיחָה נָּא
אָנָּא שְׁכִינָה הַצְלִיחִי נָּא

ana adonai hatzlicha na
ana shekhinah hatzlichi na

Please o holy nourish us

o tree of life shelter us
o fire of life shine in us

הוֹדוּ לַשְּׁכִינָה כִּי טוֹבָה
כִּי לְעוֹלָם חַסְדָּהּ

hodu lashekhinah ki tovah ki le'olam chasdah

Thanks to Shekhinah for she is good, her love runs through all worlds.

□ בְּרוּכָה אַתְּ אֱלָהּ
מַלְכָּה מְהֻלֶּלֶת בַּתִּשְׁבָּחוֹת.

□ beruchah at elah
malkah mehulelet batishbachot.

△ בָּרוּךְ אַתָּה יהוה
מֶלֶךְ מְהֻלָּל בַּתִּשְׁבָּחוֹת.

△ baruch ata adonai
melech mehulal batishbachot.

Blessed is the One to whom we ululate in praise!

HAVDALAH
FAREWELL TO SHABBAT

The havdalah ritual is a ritual of separation, marking the end of the Sabbath and the beginning of the week. It is a sensual ritual that centers on the body: the sense of taste (wine), smell (spices), sight (flame), and sound (song).

The ritual contains the elements of fire (the candle), water (earth (the wine), and air (the spices). These elements correspond to the three "mothers," water, air, and fire. The Sefer Yetzirah teaches that these elements combine to create the world.

עָזִי וְזִמְרָת יָה וַיְהִי לִי לִישׁוּעָה

ozi ve'zimrat yah, vay'hi li li'shuah

My strength, and the Divine song, will be my deliverance.

Exodus 15:3

UND DI VOCH ZAL

und di voch zal
uns kumen tzu chesed
und tzu mazal
may this week be a blessing

Taya Shere, after the traditional Yiddish prayer Gott Fun Avrohom, which Rabbi Levi Yitzhak of Berdichev prescribed to be recited three times before Havdalah, toward ensuring blessing for the week to come

LAYEHUDIM HAYTAH ORAH

לַיְהוּדִים הָיְתָה אוֹרָה וְשִׂמְחָה וְשָׂשׂוֹן וִיקָר כֵּן תִּהְיֶה לָנוּ

layehudim haytah orah vesimcha vesasson veyikar kein tihiyeh lanu

The Jews had light and joy and gladness and preciousness. So may it be for us.

Esther 8:17

beruchah at shekhinah eloteinu ruach ha'olam
boreit peri hagafen.

בְּרוּכָה אַתְּ שְׁכִינָה אֱלֹתֵינוּ רוּחַ הָעוֹלָם
בּוֹרֵאת פְּרִי הַגֶּפֶן.

beruchah at shekhinah eloteinu ruach ha'olam
boreit minei vesamim.

בְּרוּכָה אַתְּ שְׁכִינָה אֱלֹתֵינוּ רוּחַ הָעוֹלָם
בּוֹרֵאת מִינֵי בְשָׂמִים.

beruchah at shekhinah eloteinu ruach ha'olam
boreit me'orei ha'eish.

בְּרוּכָה אַתְּ שְׁכִינָה אֱלֹתֵינוּ רוּחַ הָעוֹלָם
בּוֹרֵאת מְאוֹרֵי הָאֵשׁ.

beruchah at shekhinah eloteinu ruach ha'olam
hamavdila bein kodesh lechol, bein or lechoshech
bein yom hashevi'i lesheishet yemei hama'aseh.
beruchah at shekhinah
hamavdilah bein kodesh lechol.

בְּרוּכָה אַתְּ שְׁכִינָה אֱלֹתֵינוּ רוּחַ הָעוֹלָם
הַמַּבְדִּילָה בֵּין קֹדֶשׁ לְחֹל וּבֵין אוֹר לְחֹשֶׁךְ
בֵּין יוֹם הַשְּׁבִיעִי לְשֵׁשֶׁת יְמֵי הַמַּעֲשֶׂה
בְּרוּכָה אַתְּ שְׁכִינָה
הַמַּבְדִּילָה בֵּין קֹדֶשׁ לְחֹל.

Blessed are You, Shekhinah our divinity who nourishes the world, who creates the fruit of the vine. Blessed are You, Shekhinah, our divinity who enlivens the world, who creates many kinds of spices. Blessed are You, Shekhinah, our divinity who embodies the world, who creates the lights of fire.

Blessed are You, Indwelling One, Wind of the Universe, who divides certain moments from the flow of time, raises up light in the darkness, and separates between the Sabbath and the days of work. Blessed are You, Presence who gives us the gift of pausing in the flow of time to name holiness.

ELIYAHU HANAVI

eliyahu hanavi, eliyahu hatishbi
eliyahu, eliyahu, eliyahu hagiladi
bimheira v'yameinu yavo eileinu
im mashiach ben david, im mashiach ben david

אֵלִיָּהוּ הַנָּבִיא אֵלִיָּהוּ הַתִּשְׁבִּי
אֵלִיָּהוּ אֵלִיָּהוּ אֵלִיָּהוּ הַגִּלְעָדִי
בִּמְהֵרָה בְיָמֵינוּ יָבוֹא אֵלֵינוּ
עִם מָשִׁיחַ בֶּן דָּוִד

Elijah the prophet, come to us with the anointed one, David's child.

MIRIAM HANEVIAH

miriam ha'neviah, oz v'zimra b'yadah
miriam tirkod itanu l'taken et ha-olam
bimherah v'yameynu hi tevi'eynu
el mei hayeshua (x2)

מִרְיָם הַנְּבִיאָה עֹז וְזִמְרָה בְּיָדָהּ
מִרְיָם תִּרְקֹד אִתָּנוּ לְתַקֵּן אֶת הָעוֹלָם
בִּמְהֵרָה בְיָמֵינוּ הִיא תְבִיאֵנוּ
אֶל מֵי הַיְשׁוּעָה

Miriam the prophetess, in whose hand is strength and song, Miriam dance with us to heal the world. Quickly, in our own day, bring us to the waters of transformation.

Leila Gal Berner

BORDERLINE OZI

עָזִּי וְזִמְרָת יָהּ וַיְהִי לִי לִישׁוּעָה

ozi ve zimrat yah, vayehi li lishua

Yah is my strength and my song, Yah will be my salvation

Look for three stars in the night sky
Smell the spices, pour the sweet wine
We're at the great divide, on the borderline
With Sabbath ending, gather in blessing
Cause we're going back to the fires we're tending
At the great divide, on the borderline
For every mortal the sacred portal
Nobody knows what will be tomorrow
At the great divide, on the borderline
So light it up in celebration,
Profane and holy are both revelations
At the great divide, on the borderline

So start your work week, start the action
Bring more justice, bring your passion
At the great divide, on the borderline
Find a lover, don't take cover
Wish a good week to some sweet other
At the great divide, on the borderline
Bring the Messiah, bring good intention
For soon you will be the next ancestor
At the great divide, on the borderline
There are evil forces, but there is freedom
Help us Elijah, and Prophetess Miriam
At the great divide, on the borderline

The fire's shining rainbow colors
Lift all the children high up on our shoulders
At the great divide, on the borderline
Just put your trust in the power of loving
Fill your senses, offer your skin for touching
At the great divide, on the borderline
There's still a good chance, for the big dance
The Queen is hanging on for one more romance
At the great divide, on the borderline
So, say hello, or say goodbye, just
Put your candle into the cup of wine
At the great divide, on the borderline

Shoshana Jedwab

TEKUFOT
EQUINOXES AND SOLSTICES

To be recited on equinoxes and solstices, with wine, spices, a candle, and other appropriate readings.

beruchah at shekhinah eloteinu ruach ha'olam boreit peri hagafen.	Blessed are You, Shekhinah our divinity who nourishes the world who creates the fruit of the vine.	בְּרוּכָה אַתְּ שְׁכִינָה אֱלֹתֵינוּ רוּחַ הָעוֹלָם בּוֹרֵאת פְּרִי הַגָּפֶן.
beruchah at shekhinah eloteinu ruach ha'olam boreit minei vesamim.	Blessed are You, Shekhinah our divinity who enlivens the world who creates many kinds of spices.	בְּרוּכָה אַתְּ שְׁכִינָה אֱלֹתֵינוּ רוּחַ הָעוֹלָם בּוֹרֵאת מִינֵי בְשָׂמִים.
beruchah at shekhinah eloteinu ruach ha'olam boreit me'orei ha'eish.	Blessed are You, Shekhinah our divinity who embodies the world who creates the lights of fire.	בְּרוּכָה אַתְּ שְׁכִינָה אֱלֹתֵינוּ רוּחַ הָעוֹלָם בּוֹרֵאת מְאוֹרֵי הָאֵשׁ.
beruchah at shekhinah eloteinu ruach ha'olam osah vereishit asher bit'vunah meshanah itim umachalifah et hazemanim.	Blessed are You Presence who inspires the world who makes creation whose wisdom changes the times and turns the seasons.	בְּרוּכָה אַתְּ שְׁכִינָה אֱלֹתֵינוּ רוּחַ הָעוֹלָם עוֹשָׂה בְרֵאשִׁית אֲשֶׁר בִּתְבוּנָה מְשַׁנָּה עִיתִים וּמַחֲלִיפָה אֶת הַזְּמַנִּים
od kol yemei ha'aretz zera vekatzir vekor vechom vekayitz vechoref veyom velailah lo yishbotu.	As long as the days of the earth endure planting and harvest cold and heart summer and winter day and night shall not cease.	עֹד כָּל יְמֵי הָאָרֶץ זֶרַע וְקָצִיר וְקֹר וָחֹם וְקַיִץ וָחֹרֶף וְיוֹם וָלַיְלָה לֹא יִשְׁבֹּתוּ
baruch ata yah mevarech hashanim.	Blessed are You, Breath of Life who blesses time.	בָּרוּךְ אַתָּה יָהּ מְבָרֵךְ הַשָּׁנִים.

ROSH CHODESH
NEW MOON CEREMONY

In ancient times, two witnesses had to confirm the appearance of the new moon. The exact day of this appearance was crucial because the new moon would determine when the month began and when that year's festivals would fall. The Mishnah (the earliest Jewish legal code, 200 CE) reports that two witnesses would report that they had sighted the new moon to a court of judges in Jerusalem. These judges would examine the witnesses carefully to make sure their testimonies were identical, and then confirm that the new moon had indeed appeared (Mishnah Rosh haShanah 2:6). In order to quickly transmit this knowledge to the far-flung Jewish community, bonfires were lit on hilltops around Jerusalem. Each community that saw the fires burning would light its own bonfire. Thus the news would pass from mountain to mountain and town to town, until all the Jews knew it was Rosh Chodesh, the new moon.

כָּל הַמְבָרֵךְ אֶת הַחֹדֶשׁ בִּזְמַנוֹ כְּאִלּוּ מְקַבֵּל פְּנֵי שְׁכִינָה

kol hamevarech et hachodesh bizmano ke'ilu mekabel p'nei shekhinah.

Whoever says the blessing over the new moon in its time, it is as if that person welcomes the presence of the Shekhinah.

Babylonian Talmud, Sanhedrin 42a

After everyone in the group has been given an unlit candle, a single participant lights her candle from a central flame. Then she passes the flame to the next person in the group, until all the candles are lit. The candles are then set around the central flame. Through this ritual, we recall both the ancient bonfires of the Jewish people and the light of hope and warmth that we pass from one person to another.

Jill Hammer, from ritualwell.org

ALL RECITE THE BLESSING

בְּרוּכָה אַתְּ שְׁכִינָה אֱלֹתֵינוּ רוּחַ הָעוֹלָם מְחַדֶּשֶׁת אֶת הַלְּבָנָה

beruchah at shekhinah eloteinu ruach ha'olam, mechadeshet et halevanah.

Blessed are You, Presence enlivening the world, who renews the moon.

RENEW THE WOMEN / RENEW THE PEOPLE

בְּרוּכָה אַתְּ שְׁכִינָה
שֶׁעָשְׂתָה אִשָׁה
מְחַדֶּשֶׁת אֶת הַנְשָׁמָה
עִם הַלְבָנָה

brucha at shekhinah
she'astah isha
m'chadeshet et haneshama
im halevana

You who renew the women
as you renew the moon
please renew the spirit
as you renew the womb

brucha at shekhinah
she'astah isha
m'chadeshet et haneshama
im halevana

You who renew the women
as you renew the moon
please renew the spirit
as we re-attune

Taya Shere, with re-attune lyric crafted with Keshira haLev Fife

NEW MOON CEREMONY

BLESSING THE MOON (KIDDUSH LEVANAH)

The prayer for blessing the moon is recited between the third and fourteenth days of the Hebrew month, at night, outside, when one can see the moon.

haleluyah	הַלְלוּיָהּ
halelu et havayah min hashamayim	הַלְלוּ אֶת יְהוָה מִן הַשָּׁמַיִם
haleluha bameromim	הַלְלוּהָ בַּמְּרוֹמִים
haleluha kol melacheha	הַלְלוּהָ כָל מַלְאָכֶהָ
haleluha kol tz'va'eha	הַלְלוּהָ כָל צְבָאֶיהָ
haleluha shemesh veyareiach	הַלְלוּהָ שֶׁמֶשׁ וְיָרֵחַ
haleluha kol kochvei or	הַלְלוּהָ כָל כּוֹכְבֵי אוֹר
haleluha shmei hashamayim	הַלְלוּהָ שְׁמֵי הַשָּׁמָיִם
vehamayim asher me'al hashamayim	וְהַמַּיִם אֲשֶׁר מֵעַל הַשָּׁמָיִם
yehalelu et shem havayah	יְהַלְלוּ אֶת שֵׁם יְהוָה
ki hi tzivtah venivra'u	כִּי הִיא צִוְּתָה וְנִבְרָאוּ
vetaamideim la'ad le'olam	וַיַּעֲמִידֵם לָעַד לְעוֹלָם
chok natnah velo yaavor	חָק נָתְנָה וְלֹא יַעֲבוֹר

Praise Shekhinah from the skies!
Praise Her, o heights! Praise Her, Her messengers!
Praise Her, her hosts! Praise Her, moon and sun! Praise her, stars of light!
Praise Her, heights of the heavens and water that is above the heavens!
Praise the name of the Mother, for She spoke and All became,
and the All will be forever, guided by Her laws.

Psalm 148

בְּרוּכָה אַתְּ שְׁכִינָה אֱלֹתֵינוּ רוּחַ הָעוֹלָם אֲשֶׁר בְּמַאֲמָרָהּ בָּרְאָה שְׁחָקִים וּבְרוּחַ פִּיהָ כָּל צְבָאָם חֹק וּזְמַן נָתְנָה לָהֶם שֶׁלֹּא יְשַׁנּוּ אֶת תַּפְקִידָם שָׂשִׂים וּשְׂמֵחִים לַעֲשׂוֹת רְצוֹן קוֹנָתָם פּוֹעֶלֶת אֱמֶת שֶׁפְּעֻלָּתָהּ אֱמֶת וְלַלְּבָנָה אָמְרָה שֶׁתִּתְחַדֵּשׁ עֲטֶרֶת תִּפְאֶרֶת לַעֲמוּסֵי בָטֶן שֶׁהֵם עֲתִידִים לְהִתְחַדֵּשׁ כְּמוֹתָהּ וּלְפָאֵר לְיוֹצְרָתָם עַל שֵׁם כְּבוֹד מַלְכוּתָהּ. בְּרוּכָה אַתְּ שְׁכִינָה מְחַדֶּשֶׁת הַחֳדָשִׁים

beruchah at shekhinah eloteinu ruach ha'olam asher bema'amarah barah shechakim uveruach piha kol tzeva'am chok uzman natnah lahem shelo yishanu et tafkidam sasim usmeichim la'asot retzon konatam poelet emet shepe'ulatah emet ulalevanh amrah she titchadesh ateret tiferet la'amusei vaten sheheim atidim lehitchadesh kamotah ulefa'er leyotzratam al shem kevod malchutah. beruchah at shekhinah mechadeshet hachadashim.

Blessed are You, Weaver of the universe, whose loom laid out the heavens and whose breath made the heavenly hosts, who gave them orbits that they will not change. Joyful and happy are they to do the will of their Creator, a worker of truth whose work is truth! To the moon God said; renew yourself, crown of glory for those borne in the womb, for the,y like you, are destined to renew themselves, and to give glory to their creator for the sake of God's being. Blessed are You, God, renewer of months.

EACH OF THE FOLLOWING LINES IS SAID THREE TIMES TO THE MOON
WHILE JUMPING TOWARD HER

בְּרוּכָה עוֹשָׂתֵךְ בָּרוּךְ יוֹצְרֵךְ
בָּרוּךְ בּוֹרְאֵךְ בְּרוּכָה קוֹנָתֵךְ

beruchah osateikh barukh yotzreikh
barukh boreikh beruchah konateikh

Blessed be your Maker, blessed be your Former
blessed be your Creator, blessed be your Artist.

IF DESIRED ADD

דָּוִד מֶלֶךְ יִשְׂרָאֵל חַי וְקַיָּם

david melekh yisrael chai v'kayam*

David King of Yisrael lives

EXCHANGE GREETINGS WITH THREE PEOPLE

שָׁלוֹם עֲלֵיכֶם/עֲלֵיכֶן

shalom aleikhem/aleichen

Peace to you

עֲלֵיכֶם/עֲלֵיכֶן שָׁלוֹם

aleikhem/aleichen shalom

To you peace

סִמָּן טוֹב וּמַזָּל טוֹב יְהֵא לָנוּ וּדְכָל יִשְׂרָאֵל אָמֵן

siman tov umazel tov y'hei lanu ul'khol yisra'el

A good sign and a good star for us and for all Israel

* In the kabbalah, King David is considered an embodiment of MALKHUT, Shekhinah.

TABLE BLESSINGS

BLESSING THE CHILDREN

תְּשִׂימֵךְ שְׁכִינָה כְּשָׂרָה רִבְקָה רָחֵל וְלֵאָה

tesimeich shekhinah k'sarah rivkah rachel veleah

May you be like Sarah, Rebekah, Rachel, and Leah

תְּבָרְכֵךְ שַׁדַּי וְתִשְׁמְרֵךְ
תָּאֵר שַׁדַּי פָּנֶיהָ אֵלַיִךְ וִתְחֻנֵּךְ
תִּשָּׂא שַׁדַּי פָּנֶיהָ אֵלַיִךְ וְתָשֵׂם לָךְ שָׁלוֹם

tevarcheich shadai vetishmereich
ta'er shadai paneha elayich vit'chuneich
tisa shadai paneha elayich vetasem lach shalom

May the One of Being bless you and keep you.
May the One Who Is shine the Divine faces on you and show you grace.
May the Who Is Becoming lift up the Divine faces to you,
and grant you wholeness and peace.

יְשִׂמְךָ אֱלֹהִים כְּאֶפְרַיִם וְכִמְנַשֶּׁה

yesimcha elohim k'ephraim vechimenashe

May God make you like Ephraim and Manasseh

יְבָרֶכְךָ יהוה וְיִשְׁמְרֶךָ
יָאֵר יהוה פָּנָיו אֵלֶיךָ וִיחֻנֶּךָּ
יִשָּׂא יהוה פָּנָיו אֵלֶיךָ וְיָשֵׂם לְךָ שָׁלוֹם

yevarechecha adonai veyishmerecha
ya'er adonai panav elecha viychuneka
yisa adonai panav eilecha veyasem lecha shalom

May the One of Being bless you and keep you.
May the One Who Is shine the Divine faces on you and show you grace.
May the Who Is Becoming lift up the Divine faces to you,
and grant you wholeness and peace.

RAISE YOUR HANDS/AL NETILAT YADAYIM

Oh, Raise your hands (Oh, Raise your hands) x2

Raise your hands in holiness

Oh, Raise your hands (Oh, Raise your hands) x2

Raise your hands and we'll be blessed.

Oh, Raise your hands (Oh, Raise your hands) x2

Raise your hand in holiness

Oh, Raise your hands (Oh, Raise your hands) x2

al netilat yadayim

amen

Geela Rayzel Raphael

PRIESTESS BLESSING

tivarechna b'ahava
tivarechna b'shalom
tivareychna maasaeh yadaiyich
tivarchna m'hashamayim v'tahom

We honor the work of your hands
Bless you with love and with peace
Praise the vision you bring to your task
Blessings from the heavens and the deep
Join with our voices and our hearts

Geela Rayzel Raphael

EISHET CHAYIL (A WOMAN OF VALOR)

This ancient poem from the end of the book of Proverbs, "A Woman of Valor," describes an active, wise, engaged woman who runs a family, spinning, farming, teaching and doing good deeds. While many feminists have read the poem "A Woman of Valor" as a narrow view of women, it is quite expansive for its time, imagining woman as grower of food, maker of necessities, teacher of wisdom, mother and wife, but also merchant and heroine: the word chayil, valor, can mean strength or might.

Traditionally, the poem is sung to the woman of the household on Friday night. The kabbalists imagined it as a song to Shekhinah herself, who teaches a Torah of lovingkindness and who watches over the world as if it is Her household (Raphael Patai, The Hebrew Goddess, p. 22). "Give Her of the works of Her hands" is a reminder to all gathered at the Shabbat table to honor Shekhinah through their blessings over wine and bread.

The Book of Proverbs speaks of the Divine feminine in a variety of ways, using the imagery of the Goddess Asherah as well as the language of the biblical God to create new ways to see deity. The words of Eishet Chayil may be drawn from words spoken about ancient goddesses who are spinners and dispensers of wisdom. We can imagine that the verses of Eishet Chayil address woman and Goddess as one being, a multifaceted life-force, a divine (human partnership to whom we offer praise and gratitude.

"Strength and glory are her clothing, and She laughs on the last day." The Goddess is indeed clothed in strength and glory. For Her, the last day always turns into the first, for She embodies the cycle of rebirth. All forms and beings are clothed in strength and glory, for our bodies are part of Hers, and we too can laugh on the last day, as She transforms us again and again into something new.

EISHET CHAYIL CHANT

אֵשֶׁת חַיִל מִי יִמְצָא וְרָחֹק מִפְּנִינִים מִכְרָהּ

eishet chayil mi yimtza vrachok mipninim michrah

Oracle, Oracle

טָעֲמָה כִּי טוֹב סַחְרָהּ לֹא יִכְבֶּה בַלַּיְלָה נֵרָהּ

ta'amah ki tov (ki tov) sachrah lo yichbeh balailah nerah

Healer, Healer

פִּיהָ פָּתְחָה בְחָכְמָה וְתוֹרַת חֶסֶד עַל לְשׁוֹנָהּ

piha patchah vchochma vtorat chesed al lshonah

Wisdom, Wisdom

תְּנוּ לָהּ מִפְּרִי יָדֶיהָ וִיהַלְלוּהָ בַשְּׁעָרִים מַעֲשֶׂיהָ

tnu lah mipri (mip'ri) yadeiha vihalluha vasharim maaseha

Creatrix, Creatrix

Taya Shere

EISHET CHAYIL (PROVERBS 31:10-31)

אֵשֶׁת חַיִל מִי יִמְצָא וְרָחֹק מִפְּנִינִים מִכְרָהּ	eishet chayil mi yimtza verachok mipninim michra
בָּטַח בָּהּ לֵב בַּעְלָהּ וְשָׁלָל לֹא יֶחְסָר	batach ba lev baalah veshalal lo yechsar
גְּמָלַתְהוּ טוֹב וְלֹא רָע כֹּל יְמֵי חַיֶּיהָ	gmalathu tov velo ra kol yemei chayeha
דָּרְשָׁה צֶמֶר וּפִשְׁתִּים וַתַּעַשׂ בְּחֵפֶץ כַּפֶּיהָ	darsha tzemer ufishtim vata'as bechefetz kapeha
הָיְתָה כָּאֳנִיּוֹת סוֹחֵר מִמֶּרְחָק תָּבִיא לַחְמָהּ	hayta ka'aniyot socher mimerchak tavi lachmah
וַתָּקָם בְּעוֹד לַיְלָה וַתִּתֵּן	vatakem be'od laylah vatiten
טֶרֶף לְבֵיתָהּ וְחֹק לְנַעֲרֹתֶיהָ	teref levayta vechok lena'aroteha
זָמְמָה שָׂדֶה וַתִּקָּחֵהוּ	zamemah sadeh vatikacheyhu
מִפְּרִי כַפֶּיהָ נָטְעָה כָּרֶם	mepree chapeha nata karem
חָגְרָה בְעוֹז מָתְנֶיהָ וַתְּאַמֵּץ זְרוֹעֹתֶיהָ	chagrah b'oz matneha vatametz zro'oteha
טָעֲמָה כִּי טוֹב סַחְרָהּ	ta'amah kee tov sachra
לֹא יִכְבֶּה בַלַּיְלָה נֵרָהּ	lo yichbeh balayla neyra
יָדֶיהָ שִׁלְּחָה בַכִּישׁוֹר וְכַפֶּיהָ תָּמְכוּ פָלֶךְ	yadeha shilchah bekishor vechapeha tamchu falech
כַּפָּהּ פָּרְשָׂה לֶעָנִי וְיָדֶיהָ שִׁלְּחָה לָאֶבְיוֹן	kapah parsa le'ani veyadeha shilcha le'evyon
לֹא תִירָא לְבֵיתָהּ מִשָּׁלֶג	lo tira levayta meshaleg
כִּי כָל בֵּיתָהּ לָבֻשׁ שָׁנִים	kee chol vayta lavush shanim
מַרְבַדִּים עָשְׂתָה לָּהּ שֵׁשׁ וְאַרְגָּמָן לְבוּשָׁהּ	marvadim asta la shesh ve'argaman levusha
נוֹדָע בַּשְּׁעָרִים בַּעְלָהּ	noda bashearim balah
בְּשִׁבְתּוֹ עִם זִקְנֵי אָרֶץ	beshivto im ziknei aretz
סָדִין עָשְׂתָה וַתִּמְכֹּר וַחֲגוֹר נָתְנָה לַכְּנַעֲנִי	sadin as'ta vatimkor vachagor natna laknani
עֹז וְהָדָר לְבוּשָׁהּ וַתִּשְׂחַק לְיוֹם אַחֲרוֹן	oz vehadar levushah vatischak leyom acharon
פִּיהָ פָּתְחָה בְחָכְמָה	piha patchah bechachmah
וְתוֹרַת חֶסֶד עַל לְשׁוֹנָהּ	vetorat chesed al leshonah
צוֹפִיָּה הֲלִיכוֹת בֵּיתָהּ	tzofiya halichot beitah
וְלֶחֶם עַצְלוּת לֹא תֹאכֵל	velechem atzlut lo tocheil
קָמוּ בָנֶיהָ וַיְאַשְּׁרוּהָ בַּעְלָהּ וַיְהַלְלָהּ	kamu vaneha vayashruha ba'alah vayehalelah
רַבּוֹת בָּנוֹת עָשׂוּ חָיִל וְאַתְּ עָלִית עַל כֻּלָּנָה	rabot banot asu chayil v'at alit al kulana
שֶׁקֶר הַחֵן וְהֶבֶל הַיֹּפִי	sheker hachen vehevel hayofi
אִשָּׁה יִרְאַת יְהוָה הִיא תִתְהַלָּל	isha yirat havayah hi tit'halal
תְּנוּ לָהּ מִפְּרִי יָדֶיהָ וִיהַלְלוּהָ	t'nu la mipri yadeha vayehaleluha
בַשְּׁעָרִים מַעֲשֶׂיהָ	bashe'arim ma'aseha

Who can find a courageous woman? Her worth is far above rubies.
She girds herself with strength, and performs her tasks with vigor.
She is like a great ship, bringing nourishment from afar.
Her reward is goodness; her light does not go out at night.
Her fingers work the spindle that turns the world; her hands whirl the distaff.
She gives generously to the poor, and her hands are stretched out to the needy.
No one in Her household fears the cold, for all wear Her bright colors.
Strength and glory are her clothing, and she laughs at the time to come.
She opens her mouth with wisdom and the Torah of kindness is on her tongue.
She watches over the ways of her house and does not eat the bread of idleness.
Give her of the works of her hands, and let her deeds praise her in the gates.

BLESSINGS FOR COMPANIONS

וַתֹּאמֶר רוּת אַל תִּפְגְּעִי בִי לְעָזְבֵךְ לָשׁוּב מֵאַחֲרָיִךְ כִּי אֶל אֲשֶׁר תֵּלְכִי אֵלֵךְ וּבַאֲשֶׁר תָּלִינִי אָלִין עַמֵּךְ עַמִּי וֵאלֹהַיִךְ אֱלֹהָי: וַתֵּלַכְנָה שְׁתֵּיהֶם...

vatomer rut al tifgi be le'azveich lashuv me'acharayich ki el asher telchi elech uva'asher talini alin amech ami velohayich elohai. vetelachnah shteihem.

Ruth said: Do not ask me to leave you or return from following after you, for where you go, I will go, and where you lodge, I will lodge. Your people shall be my people, and your God my God. And the two went on together.
Ruth 1:16, 19

וְנֶפֶשׁ יְהוֹנָתָן נִקְשְׁרָה בְּנֶפֶשׁ דָּוִד וַיֶּאֱהָבֵהוּ יְהוֹנָתָן כְּנַפְשׁוֹ: וְהַדָּבָר אֲשֶׁר דִּבַּרְנוּ אֲנִי וָאָתָּה הִנֵּה יהוה בֵּינִי וּבֵינְךָ עַד עוֹלָם: נִשְׁבַּעְנוּ שְׁנֵינוּ אֲנַחְנוּ בְּשֵׁם יהוה לֵאמֹר יהוה יִהְיֶה בֵּינִי וּבֵינֶךָ:

venefesh yehonatan niksherah benefesh david vaye'ehaveihu yehonatan kenafsho. vehadavar asher dibarnu ani ve'ata hineh havayah beini uveincha ad olam. nishbanu shneinu anachnu beshem havayah leimor: havaya yohiyeh beini uveincha.

Jonathan's soul became bound up with the soul of David, and Jonathan loved David as himself.... This is the word we have spoken to one another: Behold, the Eternal is between you and me forever. We have both promised in God's name: God will be between me and you.
I Samuel 18:1, 20:23

לֵךְ אֱכֹל בְּשִׂמְחָה לַחְמֶךָ וּשְׁתֵה בְלֶב טוֹב יֵינֶךָ כִּי כְבָר רָצָה הָאֱלֹהִים אֶת מַעֲשֶׂיךָ: בְּכָל עֵת יִהְיוּ בְגָדֶיךָ לְבָנִים וְשֶׁמֶן עַל רֹאשְׁךָ אַל יֶחְסָר: רְאֵה חַיִּים עִם אִשָּׁה אֲשֶׁר אָהַבְתָּ כָּל יְמֵי חַיֵּי הֶבְלֶךָ אֲשֶׁר נָתַן לְךָ תַּחַת הַשֶּׁמֶשׁ כֹּל יְמֵי הֶבְלֶךָ כִּי הוּא חֶלְקְךָ בַּחַיִּים וּבַעֲמָלְךָ אֲשֶׁר אַתָּה עָמֵל תַּחַת הַשָּׁמֶשׁ: כֹּל אֲשֶׁר תִּמְצָא יָדְךָ לַעֲשׂוֹת בְּכֹחֲךָ עֲשֵׂה...

lech echol besimcha lachmecha ushteh velev tov yeinecha ki chvar ratzah ha'elohim maasecha. bechol eit yehi vegadecha levanim veshemen al roshcha al yechsar. re'eh chayim in isha asher ahavta kol yemei chayei hevlecha asher natan lecha tachat hashemesh kol yemei hevlecha ki hu chelkecha bachayim uve'amalcha asher ata amel tachat hashamesh. kol asher timtza yadcha la'asot bekochacha aseh.

Go, eat your bread in gladness, and drink your wine in joy; for God has delighted in your works. Let your clothes be always white, and your head never lack ointment. Enjoy happiness with a woman you love all the days of your fleeting life that have been given to you beneath the sun, all your fleeting days, for that is your portion in life and in the work God has given you beneath the sun. Whatever your hand finds to do, do it with your might.
Ecclesiastes 9:7-10

TABLE BLESSINGS

FRIDAY NIGHT KIDDUSH (SANCTIFICATION OF WINE)

(וַיְהִי עֶרֶב וַיְהִי בֹקֶר) יוֹם הַשִּׁשִּׁי: וַיְכֻלּוּ הַשָּׁמַיִם וְהָאָרֶץ וְכָל צְבָאָם וַיְכַל אֱלֹהִים בַּיּוֹם הַשְּׁבִיעִי מְלַאכְתָּה אֲשֶׁר עָשָׂתָה וַתִּשְׁבֹּת בַּיּוֹם הַשְּׁבִיעִי מִכָּל מְלַאכְתָּה אֲשֶׁר עָשָׂתָה וַתְּבָרֶךְ אֱלֹהִים אֶת יוֹם הַשְּׁבִיעִי וַתְּקַדֵּשׁ אֹתוֹ כִּי בוֹ שָׁבְתָה מִכָּל מְלַאכְתָּה אֲשֶׁר בָּרְאָה אֱלֹהִים לַעֲשׂוֹת:

בְּרוּכָה אַתְּ שְׁכִינָה אֱלֹהֵינוּ רוּחַ הָעוֹלָם בּוֹרֵאת פְּרִי הַגָּפֶן.
בְּרוּכָה אַתְּ שְׁכִינָה אֱלֹהֵינוּ רוּחַ הָעוֹלָם אֲשֶׁר קִדְּשָׁתְנוּ בְּמִצְוֹתֶיהָ וְרָצְתָה בָּנוּ וְשַׁבַּת קָדְשָׁהּ בְּאַהֲבָה וּבְרָצוֹן הִנְחִילָתְנוּ זִכָּרוֹן לְמַעֲשֵׂה בְרֵאשִׁית (כִּי הוּא יוֹם) תְּחִלָּה לְמִקְרָאֵי־קֹדֶשׁ זֵכֶר לִיצִיאַת מִצְרָיִם. (כִּי בָנוּ בָחַרְתְּ וְאוֹתָנוּ קִדַּשְׁתְּ עִם כָּל הָעַמִּים) וְשַׁבַּת קָדְשֵׁךְ בְּאַהֲבָה וּבְרָצוֹן הִנְחִילָתְנוּ.
בְּרוּכָה אַתְּ שְׁכִינָה מְקַדֶּשֶׁת הַשַּׁבָּת.

(vayehi erev vayehi voker) yom hashishi. vatechulu hashamayim veha'aretz vechol tzeva'am vatekhal elohim bayom hashevi'i melakhtah asher astah vatishbot bayom hashev'i mikol melakhtah asher astah. vativarekh elohim et yom hashevi'i vatikadesh oto ki vo shavtah mikol melakhtah asher bar'ah elohim la'asot.

beruchah at shekhinah eloheinu ruach ha'olam boreit peri hagafen. beruchah at shekhinah, eloheinu ruach ha'olam, asher kidshatnu bemitzvoteha veratztah vanu, veshabbat kodsha, be'ahavah uveratzon hinchilatnu, zikaron lemaasei vereishit, (ki hu yom) techila lemikra'ei kodesh, zecher litziat mitzrayim. (ki vanu vachart, ve'otanu kidasht, (im kol ha'amim,) veshabbat kodshech be'ahavah u'veratzon hinchilatnu. beruchah at shekhinah mekadeshet hashabbat.

And there was evening and there was morning, the sixth day. heaven, earth, and all their hosts were finished. God completed on the seventh day all the work that had been done, and ceased upon the seventh day from all the work that had been done. God blessed the seventh day and made it holy, for on it God ceased from all the work that God had created to do.

Genesis 1:31-2:3

Blessed are You, Infinite Presence filling and surrounding the world, who creates the fruit of the vine. Blessed are You, Divine One who guides creation, who has made us holy with your commandments, and taken pleasure in us and the holy Shabbat, and granted it to us with love and favor as a remembrance of the work of creation. (For it is the) first of all the proclaimed holy days, a reminder of the exodus from Egypt. (For you have chosen us from (among all peoples) and give us to keep, in love and favor, your holy Shabbat.

Blessed are You, Source of Life, who makes Shabbat holy.

Some have the custom to the words in parentheses in accordance with a Kabbalistic custom that reduces this paragraph to 35 words, in parity with the 35 words of VaYechulu. This makes the resultant blessing 70 words in total, signifying the completeness of the Seventh Day.

SATURDAY MORNING KIDDUSH (SANCTIFICATION OF WINE)

וְשָׁמְרוּ בָתֵי יִשְׂרָאֵל אֶת הַשַּׁבָּת לַעֲשׂוֹת אֶת הַשַּׁבָּת לְדֹרֹתָם בְּרִית עוֹלָם: בֵּינִי וּבֵין בְּנֵי יִשְׂרָאֵל אוֹת הוּא לְעֹלָם כִּי שֵׁשֶׁת יָמִים עָשְׂתָה יהוה אֶת הַשָּׁמַיִם וְאֶת הָאָרֶץ וּבַיּוֹם הַשְּׁבִיעִי שָׁבְתָה וַתִּנָּפַשׁ:

זִכְרִי אֶת יוֹם הַשַּׁבָּת לְקַדְּשׁוֹ: שֵׁשֶׁת יָמִים תַּעַבְדִי וְעָשִׂית כָּל מְלַאכְתֵּךְ וְיוֹם הַשְּׁבִיעִי שַׁבָּת לַיהוה אֱלֹהָיִךְ לֹא תַעֲשִׂי כָל מְלָאכָה אַתְּ וּבְנֵךְ וּבִתֵּךְ עַבְדֵּךְ וַאֲמָתֵךְ וּבְהֶמְתֵּךְ וְגֵרֵךְ אֲשֶׁר בִּשְׁעָרָיִךְ: כִּי שֵׁשֶׁת יָמִים עָשְׂתָה יהוה אֶת הַשָּׁמַיִם וְאֶת הָאָרֶץ אֶת הַיָּם וְאֶת כָּל אֲשֶׁר בָּם וַתָּנַח בַּיּוֹם הַשְּׁבִיעִי עַל כֵּן בֵּרְכָה יהוה אֶת יוֹם הַשַּׁבָּת וַתְּקַדְּשֵׁהוּ:

בְּרוּכָה אַתְּ שְׁכִינָה אֱלֹהֵינוּ רוּחַ הָעוֹלָם בּוֹרֵאת פְּרִי הַגָּפֶן.

veshamru batei yisrael et hashabbat la'asot et hashabbat ledorotam berit olam, beini u'vein benei yisrael ot hi le'olam ki sheishet yamim asta adonai et hashamayim ve'et ha'aretz uvayom hashevi'i shavtah vatinafash.

zichri et yom hashabbat lekodsho sheishet yamim taavdi ve'asit kol melachtech uvayom hashevi'i shabbat la'adonai elohayich lo ta'asi kol melachah at uvanech uvitech avadech amatech uvehemtech vegerech asher besha'arayich ki sheshet yamim asta adonai et hashamayim ve'et ha'aretz et hayam ve'et kol asher bam vatanach bayom hashevi'i. al kein berchah adonai et yom hashabbat vatikadsheihu. beruchah at shekhinah boreit peri ha'gafen.

The Jewish people shall keep Shabbat, to make Shabbat throughout the generations as a covenant for always. It is a sign forever between Spirit and the people, that in six cycles Spirit created sky and earth, and on the seventh day, the day of completion, Spirit rested.

after Exodus 31:16-17

Remember the Sabbath to keep it holy. Six days shall you work and do all your labor, and on the seventh day is a Sabbath to the Eternal your God. You shall not do any labor, not you or your son or your daughter or your male or female worker or the animals that live with you or the stranger within your gates, for in six days the Eternal made heaven and earth, the sea and all within it, and on the seventh day the Divine rested. Therefore the Eternal blessed the seventh day and made it holy.

Exodus 20:8-11

Blessed are You, Infinite Presence, who creates the fruit of the vine.

TABLE BLESSINGS 226

FESTIVAL EVENING KIDDUSH (SANCTIFICATION OF WINE)

IF IT IS ALSO SHABBAT, INSERT THE FIRST PARAGRAPH OF SHABBAT KIDDUSH ON THE PREVIOUS PAGE, AND ALL WORDS IN PARENTHESIS BELOW

בְּרוּכָה אַתְּ שְׁכִינָה אֱלֹהֵינוּ רוּחַ הָעוֹלָם בּוֹרֵאת פְּרִי הַגָּפֶן. בְּרוּכָה אַתְּ שְׁכִינָה אֱלֹהֵינוּ רוּחַ הָעוֹלָם אֲשֶׁר בָּחֲרָה בָּנוּ עִם כָּל עָם וְרוֹמַמְתָנוּ עִם כָּל לָשׁוֹן וְקִדְּשָׁתָנוּ בְּמִצְוֹתֶיהָ וַתִּתְּנִי לָנוּ שְׁכִינָה אֱלֹתֵינוּ בְּאַהֲבָה (שַׁבָּתוֹת לִמְנוּחָה) מוֹעֲדִים לְשִׂמְחָה חַגִּים וּזְמַנִים לְשָׂשׂוֹן אֶת יוֹם (הַשַׁבָּת הַזֶּה וְאֶת יוֹם)

לִשְׁמִינִי עֲצֶרֶת וְשִׂ״ת	לְסֻכּוֹת	לְשָׁבוּעוֹת	לְפֶסַח
שְׁמִינִי חַג הָעֲצֶרֶת הַזֶּה. זְמַן שִׂמְחָתֵנוּ זְמַן צֵאת הַשָּׁנָה	חַג הַסֻּכּוֹת הַזֶּה. זְמַן שִׂמְחָתֵנוּ זְמַן אֲסִיפֵנוּ	חַג הַשָּׁבוּעוֹת הַזֶּה. זְמַן מַתַּן תּוֹרָתֵנוּ זְמַן בִּכּוֹרֵנוּ	חַג הַמַּצּוֹת הַזֶּה. זְמַן חֵרוּתֵנוּ זְמַן קְצִירָתֵנוּ

(בְּאַהֲבָה) מִקְרָא קֹדֶשׁ זֵכֶר לִיצִיאַת מִצְרָיִם. כִּי בָנוּ בָחַרְתְּ וְאוֹתָנוּ קִדַּשְׁתְּ עִם כָּל הָעַמִּים וּמוֹעֲדֵי קָדְשֵׁךְ בְּאַהֲבָה וּבְרָצוֹן הִנְחַלְתָּנוּ. בְּרוּכָה אַתְּ שְׁכִינָה מְקַדֶּשֶׁת יִשְׂרָאֵל וְהַזְּמַנִים.

beruchah at shekhinah eloteinu ruach ha'olam boreit peri hagafen.
beruchah at shekhinah eloteinu ruach ha'olam asher bachrah banu im kol ha'amim veromematnu im kol lashon vekidshatnu bemitzvoteha vetitni lanu shekhinah eloteinu be'ahavah (shabbatot limenuchah) moadim elsimcha chagim uzmanim lesasson et yom (hasabbat hazeh ve'et yom):

ON PASSOVER	chag hamatzot hazeh,	zman cheruteinu,	zman ketzirateinu
ON SHAVUOT	chag hashavuot hazeh,	zman matan torateinu,	zman bikkureinu
ON SUKKOT	chag hasukkot hazeh,	zman simchateinu,	zman asifeinu

ON SHMINI ATZERET
AND SIMCHAT TORAH shemini chag ha'atzeret hazeh, zman simchateinu, zman tzeit hashanah (be'ahavah) mikra kodesh zecher letziat mitzrayim. ki vanu vachart ve'otanu kidasht im kol ha'amim umo'adei kodsheich be'ahavah uveratzon hinchilatnu. beruchah at shekhinah mekadeshet yisrael vehazmanim.

Blessed are You, Infinite Presence filling and surrounding the world, who creates the fruit of the vine. Blessed are You, Infinite Presence filling and surrounding the world, who has chosen us from (with other nations, and exalted us from (with all languages, and made us holy with commandments. Divine Presence, our divinity, you have given us in love (Sabbaths for rest) seasons for joy, festivals and times for gladness, this day of:

| this Passover, season of our freedom, season of spring renewal; | this Shavuot, season of the giving of the Torah, season of first fruits; | this Sukkot, season of our joy, season of full harvest; | this Shemini Atzeret/ Simchat Torah, season of our joy, season of autumn rain; |

[In love] a sacred occasion, in remembrance of the exodus from Egypt. You have gifted us in holiness, along with with other people's, with sacred times in love and favor as an inheritance. Blessed are You, Infinite Presence, who makes the community and time holy.

FESTIVAL MORNING KIDDUSH (SANCTIFICATION OF WINE)

וַתִּקַח מִרְיָם הַנְבִיאָה אֲחוֹת אַהֲרֹן אֶת הַתֹּף בְּיָדָהּ
וַתֵּצֶאןָ כָל הַנָּשִׁים אַחֲרֶיהָ בְּתֻפִּים וּבִמְחֹלֹת

vaytikach miriyam haniviah achot aharon et ha'tof be'yadah
vateytzenah khol ha'nashim achareha be'tupim u'vim'cholot

Then Miriam took a timbrel in her hand,
and all the women went after her with timbrels and with dances. *Exodus 15:20*

וַיְדַבֵּר מֹשֶׁה אֶת מוֹעֲדֵי יהוה אֶל בְּנֵי יִשְׂרָאֵל

vay'daber moshe et mo'adei adonai el b'nei yisrael.

Then Moses declared the seasons of God to the people Israel. *Leviticus 23:44*

בְּרוּכָה אַתְּ שְׁכִינָה □	beruchah at shekhinah
אֱלֹהֵינוּ רוּחַ הָעוֹלָם	eloteinu ruach ha'olam
בּוֹרֵאת פְּרִי הַגֶּפֶן	boreit pri ha'gafen
בָּרוּךְ אַתָּה יהוה △	baruch ata adonai
אֱלֹהֵינוּ מֶלֶךְ הָעוֹלָם	eloheinu melekh ha'olam
בּוֹרֵא פְּרִי הַגֶּפֶן	borei pri ha'gafen
בְּרוּכֶה אַתֶּה הֲוָיָה ⊖	berucheh ateh havayah
אֱלֹהֵינוּ חֵי הָעוֹלָמִים	eloheinu chei ha'olamim
בּוֹרְאַת פְּרִי הַגֶּפֶן	bor'at pri ha'gafen

Blessed are You, Infinite Presence filling and surrounding the
world, who creates the fruit of the vine.

TABLE BLESSINGS 228

WASHING THE HANDS (NETILAT YADAYIM)

In Jewish tradition, hands are washed before a meal in remembrance of the custom priests had of washing hands before entering the Divine Presence in the Temple. It is the custom to remain silent between handwashing and the blessing over bread.

בְּרוּכָה אַתְּ שְׁכִינָה
אֱלֹהֵינוּ רוּחַ הָעוֹלָם
אֲשֶׁר קִדְּשַׁתְנוּ בְּמִצְוֹתֶיהָ
וְצִוְּתָנוּ עַל נְטִילַת יָדָיִם.

☐ beruchah at shekhinah
eloteinu ruach ha'olam
asher kidshatnu bemitzvoteha
vetzivatnu al netilat yadayim

בָּרוּךְ אַתָּה יהוה
אֱלֹהֵינוּ מֶלֶךְ הָעוֹלָם
אֲשֶׁר קִדְּשָׁנוּ בְּמִצְוֹתָיו
וְצִוָּנוּ עַל נְטִילַת יָדָיִם.

△ baruch ata adonai
eloheinu melekh ha'olam
asher kidshanu bemitzvotav
vetzivanu al netilat yadayim

בְּרוּכֶה אַתָּה יָהּ
אֱלֹהֵינוּ רוּחַ הָעוֹלָם
אֲשֶׁר קִדְּשֵׁנוּ בְּמִצְוֹתֶה וְצִוֵּנוּ
וְצִוֵּנוּ עַל נְטִילַת יָדָיִם.

⊖ berucheh ate yah
eloheinu ruach ha'olam
asher kidshenu bemitzvoteh
vetzivenu al netilat yadayim

Blessed are You, Source of Life, who makes us holy with your sacred acts, and commanded us concerning the washing of hands.

BLESSING OVER BREAD (HAMOTZI/YAH/YEH)

בְּרוּכָה אַתְּ שְׁכִינָה
אֱלֹהֵינוּ רוּחַ הָעוֹלָם
הַמּוֹצִיאָה לֶחֶם מִן הָאָרֶץ.

☐ beruchah at shekhinah
eloteinu ruach ha'olam
hamotziyah lechem min ha'aretz

בָּרוּךְ אַתָּה יהוה
אֱלֹהֵינוּ מֶלֶךְ הָעוֹלָם
הַמּוֹצִיא לֶחֶם מִן הָאָרֶץ.

△ baruch ata adonai
eloheinu melekh ha'olam
hamotzi lechem min ha'aretz

בְּרוּכֶה אַתָּה יָהּ
אֱלֹהֵינוּ רוּחַ הָעוֹלָם
הַמּוֹצִיאֶה לֶחֶם מִן הָאָרֶץ.

⊖ berucheh ate yah
eloheinu ruach ha'olam
hamotziyeh lechem min ha'aretz

Blessed are You, Infinite Presence surrounding and filling the world, who brings forth bread from the earth.

GRACE AFTER MEALS

BRICH RACHAMANA

בְּרִיךְ רַחֲמָנָא מַלְכָּא דְעָלְמָא
מָרֵיה דְּהַאי פִּיתָא

brich rachamana malka de'alma
marei dehai pita

You are the source of life for all that is
and your blessing flows through me.

Aramaic: Babylonian Talmud; English adaptation: Shefa Gold

GRACE AFTER MEALS

From Her Body, comes our bread
By Her Body, we are fed
From Her Waters, come our wine
By Her Grace and Love Divine

ALY/Ahavah Lilith evershYne

SHE'ACHALNU MISHELAH

שֶׁאָכַלְנוּ מִשֶּׁלָּה וּבְטוּבָהּ חָיִינוּ
בְּרוּכָה אַתְּ שְׁכִינָה הַזָּנָה אֶת הַכֹּל

she'achalnu mishelah uvtuva chayinu
brucha at shekhinah hazana et hakol

We have eaten and we bless
and we revel in Your/Her holiness!

Taya Shere

TZUR MISHELA CHANT

TZUR MISHELA describes God/dess as an ever-flowing fountain of abundance. This traditional Shabbat song (usually rendered in the masculine) lends itself well to an understanding of divinity as the life-force residing in all things. When we imagine God/dess this way, the rebuilt Temple mentioned in the last verse is the sacred earth, for whose healing we pray daily.

צוּר מִשֶּׁלָּה אָכַלְנוּ בָּרְכוּ אֱמוּנַי שָׂבָעְנוּ

tzur mishela achalnu barchu emunai savanu

Oh faithful friends, let us bless our foundation
All we have eaten, the great Mother's creation

הַזָּנָה אֶת עוֹלָמָהּ רוֹעָתֵנוּ אִמֵּנוּ

hazana et olama roateynu imeynu

She nourishes our world, our shepherd and mother
She nourishes our world, She is like none other

בְּשִׁיר וְקוֹל תּוֹדָה נְבָרֵךְ לֵאלֹהֵינוּ
עַל אֶרֶץ חֶמְדָּה טוֹבָה שֶׁהִנְחִילָה לְהוֹרֵינוּ

b'shir v'kol todah n'varech leloheynu
al eretz chemda tova sh'hinchila l'horeynu

With song and thankful voice, we praise God in chorus
What abundant land, She gave us and those before us

מָזוֹן וְצֵדָה הִשְׂבִּיעָה לְנַפְשֵׁנוּ
חַסְדָּהּ גָּבַר עָלֵינוּ

mazon v'tzedah hisb'ia l'nafsheynu
chasda gavar, gavar aleynu

With food and sustenance, our souls are overflowing
Through her love and grace, we are infinitely growing

Taya Shere and Jill Hammer

TZUR MISHELA

tzur mishela achalnu barchu emunai	צוּר מִשֶּׁלָה אָכַלְנוּ בָּרְכוּ אֱמוּנַי
savanu vehotarnu kidvar tzimtzemai*	שָׂבַעְנוּ וְהוֹתַרְנוּ כִּדְבַר צִמְצְמַי
hazana et olama roateynu imeynu	הַזָּנָה אֶת עוֹלָמָהּ רוֹעָתֵנוּ אִמֵּנוּ
achalnu et lachmah, veyeynah shatinu	אָכַלְנוּ אֶת לַחְמָהּ וְיֵינָהּ שָׁתִינוּ
al ken nodeh lishmah unehalelah befinu	עַל כֵּן נוֹדֶה לִשְׁמָהּ וּנְהַלְלָהּ בְּפִינוּ
amarnu ve'aninu ain kedoshah keshaddai	אָמַרְנוּ וְעָנִינוּ אֵין קְדוֹשָׁה כַּירוהה
b'shir v'kol todah n'varech lelohcynu	בְּשִׁיר וְקוֹל תּוֹדָה נְבָרֵךְ לֵאלֹהֵינוּ
al eretz chemda tova sh'hinchila l'horeynu	עַל אֶרֶץ חֶמְדָּה טוֹבָה שֶׁהִנְחִילָה לְהוֹרֵינוּ
mazon vetzeidah hisbi'ah lenafsheinu	מָזוֹן וְצֵדָה הִשְׂבִּיעָה לְנַפְשֵׁנוּ
chasdah gavar aleinu ve'emet tzimtzemai	חַסְדָּהּ גָּבַר עָלֵינוּ וֶאֱמֶת ירוהה
rachami bechasdeich al ameich tzureinu	רַחֲמִי בְחַסְדֵּךְ עַל עַמֵּךְ צוּרֵנוּ
al tzion mishkan kevodeich zevul beit tifarteinu	עַל צִיּוֹן מִשְׁכַּן כְּבוֹדֵךְ זְבוּל בֵּית תִּפְאַרְתֵּנוּ
tzmichat rut amateich tavo vetigaleinu	צְמִיחַת רוּת אֲמָתֵךְ תָּבוֹא וְתִגְאָלֵנוּ
ruach apeinu mashiach tzimtzemai	רוּחַ אַפֵּינוּ מְשִׁיחַ ירוהה
yibaneh hamikdash ir tzion temalei	יִבָּנֶה הַמִּקְדָּשׁ עִיר צִיּוֹן תְּמַלֵּא
vesham nashir shir chadash uvirnana na'alei	וְשָׁם נָשִׁיר שִׁיר חָדָשׁ וּבִרְנָנָה נַעֲלֶה
harechem hamikdash titbarach vetitaleh	הָרֶחֶם הַמִּקְדָּשׁ תִּתְבָּרֵךְ וְתִתְעַלֶּה
al kos yayin malei kevirkat tzimtzemai	עַל כּוֹס יַיִן מָלֵא כְּבִרְכַּת ירוהה

My faithful friends, let us bless the Rock,
for we have eaten what belongs to Her
We have been filled and have left over,
just as the word of God/dess promised.
She nourishes her world, our shepherd and mother.
We have eaten her bread and drunk Her wine.
Then we shall praise her name and fill our mouths
with Her glory, saying; None is holy like Her!
With song and thankful voices, we will bless our God,
for the good land that our ancestors received.
With food and sustenance our souls have been satisfied.
Her lovingkindness and truth enfolds us.

*Tzimtzemai is a God-name we use in the Kohenet community, deriving from a Talmudic tale about a mysterious queen named Tzimtzemai. See page 142 for further commentary.

GRACE AFTER MEALS 232

The Kohenet Hebrew Priestess Institute (2005-2023) had the evolving mission to revive and re-embody Judaism through the gifts of women and non-binary people, and through experiences of the sacred feminine. In that context, we and the many who wove with us facilitated the creation of embodied, earth-based, feminist Jewish ritual inspired by earlier traditions of feminine-centered earth-based spiritual leadership, and trained kohanot—priestesses and priestexxes–in this tradition. The work of the Kohenet Hebrew Priestess Institute gave rise to a movement of people embracing these values and practices and drawing on ancient Israelite sources, Jewish texts and folklore, women's practices, kabbalah and contemporary creativity to transform Jewish life, and now informs many individuals and communities. **kohenet.org**

Rabbi Jill Hammer, Ph.D., is the co-founder of the Kohenet Hebrew Priestess Institute (2005-2023), the Director of Spiritual Education at the Academy for Jewish Religion, and the co-founder of Beit Kohenet, a house of Jewish, mystical, earth-based, feminist seeking. She is the author of *Undertorah: An Earth-Based Kabbalah of Dreaming, Return to the Place: The Magic, Meditation, and Mystery of Sefer Yetzirah, The Hebrew Priestess: Ancient and New Visions of Jewish Women's Spiritual Leadership* (with Taya Shere), *The Jewish Book of Days: A Companion for All Seasons, The Omer Calendar of Biblical Women, Sisters at Sinai: New Tales of Biblical Women,* and *The Book of Earth and Other Mysteries,* and a novel called *The Moonstone Covenant.* She lives in Manhattan with her family. **jillhammer.net | beitkohenet.org**

Taya Mâ Shere is the co-founder of the Kohenet Hebrew Priestess Institute (2005-2023), professor of Organic Multi-Religious Ritual at Starr King School for the Ministry, and co-weaver of Makam Shekhina, a spiritual community of Jewish priestexxes and Sufi dervishes committed to counter-oppressive devotion. Taya Mâ hosts the acclaimed *Jewish Ancestral Healing* podcast and *The Sarah & Hajar Series,* and co-authored *The Hebrew Priestess: Ancient and New Visions of Jewish Women's Spiritual Leadership* (with Jill Hammer). Her five albums of Hebrew Goddess chant have been heralded as "cutting-edge mystic medicine music." Taya Mâ tends and teaches liberatory ritual arts through *From the Deep*, an emergent mystery school of earth, sea and soma. **www.taya.ma | fromthedeep.earth**

Shoshana (Batshemesh) Jedwab is a percussionist, singer-songwriter, worship leader, liturgist, prize-winning educator and the Jewish Life Coordinator at the A.J. Heschel Middle School with more than 34 years of experience bringing sacred Jewish texts to life. Shoshana served as founding faculty member and sacred drummer for the Kohenet Hebrew Priestess Institute where she facilitated powerful primal prayer, vibrant Torah service ritual translations, and taught Jewish sacred foolery, contemporary mystical experience, Jewish spiritual practices, and Jewish history. The original songs of Shoshana's debut album, "I Remember," and her love-and-inclusion anthem, "Where You Go," are now being sung, and danced to, in churches, synagogues, weddings and protest marches around the globe. She was included in Jewish Rock Radio's Jewish Women Who Rock the Worship World. **shoshanajedwab.com**

SIDDUR HAKOHANOT CREDITS

GRAPHIC DESIGN

Shir Meira Feit, Kohenet's levitical magician. **shirmeira.com**

ARTWORK

Yosefa Strouss, Kohenet of blessed memory: Cover Illustration, Netivot p. xi, Waves p. 53, Hamsa p. 191

Nomy Lamm: Magic Tree p. 6, Healing Breath p. 100, Chai Fem p. 122, How Good p. 176

Sarai Shapiro: Elemental Directions p. 12, Nurture/Nature p. 21, Moon Angel p. 32, Grapes p. 81/104, Four Directions p. 110

Tamuz Shiran: Three Mothers Papercut p. 188

Bekah Starr: Shrinekeeper Hamsa p. 152, Maiden Hamsa p. 157, Seeker Hamsa p. 164

POETRY AND TEXT

All work in this siddur is copyright by the individual liturgist, poet, musician, or artist. Most attributions appear in the body of the siddur. Texts not otherwise attributed, if not traditional prayerbook texts, are © Rabbi Jill Hammer, 2007. All unattributed Shabbat table material first appeared in *Birkon Tel Shemesh*, © Jill Hammer 2004.

The poem on p. 4 by Jill Hammer has appeared as "The Unfolding One" in *Stepping into Ourselves: An Anthology of Writings about Priestesses* (eds. Anne Key and Candace Kant, Goddess-Ink, 2014), and in *The Book of Earth and Other Mysteries* (Jill Hammer, Dimus Parrhesia Press, 2016).

"Revelation" and "Singing," by Joy Ladin both appear in her book *Shekhinah Speaks* (Selva Oscura, 2022).

"Grace" and "We Live in the Smallest House," by Nina Pick both appear in her book *A Luz* (Dancing Girl Press, 2015).

"Tehomot Rolls," "What is in the Goddess's Tefillin?, "Blessing for Diversity", "Prayer for Sight", untitled poem in shaded bar on p. 145, "Labyrinth", "Elemental Amidah", "Crossroads" all by Jill Hammer, appear in similar forms in *The Book of Earth and Other Mysteries*.

Excerpt from *The Volcano Sequence* by Alicia Ostriker (University of Pittsburgh Press, 2002).

"A Prayer to the Shekhinah" was first published in Alicia Ostriker's book *The Nakedness of the Fathers: Biblical Visions and Revisions* (Rutgers University Press, 1994), p. 253-254.

SONG INDEX

Meditation
  for Tzitzit 139
  on the Tallit 102
  Shabbat Meditation 59
Mehulelet 118
Mi Chamocha 45, 148
Mimainei/Barchu 132
Min hametzar karati yah 209
Miriam ha-neviah 211
Mizmor Shir leYom HaShabbat 30
M'kimi me'afar dal 207
Modah/eh/et Ani 96
Morning Blessings 107
Mourner's Kaddish 91

N

Nechoshet bemarot 133
Netilat Yadayim 228
Nishmat kol chai 127

O

Openings 99
Or Zarua 20
Osah Shalom 63
Ozi ve'zimrat yah 208, 210

P

Peace Be To You 9
Peace Be With You 9
Peace To You Angels 9
Praise Elah 126
Prayer before the Amidah 55, 153
Prayer for Oneness 38, 140
Prayer for Sight 134
Prayer for Words 118
Prayer of Love 138
Priestess Blessing 219
Priestesses' Kaddish 114
Psalm 29 25
Psalm 33 120
Psalm 96 17
Psalm 97 19
Psalm 148 124
Psalm 150 126
Pure Heart 119
Putting on the Tallit 101

R

Ranenah tzadikot bahavaya 120
Raise Your Hands 219
Reishit chochmah 174

Renew The Women 215
Roiza's Niggun 97
Ruach Assiyah 52

S

Sabbath Poem of the Skies 136
Seals of the Seven Directions 202
Self Gives Thanks 102
Seven Blessings Amidah 166
Seven Breath Meditation 55, 153
Shabbat Amidah 56, 154
Shabbat haMalkah 8
Shalom Alayich 9
Shalom Aleichem 9, 11
Shalom Aleichen 10
Sham'ah vatismach tzion 20
She'achalnu Mishelah 229
She began to contract her womb 119
She Creates 118
She is Free 106
Shehecheyatnu 207
Shekhinah El Shaddai 105
Shekhinah Thank You for Blessing This Day 97
Shemesh tzedakah 183
She Who Makes Peace 63
Shielding Prayers 191
Shimi Yisrael 40
Shirat haParochet 93
Sh'ma 38, 140
Sh'ma u'birkoteha 134
Shnirele Perele 82
Shrine Meditation 164
Siman tov umazel tov 217
Sing to Goddess a new song 16
Sister 75
Song for My Sisters 175
Song of the Archetypes 112
Spirit is Flowing 46, 149
Spirit of the World 52
Spirit practice a song through me 128
Standing Like a Tree 174
Stretching Our Hands 87
Sukkah of Shekhinah 50
Sun and moon and stars 125
Sun Haleluyah 125

T

Tehom 31
Tehomot Rolls 31

Three Mothers 90
Torah Orah 175
Tree of Life Meditation 175
Tzimtzemai Sh'ma 40, 142
Tzur Mishela 231
Tzur Mishela Chant 230

U

Und di voch zal 210

V

Vatikach Miriam 47, 149
Vayehi binsoa ha'aron 177
Vehasheivota 86, 189
Verses of Song 117
Viene para sanarte milesinarte 182

W

Washing the Hands 228
We Are a Spiral 92, 192, 193
We are the earth, wind, water and fire 95, 199
We are the women tending shrine 133
We are writing 47
Weaver's Song 93
Weaving the Circle 95
We have eaten and we bless 231
Welcoming the Elements 110
We live in the smallest house 116
We shall lift each other up 138
What Is In The Goddess's Tefillin? 104
When the Ark Would Travel 177
Where were you? 174
Where You Go 197
Whole Wide World 93
Wind that Blows Through Me 87
Wise Woman chant 179
Woman of Valor 220

Y

Yihiyeh adonai echad 189
Yismechu hashamayim vetagel h'aretz 19
You Shall Love 142

Z

Zacharti 27

A

Achoteynu at hayi 75
Ahavah Rabah 138
Ahavat Olam 37
Al netilat yadaim 219
All of It, Always, Earth 192
Amidah 152
Ana adonai hoshia na 209
Ana b'Choach 26
Ana el nah 182, 184, 185
Ancestor Chant 55, 153
And We Will See Shekhinah 189, 206
Angels of Fire 12
Angel Song 88
Ani Kratich 134
Anu Matzanu 50
Arigat haMa'agal 95
Ashrei 122
Azkirah Shekhinah 112

B

Barchi nafshi 102
Barchu 33
Beginning of Wisdom 174
Behold how good 8
Bereisheet bara elohi 119
Betzeit yisrael mimitzrayim 208
Birchot haShachar 107
Birchot haShachar Chant 109
Birth of the Elements 13, 110
Blessing
  for Diversity 111
  for Love 37
  for Protection 49
  for Redemption 45, 148
  for Tefillin 103
  for Time 34
  over Bread 228
  over Torah Study 105
  the Children 218
  the Moon 216
Blessings for Torah Reading
  Feminine 180
  Masculine 181
Bless the Goddess/Barchu 132
Boi Kallah 30
Borderline Ozi 212
Brich Rachamana 229

C

Candle Lighting for Shabbat 15
Circle of Life Amidah 168
Circle of Love 198
Come, Beloved 28
Come to the Well 196
Copper Mirrors 133
Creation 119
Crossroads 178

D

David melekh yisrael 217
Dor Holech 111

E

Earth-Based Amidah 171
Eishet Chayil 220
Eit Dodim 7
Elah beruchah gedolah deah 135
Elah eden lekhol hama'asim 136
Elah Malkah 176
Elemental Amidah 167
Elemental Meditation 13
Eliyahu hanavi 211
Elotai/Elohai Neshama 105, 106
El Shaddai 50
Elemental Amidah 167
Etz chayim hee 187
Evening Prayer 32
Eyl malei 193

F

Four Worlds Chant 110

G

Generous Sun 183
Goddess, my Soul 105
God Is All 52
Grace 26
Grace After Meals 229
Grove song 46, 149
Guardian Song/Barchu 131

H

HaMotzi/Yah 228
Happy People 123, 201
Hashkivinu 49
Hatzi Kaddish 51
Here and Now 26
Here I come 36
Hinei mah tov u'manyim 8
Holy Holy 36, 137
How Good 101

I

I Am Grateful 96
I Call Out to You 134
I can't believe all you have done for me 183
Ilu finu 129
Inculcation 147
I place my hands on the roots of the tree of life: 145
I Remember 27
It is the time of love 7

J

Journey 48, 150

K

Kaddish chant 92
Kaddish D'kohanot 114
Kadosh kadosh 137
Katonti m'kol hahasadim 183
Kein tihiyeh lanu 210
Ki Afar At 92, 192
Kiddush Levanah 216
Kiddush (Blessing of Wine)
  Festival Evening 226
  Festival Morning 227
  Friday Night 224
  Saturday Morning 225
Kivvun haYesodot 110
Knower of Secrets 7

L

Labyrinth 151
La Orasion De La Mujer 14
Layehudim haytah orah 210
L'cha Dodi 28
Lean Back 193
Lev Tahor 119
Life is Born 111
Lishmah lishmo 95, 199

M

Maalah Mata 89
Ma'arivah 32
Ma'arivah Aravim 34
Mah norah 8, 106
Mah Tovu 101
Mama Tovu 98
Master Key 84
May our souls circle 95, 199

SIDDUR HAKOHANOT CREDITS

OUR GRATITUDE GOES TO

Kohenet Rae Abileah
Tziona Achishena
Penina Adelman
Kohenet April N. Baskin
Rabbi Leila Gal Berner
Joshua Blaine and Kohenet Keshira haLev Fife
Kohenet Annabel Gottfried Cohen
Kohenet Elana Brody
Kohenet ALY/Ahavah Lilith evershYne
Rabbi Shir Meira Feit
Kohenet Renee Finkelstein/Radharani
Kohenet Sarah Bracha Gershuny
Rabbi Shefa Gold
Rick Hamouris
Yael Kanarek and Tamar Biala
Shoshana Jedwab
Kohenet Jo Kent Katz
Kohenet Sharon Shosh Lulyanit
Dr. Joy Ladin
Kohenet Nomy Lamm
Kohenet Yocheved Landsman
Kohenet Ketzirah Lesser
Rabbi Justin Lewis
Kohenet Annie Matan
Kohenet Traci Marx
Dr. Alicia Ostriker
Kohenet Nina Pick
Rabbi Geela Rayzel Raphael
Kohenet Angelique Rivera
Kohenet Ruach-El Rachel Rose Reid
Kohenet Sarah Salem
Kohenet Yael Schonzeit
Kohenet Avra Shapiro
Sarai Shapiro
Rakia Shemaya
Tamuz Shiran
Kohenet Bekah Starr
Kohenet Ilana Streit
Kohenet Yosefa Strouss *z"l*
Kohenet Ri J. Turner
Rabbi Melissa Weintraub
Kohenet Liviah Wessely
Kohenet Harriette Wimms

for their powerful spiritual and artistic contributions to this siddur.